# CANCER, INCORPORATED

Ralph W. Moss, PhD


Equinox Press
Blue Hill, ME 04614

EQUINOX

## Advance Comments

"At first I was appalled. Then I cried. Now I am angry and want to do something about this. Unless those of us impacted by cancer (and that is the majority of us) do the same, the cancer profit engine will continue to suck money out of the suffering. Read this book. Cry and yell. Then demand that national policies change before you, too, suffer and die for the benefit of Big Pharma."

*—Wayne Jonas, MD*
*Clinical Professor of Family Medicine, Georgetown School of Medicine; Former Director, Office of Alternative Medicine (1995-1999), National Institutes of Health*

"Ralph Moss has nailed his protest to the cathedral door of Big Pharma for its corruption of oncology. *Cancer, Incorporated* is a very important document that could spark a revolt reverberating far into the future."

*—Tibor Bakacs, MD, PhD, DSc*
*Alfréd Rényi Institute of Mathematics*
*Hungarian Academy of Sciences, Budapest*

"An extremely important book, which reveals the profoundly corrupting influence of money on cancer research and treatment. Everyone involved in cancer care needs to read this book and to act on its recommendations."

*—Dwight L. McKee, MD*
*Diplomate, American Board of Medical Oncology*

"*Cancer, Incorporated* presents an amazing array of historical facts on the relationship of Big Pharma to cancer care in America. I applaud Ralph Moss's courage."

*—Damian Dupuy, MD*
*Professor of Diagnostic Imaging, Warren Alpert School of Medicine, Brown University*
*Providence, Rhode Island*

"If you care about cancer research and treatment, read this powerful critique. When the history of cancer treatment is written, Moss will be remembered as one of the leading science journalists of our time."

*—Michael Lerner, PhD*
*Author of* Choices in Healing
*Director of Commonweal, Bolinas, CA*

"Strong and convincing! It is about time that the hard facts are presented to the public and the oncology profession. I congratulate Moss for his courage in showing that sometimes—the king is naked."

—*Professor Shimon Slavin, MD*
*Biotherapy International, Tel Aviv, Israel*

"A well-documented analysis linking Big Pharma with the outrageous cost of cancer medicine. At the end, Moss suggests potential ways to reduce the problem."

—*Michael Retsky, PhD*
*Harvard T.H. Chan School of Public Health*
*Boston, Massachusetts*

"Ralph Moss has illuminated the dark side of the cancer industry, where revenue generation trumps patient outcome."

—*Thomas Seyfried, PhD*
*Professor of Biology, Boston College*
*Chestnut Hill, Massachusetts*

"This is an amazing piece of work! Ralph Moss has eloquently delivered a no-holds-barred, tell-all synopsis of the corruption of the cancer business. He poses a question to the reader at the end of this book, 'How would you propose to improve such a broken system?' My answer is to begin by making Moss' book required reading for all individuals involved in the cancer industry."

—*Mark A Rosenberg, MD*
*President and Medical Dir*ector, *Advanced Medical Therapeutics*
*Boca Raton, Florida*

"This groundbreaking book will leave the reader in awe. I strongly recommend it to anyone who has cancer, who cares for cancer patients, or simply cares for humanity and good health."

—*Ferre Akbarpour, MD*
*Chief Medical Officer, Orange County Immune Institute*
*Huntington Beach, California*

"Thank you, Ralph Moss, for exploring and exposing distortions in drug company data and the potentially painful consequences for cancer patients."

—*James S. Gordon, MD*
*Former chair of the White House Commission on Complementary and Alternative Medicine Policy*
*Washington, DC*

Published by

The Moss Report

Stamford, CT



Photographs are from iStockPhoto or in the public domain from Wikimedia Commons.

Library of Congress Cataloging-in-Publication Data
Moss, Ralph W.

Cancer, Incorporated / Ralph W. Moss, PhD. — First edition. p. cm.

Includes bibliographical references.

ISBN 978-1-881025-15-3

1. Oncology.
2. Cancer—Chemotherapy—Research—United States.
3. —Immunotherapy–Research–United States.
4. —Drugs—Research—Corrupt practices—United States.
5. Pharmaceutical policy—United States.
6. American Society of Clinical Oncology.
7. United States Food and Drug Administration.

I. Title.

616.99

Library of Congress Control Number: 2020902007

Printed in the United States of America

ISBN 978-1-881025-15-3

Cover art: Ben Moss

# Table of Contents

To Martha

*For nothing is greater or better than this,*
*than when a man and a woman keep house together*
*sharing one heart and mind,*
*a great grief to their foes*
*and a joy to their friends.*

Homer, *The Odyssey*

A.T. Murray, translator / Loeb Classical Library, Book VI, lines 182–185

# Preface

> **"We landed in our present mess because of innumerable mistakes in the past.... They include failure of clinical scientists, their institutions and the editors of the journals publishing their science.... I believe it will take a revolution to sweep away decades of self-dealing by industry."**
>
> *—Drummond Rennie, MD, Deputy Editor, Journal of the American Medical Associaton*

To the average person, cancer needs no introduction. It is now one of the predominant causes of illness, suffering and death in most countries, including the United States of America. In 2020, the American Cancer Society (ACS) estimated that there would be more than 1.8 million new cases of invasive cancer. Over 600,000 Americans die of cancer in a given year, or 1,660 deaths per day.

Worldwide, the picture is just as bad. This disease accounts for one in six deaths. Each year there are an estimated 17 million new cases of cancer diagnosed, and 9.5 million deaths. By 2040, says the ACS, the global burden is expected to reach 27.5 million new cases and 16.3 million cancer deaths annually. But bad habits, especially cigarette addiction fostered by the tobacco industry, will almost certainly multiply that effect.

In response to this catastrophe, many countries (led by the United States) have committed significant resources to the search for reliable cures for cancer. However, despite federal spending of over six billion dollars in 2019, progress has been painfully slow. We are told that steady progress is being made. In particular, it is said that the current system is producing effective 'targeted' drugs almost every day. New drugs are bringing a supposed "world without cancer" into view. The giant M.D. Anderson Cancer Center in Houston, Texas has even crossed out the word "cancer" from its logo, to indicate the imminent demise of the disease.

**Disclaimer:** *The information provided in this book is for general educational purposes only. Neither the author nor the publisher makes warranties, expressed or implied, that this information is complete nor do they warrant the fitness of this information for any particular purpose. This information is not intended as medical advice. We encourage all cancer patients to be under the care of licensed medical providers.*

**Note to readers:** *Rather than interrupt the flow of the narrative with footnotes, we have placed all references in the Endnotes section.*

This is wishful thinking. In fact, as I shall present in this book, there is massive deception and manipulation underway, to convince us that steady progress is being made. This is to get us to continue to consume—in fact, to demand—the products of the pharmaceutical industry, and to keep us from investigating less profitable treatments that could upset the multi-billion dollar plans and ploys of the drug industry. Even those who now criticize traditional chemotherapy foster unreasonable claims for so-called 'targeted therapies' or 'precision medicine.' As this book shows, such claims are like a house built on sand. They do not stand up to critical scrutiny.

Other books and articles, all excellent in their own ways, have drawn similar conclusions to this one. I would point for example to three listed in my bibliography, Marcia Angell's *The Truth About the Drug Companies* (2005), Peter Gøtzsche's *Deadly Medicine and Organized Crime* (2013), and Sergio Sismondo's *Ghost-Managed Medicine* (2018). But I would suggest that this book is different in a number of important respects. In contrast to those works, *Cancer, Incorporated* is exclusively focused on a single disease. It also brings into sharp relief the corruption of the oncology profession. Millions of dollars now flow from pharmaceutical companies to the oncologists who oversee the clinical trials that supposedly validate the safety and effectiveness of new drugs.

*Cancer, Incorporated* is in a sense an extension of my career-long project of exposing the economic system that underpins oncology and shows how the relentless drive for profit and growth (the imperatives of capitalism) turns Big Pharma's wishes into the decisions of cancer doctors.

This project began with publication of *The Cancer Industry* in 1980, in which I identified interlocks between my former employer, Memorial Sloan-Kettering Cancer Center, and top echelons of the pharmaceutical industry. It continued through many articles in newspapers, magazines and newsletters, an analysis that I further developed in another book, *Questioning Chemotherapy,* in 1995.

My writings on complementary therapies flow not from sentimental attachment to natural treatments, but from my belief that the key characteristic of an accepted treatment is its profitability for Wall Street. Some good treatments get left behind simply because they do not meet the financial requirements of Big Pharma or actively threaten the status quo. I give three such examples in this text.

It is not my intention to discourage cancer patients from seeking effective treatments, but I also cannot be silent about Big Pharma's corruption of the oncology profession. Patients and caregivers deserve recommendations that are based on unimpeachable science, and not on research that has been compromised by the shady practices of giant drug companies.

As a patient myself, who has faced life-threatening cancer, I know that hope and morale are very important to one's peace of mind, and possibly to one's recovery as well. In fact, four years ago, when my highly skilled and dedicated doctors were actively battling my cancer with me, the last thing I wanted to hear was anything negative about my treatment choices. But this story needs to be told. I sincerely believe that we will never reach that universally desired "world without cancer" unless we root out the corruption that has overtaken much of the leadership of the oncology profession. The corruption in oncology has become so pervasive that it is now the rule rather than the exception. As the *Journal of the American Medical Association* editor Drummond Rennie, MD, has said, it will take a political revolution to correct this.

I recently performed jury duty in the Superior Court of the county where I live. The judge spent six hours examining a pool of potential jurors. In the course of that day we were required to fill out written surveys about our attitudes and opinions and were quizzed about anything at all that might prejudice us for or against a defendant. One potential juror was excused because she babysat for a defendant 25 years earlier!

We would certainly not tolerate a judge or a juror receiving payments from one of the parties in a legal case. Why then do we tolerate egregious examples of corruption on the part of those who carry out *clinical* trials of drugs? Some oncologists may be outraged to see their "dirty little secret" (as one doctor called it) exposed to public view. But, once they get over their shock, they should understand that it is simply unacceptable that cancer drugs are evaluated by those financially beholden to that modern-day octopus known as Big Pharma.

## Table 1. Drugs with trade and generic names

Approved drugs normally have a generic and a trade name. Scientific writings generally identify them by their generic names. But for the sake of readability, we have mainly used the trade names.

| Trade Name | Generic Name |
|---|---|
| Adriamycin | doxorubicin |
| Aldesleukin | interleukin-2 |
| Alecensa | alectinib |
| Angiostatin | no other name |
| Avastin | bevacizumab |
| BCG | Bacillus Calmette-Guérin |
| Brilinta | ticagrelor |
| Endostatin | no other name |
| Ganetespib | no other name |
| Gleevec | imatinib |
| Herceptin | trastuzumab |
| Imfinzi | durvalumab |
| Interferon | no other name |
| Keytruda | pembrolizumab |
| Kymriah | tisagenlecleucel |
| Laetrile | amygdalin |
| Glucophage | metformin |
| Nexavar | sorafenib |
| Novantrone | mitoxantrone |
| Opdivo | nivolumab |
| Platinol | cisplatin |
| Proleukin | interleukin-2 |
| Revlimid | lenalidomide |
| Rituxan | rituximab |
| Sutent | sunitinib malate |
| Taselisib | no other name |
| Taxol | paclitaxel |
| Taxotere | docetaxel |
| Tecentriq | atezolizumab |
| Trisinox | arsenic trioxide |
| Vitrakvi | larotrectinib |
| Xalkori | crizotinib |
| Xeloda | capecitabine |
| Yescarta | axicabtagene ciloleucel |
| Zaltrap | aflibercept |

# Section I: Conventional Therapy

## Chapter 1. The limits of chemotherapy

**"People go where the money is. You'd like to believe it's different in medicine, but it's really no different. When you start thinking of oncology as a business, then all these decisions make sense."**

*—Robert B. Geller, MD, medical oncologist*

If you have been touched by cancer, and the majority of families have, you probably are aware that cancer drugs rarely perform as the public imagines. You may know some cancer patients who have significantly benefited from these agents given in the conventional way. But how many others have suffered serious side effects, or been thrown into debt by their outrageous cost? For most of the advanced solid tumors of adults, chemotherapy has reached the limits of its usefulness. Even modern drugs, such as targeted and precision therapies, do not always perform as promised.

This is not to deny the benefit of conventional therapy in certain situations. The most obvious example is in the treatment of pediatric cancers, and particularly acute lymphoblastic leukemia, where 85 percent of American children are alive at least five years after receiving treatment for this diagnosis. Other diseases that are substantially benefited by chemotherapy are testicular cancer, choriocarcinoma, Hodgkin and non-Hodgkin lymphoma. Chemotherapy also plays a significant role in preventing the recurrence of several common cancers, including of the breast and colon.

The benefit of drugs in the final stages of the most common cancers is typically measured in months, rather than years. There are exceptions, of course. There are certainly individuals who have had long-term survival, with minimal side effects, after receiving targeted agents for some types of cancer, including melanoma patients responding well to immunotherapy. Nor am I speaking about innovative ways of giving cancer drugs, some of which hold great promise. But, by and large, the picture remains downbeat, as it was in 1995, when I wrote *Questioning Chemotherapy.*

Of course, you may have the opposite impression. No surprise, as hardly a day goes by that a news outlet somewhere doesn't announce another "breakthrough" in cancer treatment. According to a search of Google News, there have been thousands of such articles over the years. But there is often a huge disconnect between what we are told and stark reality.

"Cancer journalism usually hails alleged advances," while ignoring the limitations of treatment, according to an article in *Scientific American.* I learned this on my first day on the job as science writer at Memorial Sloan-Kettering Cancer Center in 1974. People, I was told, want to hear good news about what our ancestors called the dread disease, no matter how tentative the findings. But the vast majority of such breakthroughs never pan out. The veteran *New York Times* science writer Gina Kolata has remarked on how the public is deluged with:

> "...positive messages from the news media, advocacy groups and medical centers, and even labels on foods and supplements, hinting that they can fight or prevent cancer."

Meanwhile, the overall death rate from cancer—adjusted for the aging of the population—fell by just 5% between 1950 and 2013. Yes, a 5% decline in over 60 years. And most of that gain, said Kolata, was not due to better drugs:

> "The much touted recent drops in some cancer rates were mostly attributable not to cancer breakthroughs but to a decline in smoking that began decades ago—propelled, in part, by federal anti-smoking campaigns that began in the 1960s."

There are many stories in the mainstream media and on the internet intended to make cancer patients feel optimistic about their prospects, which is psychologically uplifting. But it is also important that we (as individuals and as a society) periodically take stock of our situation and look reality in the face.

James P. Allison, PhD, chair of immunology at the M.D. Anderson Cancer Center, Houston, did just that in his 2018 Nobel Prize acceptance speech. In the course of his presentation on the use of the immune system to fight cancer, Professor Allison exposed the inadequacy of most conventional drug treatments.

James P. Allison, PhD,
2018 Nobel Prize ceremony.
Photo by Bengt Nyman

Professor Allison stated:

> "This is what we are used to looking at in cancer therapy over the last 30 years or so. We treat a large number of patients and compare the median survival to the standard of care and, if you move it over for a few months, that's success."

This was in line with a 2017 report in *JAMA Oncology* showing that cancer drugs approved between 2003 and 2013 increased overall survival by an average of 3.4 months. And even that may have been an exaggeration, since the report's authors also stated:

> "There may be reasons to doubt that claims of efficacy reflect real-world effectiveness exactly."

What the authors are alluding to is the difference between efficacy, which refers to results achieved in clinical trials, and effectiveness, which are results seen in the general population. Efficacy is an artificial construct, while effectiveness represents the unvarnished truth.

In his Nobel Prize speech, Professor Allison contrasted the limited efficacy of most previous drugs with the success of Yervoy, the immune checkpoint inhibitor drug that he himself invented. Overall, I agree with his positive assessment of immunotherapy. In fact, years ago, I called treatments that enhance the immune response to cancer the sum of our hopes. But, according to the same *JAMA Oncology* article, the actual gain from Yervoy for the overall patient population was also quite modest: a "marginally larger overall survival benefit" of just 5.7 months.

Unfortunately, the great majority of cancer patients, worldwide, do not have access to these new immune treatments.

This is so for three main reasons:

1. These drugs are limited in the number of cancers they can treat. While the percentage of patients who are theoretically eligible for such therapy is currently 44%, the estimated percentage of responders is just 12%. And this is in an ideal world, where everyone has equal access.

2. Immune checkpoint inhibitors at standard doses can cause a wide variety of side effects, which can run the gamut from mild to extreme, sometimes including life-threatening events.

3. These drugs are also insanely expensive, sometimes costing over one million dollars per patient.

In the first randomized trial of Yervoy, 80% of patients suffered immune-related adverse events (irAEs), a previously rare category of side effects, of which 19% were severe and 4% life-threatening. There were even seven deaths associated with the treatment, which was more than the number of patients who had a complete response.

Professor Allison has suggested that such extreme reactions are now uncommon, as oncologists have become more familiar with Yervoy and similar drugs. Yet according to a 2019 report from melanoma specialists at Memorial Sloan-Kettering Cancer Center, severe reactions continue to occur, especially when two of these new drugs are used together:

> "We observed a 91% incidence of clinically significant immune-related adverse events, leading to frequent emergency department visits, hospitalizations, and systemic immunosuppression.... Within 90 days of an irAE, patients who were hospitalized as inpatients had a 23% mortality rate."

In other words, one-quarter of that group of hospitalized patients died as a result of the treatment. According to a comprehensive review of these side effects:

> "In patients receiving immune checkpoint inhibition treatment, every symptom has to be suspected to represent a sign of a possible irAE, and patients should...contact the hospital once a possible side effect occurs...."

But how many hospitals have, as these doctors suggest, an interdisciplinary team ready to assess and manage side effects of immunotherapy? There is such a team at M.D. Anderson Cancer Center and at other comprehensive cancer centers. But how many smaller hospitals or community practices, where about 85% of American cancer patients are treated, have teams trained to identify and counter immune-related adverse events? I have not found a single one.

The University of Texas MD Anderson Cancer Center in Houston, Texas. It is one of the original three comprehensive cancer centers in the U.S.

## Chapter 2. It began with Ehrlich

The systematic testing of purified chemicals against cancer was begun by Paul Ehrlich, MD (1854-1915), director of the Royal Institute for Experimental Therapy in Frankfurt. Ehrlich coined the term chemotherapy, to denote the treatment of diseases with chemicals of known constitution.

Because of his close ties to the German dyestuffs industry, Ehrlich's main interest was in exploring the use of synthetic pigments both as stains for microscopic specimens and as treatments for various diseases.

Paul Ehrlich, MD, 1854-1915

In doing so, he co-invented Salvarsan 606, the first effective medication for the age-old scourge of syphilis. Ehrlich was also the first to systematically test synthetic chemicals against cancer. In 1898, he and his team discovered alkylating agents, which killed cancer cells in the laboratory. Half a century later, chemicals of this type became the first conventional chemotherapy drugs.

For his many accomplishments, in 1908 Ehrlich was awarded the Nobel Prize for Medicine. But to be clear, he himself was not optimistic about curing cancer. In fact, above the door of his laboratory was the famous line from Dante's *Inferno*, "Abandon all hope, ye who enter here."

Not an auspicious beginning for cancer chemotherapy!

Ehrlich called his new type of drugs magic bullets, which theoretically could home in on a causative organism, while leaving normal cells unharmed. And, a century or so later, Ehrlich's magic bullets reappeared in oncology in the guise of monoclonal antibodies, targeted therapies and precision medicine.

These are fine terms with which to launch a fund-raising drive or publicize a cancer program. But, so far, most effective cancer drugs remain quite toxic. In particular, the bullets of chemotherapy are anything but magical: they indiscriminately kill a great many normal cells, sometimes wreaking havoc on the immune, digestive, and other bodily systems.

## Chapter 3. Drug company indifference

Cancer drug therapy was slow to develop and had to overcome many obstacles. One problem was that, until the 1940s, there was no drug company interest in the topic, and the U.S. government on the whole remained indifferent to the plight of cancer patients.

A few intrepid researchers at scattered laboratories depended on the generosity of philanthropists, but such funds often dried up after a benefactor passed away. This is what happened when the railroad tycoon E.H. Harriman himself died of stomach cancer in 1909, and his heirs pivoted towards politics and other pursuits.

Kanematsu Sugiura, DSc (1890-1979), a founding member of Sloan-Kettering Institute, lived through those trying times. In the early days of chemotherapy research, he personally had to trap rodents in the basement of Roosevelt Hospital just to conduct his experiments.

Throughout the twenties and thirties, the U.S. Congress repeatedly rejected calls to fund a national cancer research laboratory. Even a major Public Health Service advisory council opposed creating a national cancer center. The National Cancer Act of 1937, which established the federal cancer center in Bethesda, Maryland, had to overcome powerful opposition from the medical community.

In fact, the American Medical Association campaigned against any government involvement, while itself doing nothing to find a cure for the disease. Morris Fishbein, MD, the "iron-fisted editor" of the *Journal of the American Medical Association,* railed against the cancer bill as a menace to the AMA's dominance:

> "Our government has already voted $750,000 a year for the control of cancer and suggestions have been added for the control of infantile paralysis, syphilis and other diseases. The danger of putting the government in the dominant position in relation to medical research is apparent."

More shocking still, James Ewing, MD (1866-1943), the director of New York's Memorial Hospital, and author of the first American textbook on cancer, wrote in his Congressional deposition:

> "There are abundant reasons for dissuading the federal government from entering any further into the field of pure cancer research. It would mean merely another futile effort to discover the ultimate cause of cancer, which is an unsolvable problem.

This solution will come when science is ready for it and cannot be hastened by pouring sums of money into the effort."

In fact, a major cause of cancer, tobacco, had already been discovered, but Ewing chose to ignore that in his public statements. In essence, this was a battle between the broad public, alarmed at the growing rates of cancer, and a narrow-minded guild of professionals, defending its turf. Put mildly, it was not organized medicine's finest hour. Then, in 1936, President Franklin D. Roosevelt and the Democrats won a landslide victory. And progressive lay people in Congress, such as the well-named Maury Maverick, finally overcame the opposition of organized medicine and passed the National Cancer Act of 1937.

But the war against cancer was slow in starting. In fact, the first cancer chemotherapy drugs emerged not from the National Cancer

American, British, French and German gas masks from World War I

Institute but from a totally unexpected quarter. Because poison mustard gas had maimed or killed so many soldiers in the World War I, the major combatants were urgently preparing for future attacks. Along these lines, Memorial Hospital's research director, Cornelius P. "Dusty" Rhoads, MD, was made chief of medicine for the Chemical Weapons Division of the U.S. Army.

A patient with advanced cancer of the lymphatic system, identified only as J.D., was being treated at Yale University in the summer of 1942. At the same time, two chemists, Louis S. Gilman, PhD (1908-1984), and Alfred Goodman, MD (1906-2000), were carrying out classified government research on the biological effects of mustard gas.

Gilman and Goodman had found that poison gas depleted white blood cells, the source of J.D.'s illness. So, in conjunction with a

New Haven doctor, they gave the man a new drug fashioned from poison gas, later called Mustargen, and noted some transient relief. Although J.D. died a few weeks later, the date of his first treatment, August 27, 1942, is now considered the birth date of chemotherapy. However, for security reasons, the incident was kept secret for years.

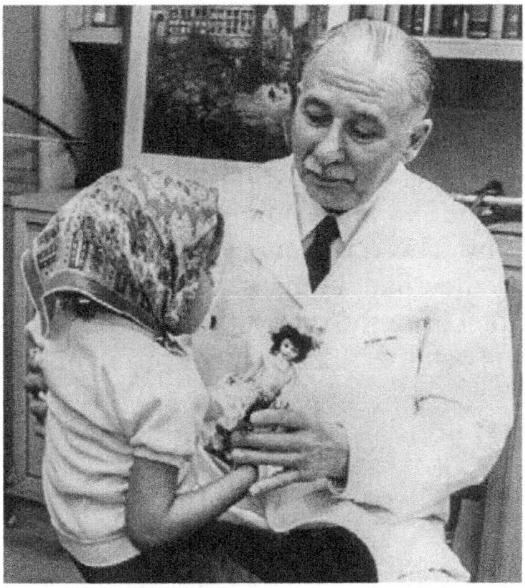

Sidney Farber with a leukemia patient

Using another early chemo drug, aminopterin, in 1948 Sidney Farber, MD, arrested the spread of acute leukemia repeatedly and at will for the first time in medical history, in 12 young patients at the Children's Medical Center of Boston.

Aminopterin was not simply a cellular poison, but an ingenious anti-nutrient, which blocked the body's uptake of a necessary B vitamin, folic acid. Unfortunately, it too was highly toxic and only resulted in temporary remissions. But this time Farber's landmark achievement made front-page news. This was how the public learned for the first time of the emergence of cancer chemotherapy.

There followed a glimmer of interest from a few drug companies into producing other anti-vitamins, such as methotrexate, which is still in use. Gertrude Elion of Burroughs Wellcome, along with scientists at Sloan-Kettering Institute, discovered the drug 6-MP in 1953. But Elion, a woman researcher in a man's world, dhad to wait 35 years to finally share a Nobel Prize in recognition of her work.

Increasingly positive results in acute leukemia, Hodgkin and non-Hodgkin lymphoma, and rare solid tumors, such as testicular cancer and choriocarcinoma (a cancer associated with pregnancy), helped bring a few companies into the field. By and large, though, this effort generated little commercial interest.

Despite Big Pharma's claim that it is the indispensable element in the fight, most drug companies stood aloof from the whole cancer problem. They looked to their bottom line and saw cancer as a money loser. Far better to promote a host of dubious over-the-counter remedies with claims that differed little from the advertising quackery of the previous century.

A few rare exceptions were Lederle Laboratories, Bristol-Myers Squibb, and Burroughs Wellcome. But most of the Big Pharma firms stood idly by. There was more money to be made from over-the-counter remedies like Tums for the Tummy, or Speedy Alka-Seltzer. They had neither the motivation nor the scientific know-how to launch a serious attack on the cancer problem.

From the Fifties...Alka-Seltzer advertisement

## Chapter 4. A proper and pleasing effect

The cigarette has justly been called the deadliest artifact in the history of human civilization. Cigarettes cause one lung cancer death per 3 or 4 million smoked, which explains why the scale of the epidemic is so large today. Worldwide, cigarettes cause a staggering 1.5 million deaths from lung cancer alone per year.

Many Americans first got hooked on cigarettes during World War I, when they were provided free to American infantrymen in the European theater. In the interwar period, cigarettes were touted as alluring for men and a sign of liberation in women.

In World War II, the U.S. Armed Forces provided each soldier with a dozen cigarettes per day as part of his basic K-rations. After the war, Big Tobacco engaged in psychologically astute and sexually-tinged advertising campaigns. At its peak, almost 50% of the adult population in America was smoking Lucky Strikes, Chesterfields, Old Golds, and other top brands. No surprise, then, that lung cancer incidence and death rates rose rapidly, due to a massive increase in tobacco use.

It is a common misconception that the realization that tobacco causes cancer was a result of *Smoking and Health,* Surgeon General Luther Terry's Report of 1964. This was certainly a major factor. But there were many references to the tobacco-cancer link in medical journals and newspapers throughout the 20th century.

It is often stated that doctors of the time did not know that tobacco products were harmful, much less that they were associated with cancer. But, if so, this was willful ignorance. A famous American surgeon, Robert Abbe, MD, published a study of 100 patients, titled "Cancer of the Mouth: The Case Against Tobacco"... in 1915! In 1928, in the third edition of his textbook, *Neoplastic Diseases*, James Ewing, MD, then chief pathologist of New York's Memorial Hospital, wrote in no uncertain terms about what he called tobacco cancers:

> "Tobacco has a predominant influence in the development of cancer of the buccal mucosa [inner lining of the lips and cheeks].... Many of the tobacco cancers arise at the base of the tongue, on the palate, tonsils, or pharynx, while the relation to laryngeal [voice box] cancer is well known."

Ewing even mentioned the influence of tobacco smoking on the rising rates of lung cancer, which had previously been a rare disease. This link was slower to emerge, because lung cancer only developed after several decades of exposure. Nevertheless, according to a historian of the tobacco plague, Robert N. Proctor, PhD, of Stanford University (2013):

> "Cigarettes were recognised as the cause of the [lung cancer] epidemic in the 1940s and 1950s, with the confluence of studies from epidemiology, animal experiments, cellular pathology and chemical analytics. Cigarette manufacturers disputed this evidence, as part of an orchestrated conspiracy to salvage cigarette sales."

As Professor Proctor has shown, this link was common knowledge in Germany before World War II. But it wasn't until the 1950s and 1960s that the American public became aware of such research. Ernst T. Wynder, MD (1922-1999), himself a German refugee, demonstrated this connection in his research at Sloan-Kettering Institute in the postwar years. According to internal documents of the tobacco industry, released via a court settlement:

> "Ernst Wynder led the anti-cigarette attacks. He exploited his Sloan-Kettering association to the industry's distinct disadvantage."

Dr. Wynder once told me how his work on tobacco had been undermined by a past president of Sloan-Kettering Institute, Frank Horsfall, MD. Horsfall, himself a Marlboro smoker, posed as an ardent supporter of Wynder's research. But internal documents later revealed that he was secretly reporting to the tobacco industry on Wynder's latest findings. In gratitude, starting in 1961, Philip Morris began making regular $25,000 contributions to Sloan-Kettering Institute. Then, according to a company memo, Horsfall:

> "...began subjecting Wynder to more rigorous screening procedures before letting him speak in the name of the Institute. This has had a proper and pleasing effect."

Wynder eventually left Sloan-Kettering in frustration over its foot-dragging on tobacco and started the American Health Foundation. Horsfall himself died of an unspecified cancer in 1971.

According to another internal tobacco industry document:

> "Between 1962 and 1979 R.J. Reynolds contributed over $1 million to the Memorial Sloan-Kettering Cancer Center for a variety of programs, the last program dealing with basic biomedical research."

Basic biomedical research is necessary, but it also kept the focus far away from tobacco. In 1975, John S. Reed, CEO of Citibank, was made a member of the Memorial Sloan-Kettering Cancer Center's board of overseers. Reed was also a paid director of Philip Morris. He claimed he brought "some of the realism of the cigarette world" to the nation's largest private cancer center. Philip Morris's idea of realism included denying any links between tobacco and cancer for the next quarter century. During that period, Reed parroted the tobacco industry line on the MSKCC board:

> "Reed says he does not believe that the statistics suffice to incriminate smoking and stresses his view of it as a matter of 'personal choice,' particularly for Americans who are aware of the possible risks."

Some MSKCC scientists, to their credit, protested against Big Tobacco's representation on the board. These doctors' spokesperson was Edward J. Beattie, Jr., MD, a thoracic surgeon who served as president of Memorial Hospital. He declared in 1982:

> "What Philip Morris does not state, is that we have...an epidemic of cancer that occurs many times more frequently in cigarette smokers than in nonsmokers. Clearly, cigarette smoking has a disastrous influence on United States cancer statistics, to say nothing of its disastrous effect on heart disease and blood-vessel disease."

Beattie died of malignant melanoma a few years afterward. Reed stayed on at MSKCC for the next quarter of a century. But at least he was not taken in by his own tobacco propaganda. He admitted to the *Washington Post* that he was a non-smoker, after having watched his own father, a life-long cigarette addict, die of lung cancer.

Albert Lasker, husband of the anticancer crusader, Mary Lasker, was another cancer warrior with close ties to the tobacco industry. Albert was known as the father of modern advertising. His firm, Lord & Thomas, thought up the clever idea of associating cigarette smoking with weight control, in its "Reach for a Lucky Instead of a Sweet" campaign.

Such ads enticed thousands of young women (as well as men) to take up cigarette smoking in order to keep their attractive figures. What they got instead, of course, were lung and throat cancer, heart attacks, chronic obstructive pulmonary disease (COPD), and many other painful and fatal diseases. In fact, this promotion of tobacco triggered the greatest single health disaster in American history. Albert Lasker himself died of cancer in May 1952. For decades, the medical profession, which should have led the anti-smoking campaign, was complicit in this ongoing catastrophe. The American Tobacco Company claimed that "20,679 physicians" endorsed its lead brand, *Lucky Strike,* because it allegedly offered "throat

Albert Lasker's 1928 ad campaign for Lucky Strike, featuring claim of "No Throat Irritation—No Cough."

protection" against irritation and smoker's cough.

Another big tobacco firm, R.J. Reynolds, created a Medical Relations Division and advertised its findings in professional journals. It paid doctors to take part in rigged studies, and then touted these in ads for its Philip Morris cigarettes. This pseudo-scientific campaign transformed Philip Morris into a major brand. A 1943 advertisement in the *Saturday Evening Post* proclaimed that Philip Morris provided "[f]ull reports in medical journals by men, high in their profession—regularly offered to physicians on request." Similarly

> "In 1946, R.J. Reynolds launched an ad campaign with the slogan, 'More doctors smoke Camels than any other cigarette.' They had solicited this 'finding' by giving doctors a free carton of Camel cigarettes, and then asking what brand they smoked."

Why then didn't the AMA blow the whistle on this orchestrated conspiracy, as Professor Proctor called it, and lead a vigorous campaign against tobacco consumption? One reason was that the editor of *JAMA*, Morris Fishbein, MD, was secretly in the pay of tobacco companies:

> "Fishbein helped stave off efforts to have the journal refuse tobacco ads and, in the mid-1950s, received about $100,000 from Lorillard to write industry-friendly articles on smoking and health. Fishbein also helped place ads for Kent cigarettes in medical magazines.... Fishbein worked for Lorillard throughout the 1960s and into the 1970s, receiving $10,000 per year from 1957 through 1969."

We live today with the legacy of the AMA's complicity. According to U.S. government figures:

> "Cigarette smoking is responsible for more than 480,000 deaths per year in the United States, including more than 41,000 deaths resulting from secondhand smoke exposure. This is about one in five deaths annually, or 1,300 deaths every day."

To put this in perspective, more people die of smoking-related deaths in the U.S. each year than the total American casualties in World War II from 1941 to 1945. According to Professor Proctor:

> "About 100 million people died from smoking in the 20th century, whereas several times that are likely to die in the present century, even if current rates of smoking fall dramatically. Most of the tobacco epidemic remains in the future, with the total global toll likely to approach two million lung cancer deaths per year in the 2020s or 2030s."

## Chapter 5. The War on Cancer

In the 1950s and 1960s, a group of individuals centered around Mary Lasker and her husband's successor at Lord & Thomas, Emerson Foote, created support for an enhanced cancer research program. It may seem strange, or even a bit suspicious, that the anticancer campaign was led by people close to the tobacco industry. But Foote was a brave and honest man. Although he had made his name promoting American tobacco products, in 1948 he stirred the industry by abruptly resigning all his company's tobacco accounts, worth $12 million in billings ($128 million today), because of his acerbic views of tobacco advertising.

Foote then quit the advertising business entirely, broke a lifelong smoking habit, and became a director of the American Cancer Society. As such, he played a pivotal role in countering the industry's advertising and propaganda. But the strain of fighting Big Tobacco proved too much for him. In 1949, according to Mrs. Lasker, he had a nervous breakdown and quit his anticancer work entirely. (Foote served as a model for the lead character, Don Draper, in the hit television series, *Mad Men*.)

The antismoking effort by the self-described benevolent plotters ultimately morphed into a full-scale war on cancer, which President Nixon signed into law on December 23, 1971. Aides called it his Christmas present to the nation. There was also a public relations campaign, complete with ads suggesting we could cure cancer by the bicentennial, July 4, 1976.

Along the way, something momentous happened. The benevolent plotters got their greatly enhanced, federally funded war on cancer. But it no longer included a fight against the tobacco industry. Prevention was edged out and treatment became the order of the day. In the text and supporting documents of the 1971 Cancer Act one cannot find a single mention of tobacco or smoking. In fact, the first mention of tobacco in NCI's timeline of important events was in 1982, a decade after passage of the National Cancer Act, when NCI supported a small pilot program to test educational interventions to prevent tobacco use.

Overwhelmingly, the emphasis of the war on cancer was on treatment, not on primary prevention. The designated leader of the enterprise (the so-called Cancer Czar) was a lawyer and investor named Benno Schmidt, Sr. After a brief foray as a law school professor, Schmidt's career-long employer was John H. "Jock" Whitney (1904-1982), who had inherited $200 million in 1927, $50 million of which was in tobacco shares. Under Schmidt's direction, the cancer war pivoted away from combating smoking and went towards money-making opportunities in treating the disease. This was a logical direction for a self-described venture capitalist.

The problem was that, in 1971, no one knew where cancer cures were supposed to come from. The main idea at the time was to identify some putative cancer-causing viruses and make vaccines against them. In pursuit of this, the NCI provided enormous sums to a Columbia University researcher, Sol Spiegelman, PhD, in a frenzied hunt for human cancer retroviruses. But, in the end, "the hoped-for human virus slipped quietly away into the night. The rocket never left its launching pad," to quote Robert A. Weinberg, PhD, of the Broad Institute at MIT. No surprise, then, that by the late 1970s there was widespread disillusionment with the war on cancer. According to the *ASCO Post:*

> "By the end of the decade...Mary Lasker's influence on the 'war on cancer' began to decline, as new cures for the disease failed to materialize and the public's skepticism of impending scientific breakthroughs in cancer research and treatment grew."

## Emergence of oncology

Promising a quick cure was a vote-getter, but it created unrealistic expectations. Medical oncology barely existed as a board-certified specialty, and cancer treatment was in its infancy. In fact, well into the 1970s, "talk of curing cancer with drugs was not considered compatible with sanity," the future NCI director, Vincent T. DeVita, Jr., MD, later remarked.

Dr. DeVita recalled that the prevailing attitude to chemotherapy among his fellow doctors could "only be described as hostile." Chemotherapy was considered a wasteful sideline to surgery and radiation, and "poison was the term in general use for anticancer drugs." Even top internists of the time publicly insulted doctors who championed chemotherapy as "the lunatic fringe."

When I began work at Memorial Sloan-Kettering Cancer Center in New York City in 1974, the *medical* treatment of the common cancers of adults was still a very new concept. I remember hearing surgeons say that trying to cure cancer with drugs was like trying to dissolve a person's left ear while leaving their right ear intact. I also heard doctors mockingly refer to the early cancer drug 5-FU as Five Feet Under, and another drug, BCNU, as Be Seein' You.

## Rise of ASCO

The evolution of cancer treatment parallels the rise of the American Society of Clinical Oncology. ASCO was conceived at a meeting of seven cancer physicians at Chicago's Edgewater Beach Hotel in 1964. As the society's historian put it:

> "At the time, cancer was viewed as a monolithic and frequently incurable disease, with only a handful of hard-to-tolerate and mostly ineffective therapies available."

Half a century later, ASCO has become an institutional powerhouse, with 45,000 members, 25,000 of whom attend its annual meeting in Chicago. Towering over it all is Big Pharma, a few giant firms that dominate the convention floor and the world of oncology.

In 1975, a sliver of clinical trials (4%) were sponsored by the industry. But by 2004 that number had risen to more than half (57%), and this included most of the key ones that affected the approval of new cancer drugs. By 2015, according to a Johns Hopkins University report, drug companies were funding six times as many clinical trials as the federal government. The *Baltimore Sun* spelled out the implications:

> "That means companies with financial interests in the studies now have more control over what doctors and patients learn about new treatments."

Given ASCO's present-day clout, it is hard to realize that not long ago, medical oncologists were a small embattled minority, fighting for their place in the sun. But after passage of the National Cancer Act of 1971, federal funds began to flow into the search for a cure. Biomedicine was also beginning its long transition from reliance on a few crude drugs that could kill fast-growing cells (both normal and malignant) to so-called targeted agents.

The drug industry still remained conspicuously absent from the fight. In the U.S., for most of the 1970s, the federal government, academia and nonprofit agencies shouldered about 95% of the burden of cancer drug development. They paid for and performed the basic research, formulated new agents, tried them out in laboratories, and organized human clinical trials.

In one glaring example of Big Pharma's apathy and neglect, in the mid-1970s NCI researchers wanted to bring a new Italian drug, Adriamycin (doxorubicin), to the U.S. But not a single American pharmaceutical company showed the slightest interest in pursuing this, and so the drug remained in short supply.

Finally, a new Italian-American collaboration, Adria Laboratories, was established to market the drug in the U.S. But because of the lack of interest by Big Pharma, the American side was represented by a chemical company, Hercules, that had no prior experience with drugs at all. In fact, Adria's executives were so inexperienced that NCI employees had to help fill out the New Drug Application (NDA) for the company's lone product.

Adriamycin, which 40 years later is still in widespread use, was a government project from start to finish in the U.S., except that all the profits went to Adria's private investors. This was a prime example of what the Nobel Prize-winning economist Joseph Stiglitz, PhD, has called "socializing the costs while privatizing the gains."

Benno Schmidt was concerned about this lack of drug industry involvement. It was not their fault, he said. There simply was not enough money to be made in cancer, due to an excess of competition. As he explained:

> "No pharmaceutical firm is going to take on a cancer drug if there's a chance of competition.... The cancer market is too small for competition."

Schmidt identified the problem from the point of view of Wall Street. The obvious solution to him was to make sure that new cancer drugs were properly patented, in order to guarantee companies a legal 20-year monopoly over the market. The veteran researcher Michael Retsky, PhD of the Harvard T.H. Chan School of Public Health is one among many who have noted this central problem of new drug development. On the failure of oncology to develop low-dose and low-cost treatments, he commented in 2019:

> "For better or for worse, that's the business model for oncology; the payback on investment is what drives new therapies. It's not a good situation, but that's the way it is."

And, to this day, not one of over 500 cancer drugs approved by the Food and Drug Administration has been an unpatented, natural or non-toxic treatment. The reason for this is the difficulty of patenting, or otherwise monopolizing, agents in the public domain. One drug that challenged this paradigm was Taxol, which is derived from the bark of the Pacific yew tree. But in that case, the National Cancer Institute's solution was to license all rights to market this substance to a single company. This focus on patented drugs also creates a problem for patients. Not only are they more expensive than generics, but by their nature as unique entities they tend to be foreign to the human host, and therefore prone to greater toxicity than, say, food-derived compounds.

Schmidt's statement was revealing in another way. Prior to this, the phrase "cancer market" was only used in reference to blatant quackery. In fact, even in the 1970s, people were still leery of cancer becoming a money-making opportunity.

## The Reagan era

With the election of Ronald Reagan as president in 1980, much changed. The U.S. veered to the right, as many Americans embraced conservatism in social, economic and political affairs. In particular, the relationship of academia to big business was fostered, as Reagan pushed privatization across the board, while simultaneously defunding many public programs.

Big business became unapologetically profit-driven. According to Reagan's intellectual guru, the University of Chicago economist Milton Friedman, PhD:

> "There is one and only one social responsibility of business, to engage in activities designed to increase its profits."

According to *Fortune* magazine,

> "Companies must obey the law. But beyond that, their job is to make money for shareholders."

Such sentiments seemed more appropriate to the mid-Victorian era than to the postwar welfare state, as many called it. But because of numerous social and economic problems of the 1970s, which were blamed on the permissiveness of liberals, Reagan's anti-government rhetoric gained a popular foothold.

Naturally, this also affected the world of medicine. According to Professor Gary Gaumer of Simmons College School of Business:

> "The culture of health care delivery began to change.... Hospitals and other providers began to behave more like businesses."

One result was that many scientists, who formerly felt secure in their academic positions, now had to raise their own funds for basic research. As one Harvard researcher put it:

> "I spent about 40% of my time chasing after funding.... It is a huge investment of time that does

> not always contribute directly to your research agenda—just something you have to do to keep the wheels turning."

According to Professor John McConough of the Harvard T.H. Chan School of Public Health:

> "'Greed is good' was more than a catchy movie line—it was the Me Decade's dominant theory. No other advanced democracy embraced deregulated health care markets in the way that the U.S. did. It swept through health care as it did every other part of the U.S. economy."

Increasingly, year by year, cancer therapy became a lucrative area of investment for entrepreneurs. In the late 1970s and 1980s, a booming cancer marketplace emerged. It became common to hear the dread disease described, not as a medical mystery or personal tragedy, but as an exciting investment opportunity. Exploiting cancer for financial gain was no longer the hallmark of the advertising quack, but became the new normal.

A class of self-described entrepreneurial oncologists emerged, seeking money-making opportunities at every turn. Some offered risky procedures at extortionate prices. This is not a reference to Tijuana cancer clinics with their alternative offerings, but about mainstream American hospitals and board-certified doctors.

In particular, hundreds of oncologists got caught up in newly hatched money-making schemes, either as practitioners or investors. The stocks of companies engaged in developing new and untested cancer treatments became hot items on Wall Street. Their price gyrations were reminiscent of the speculative bubbles of previous eras. To quote one journalistic account:

> "All of a sudden the world seemed bio-crazy. Biotech stocks doubled and tripled in a matter of months, fueled by media hype of medical discoveries on the horizon. Biotech ruled Wall Street...."

## The interferon saga

In the late 1970s and early 1980s, a new class of drugs came to the fore. These were called "biological response modifiers" (BRMs). There were many BRMs, but the lead items were two hormone-like chemicals called interferon-alpha and interleukin-2 (Il-2).

Interferon was discovered in the late 1950s and was so named because it was thought to interfere with the activity of harmful viruses in cells. As drugs, they represented a historic shift away from traditional cell-killing chemotherapy, with its daunting toxicity, to what was thought to be a more natural form of treatment, based on substances isolated from the body itself.

Starting in the late 1970s, interferon was ballyhooed as a virtual cure-all and in 1980 was featured on the cover of *Time* magazine. Here are some typical newspaper headlines of the time:

- Interferon shot cures high blood pressure.
- Are interferons the cure for the common cold?
- Interferon cures hepatitis.
- Can virus-fighting interferon cure cancer?

A stock market bubble formed around companies researching and manufacturing BRMs. For example, Interferon Sciences, founded in Houston in 1980, raised over $70 million in funding and was traded on the Nasdaq stock exchange. Its price soared throughout the 1980s and into the 1990s, based on unrealistic expectations of using interferon as a treatment for various conditions, including HIV/AIDS. But when the FDA refused to grant the company a key approval, the stock plummeted 70% in a single day. In 1998, shares were trading at $7 apiece; by 2001, they were worth one penny.

Today, interferon is approved by the FDA to treat hairy cell leukemia and a few other rare conditions. But even in kidney cancer, which was once the poster child of this type of therapy, most tumor responses were partial and rarely lasted one year.

Other magic bullet drug promotions during those years raised expectations sky-high but quickly fizzled when given to actual patients. At the time there was even a nickname for this phenomenon: the cure du jour.

But nothing raised greater hopes than interleukin-2.

### Interleukin: the land of opportunity

Interleukin-2 was discovered by Steven A. Rosenberg, MD, PhD, at the National Cancer Institute in 1977. Since it transmitted messages between white blood cells, or leukocytes, he named it inter-leukin. Rosenberg's fame rests on the successive development of a new form of cancer treatment known as adoptive immunotherapy. In the 1970s, immunotherapy garnered little respect in conventional circles. According to the *Washington Post,* it was looked on as something of a crackpot notion. When Rosenberg began his career, the work of the great founder of the field, William B. Coley, MD (1862-1936), was still on the blacklist of alternative treatments, the American Cancer Society's *Unproven Methods of Cancer Management.* As late as 1989, a student of the field could write:

> "Immunologists have remained until recently erudite but therapeutically effete. Indeed anyone purporting to treat disease by immunological methods has been in danger of being labelled a quack or a crackpot."

Initially Rosenberg began with a focus on interleukin-2 (IL-2). IL-2 is a molecule, called a cytokine, isolated from white blood cells. Starting in 1982, Rosenberg began culturing a specific anti-cancer white cell, called a T lymphocyte, in test tubes along with a synthetic (or recombinant) form of IL-2. This culturing process created what he called lymphokine activated killer cells. These LAK cells were then expanded to vast numbers in the laboratory, and re-infused into a cancer patient.

A year or so later, in 1986, Rosenberg discovered another very special kind of T cell, one that had on its own begun invading and destroying cancers. He called these cells tumor infiltrating lymphocytes. By 1988, he and his team had extracted, expanded and reintroduced these cells into patients, in one case at least causing a regression of melanoma.

Over the years, Rosenberg's methods had become ever more sophisticated. But here we shall focus on the work that made Rosenberg famous, which was the use of high-dose IL-2, both as a culturing medium for T lymphocytes, and as an anticancer agent in its own right. Rosenberg's clinical experiments with IL-2 first came to public notice in the summer of 1985, when there were rumors that the NCI had developed an effective new treatment for previously incurable cancers. Interest built in October 1985, when he received the General Motors Cancer Research Award. In November, his treatment was discussed in *Fortune* magazine. Finally, in December results were published in the *New England Journal of Medicine.*

The NCI Director, Vincent T. DeVita, MD (who, since 1982, has been co-editor with Rosenberg of the world's leading cancer textbook), declared that the new treatment was "the most interesting and exciting biological therapy we've seen so far."

These events unleashed a torrent of favorable publicity for the NCI and for Rosenberg personally. They seemed finally, after a decade and a half of false starts, to fulfill the promise of the war on cancer and the hopes of millions of people around the world. In fact, for many, the end of cancer seemed to be in sight. And the new cure didn't come from dangerous synthetic chemicals but from one's own white blood cells.

Rosenberg was featured on the cover of *Newsweek* magazine. He appeared on NBC's *Today Show*, and other major TV shows, enthusiastically describing his new treatment to nearly universal acclaim. The *Wall Street Journal* demanded that the Food and Drug Administration abandon its strict drug approval process and speed delivery of Rosenberg's medicine to thousands of desperate patients.

In fact, the entire stock market rose on the news of IL-2's successes. Cetus, which manufactured the IL-2 used in Rosenberg's study, saw its stock price double. The business press enthused:

> "The pharmaceutical branch of the biotech business is once again a sort of entrepreneurial Land of Opportunity, complete with Wall Street glamor and dazzling new products in the works."

Everyone involved in IL-2's development was besieged by reporters, desperate patients and would-be investors. According to Cetus's communications director:

> "No one here had quite predicted how the media and the general public would react. We had eight television crews and 80 press calls to deal with."

Hundreds of newspaper and magazine articles followed. Here are some typical headlines of the day:

- Cancer killing wonder drug.
- First new cancer treatment in decades found.
- Ordinary white blood cells turned into cancer killer.
- New therapy helps victims fight cancer.

The NCI was deluged with phone calls from patients seeking the therapy. As its chief of public inquiries told reporters:

> "What they're saying is our mother, our brother, our sister, is dying at this very moment. We have nothing to lose. We want to be a candidate."

Rosenberg himself received several hundred inquiries per day. But because of production difficulties, Cetus could only supply enough IL-2 to treat eight patients a month. Thus, only about one percent of desperate patients could get into the program.

In his media appearances, Rosenberg repeated the story of one remarkable complete response:

> "One 29-year-old woman whose melanoma had spread to several skin sites went through nine killer cell infusions and 47 doses of interleukin-2 and had been free of the cancer since December 1984."

What had Rosenberg and his NCI colleagues actually achieved? In their 1985 *New England Journal of Medicine* article, they revealed that so far they had treated just 25 patients with metastatic cancer. Twenty-five patients, under normal circumstances, would barely qualify as an early phase I clinical trial.

Here is how their scientific paper summarized the effects:

> "Objective regression of cancer...was observed in 11 of the 25 patients: complete tumor regression occurred in one patient with metastatic melanoma... and partial responses occurred in nine patients with pulmonary [lung] or hepatic [liver] metastases from melanoma, colon cancer, or renal-cell [kidney] cancer and in one patient with a primary unresectable lung adenocarcinoma."

So, all the favorable publicity over the combined IL-2 and LAK treatment was based on tumor shrinkages in 11 out of 25 carefully chosen patients, with just a single complete response in that one 29-year-old woman with melanoma. How would this compare to standard treatment? As the immunologist and medical historian Ilana Löwy, PhD, put it in her detailed study of the IL-2 saga:

> "Rosenberg and his collaborators ended their article with a warning about the dangers of premature conclusions and stressed that their study had involved a small number of patients who were followed for only a short time (eight months). Nevertheless, the impression conveyed by the first publication of the therapeutic effects...was one of an important breakthrough in cancer treatment."

The cost of the new treatment also became a matter of concern. IL-2 was very expensive and difficult to produce. *The New York Times* reported that HIV/AIDS patients were being offered the treatment at a cost of $125,000 per patient, or $300,000 in today's dollars. This was the world's first exposure to very expensive drugs for cancer and AIDS. At the time, a more typical cost of chemotherapy was around $500 per patient.

Dr. Rosenberg described his treatment as the first new kind of approach to cancer in perhaps 20 or 30 years. He further claimed:

> "This is really the first step. But it demonstrates that it is possible to manipulate the immune system and make a variety of cancers in a variety of locations disappear."

Rosenberg conveyed an exaggerated picture of IL-2/LAK's benefits. Most patients (14 out of 25) had no response at all and only one cancer disappeared (presuming that by cancer one means the overall condition, and not just an isolated metastatic growth).

But, as time went by, the significance of the IL-2/LAK results diminished further. Skepticism began early. In a commentary in the *Journal of the American Medical Association* in 1986, Charles Moertel, MD, the Mayo Clinic oncologist, described:

> "...the high costs, severe side effects, and limited clinical results of the new therapy. Most of the tumor regressions attributed to it had been partial and transitory."

In 1987, Rosenberg published a progress report on the treatment. That paper is actually two studies, one of high-dose IL-2 alone, the other of the IL-2/LAK combination. Among the 46 patients who received IL-2 alone, there was again only a single complete response (2.2%), which lasted just four months. In the 106 patients who received the combination treatment, eight had complete responses (7.5%). What the paper's Abstract fails to mention, but is revealed in the body of the text, is that four patients died as a result of the treatment itself.

In 1999 there was a follow-up study in the *Journal of Clinical Oncology* of 270 patients who had been treated with IL-2/LAK for advanced melanoma between 1985 and 1993. Let's focus on the main outcomes in that larger study, especially on the durable complete responses, which was the key finding that had fired up the public's imagination in 1985. Here are the basic facts as revealed in this longer paper:

- Out of 270 melanoma patients, there were 43 responders.
- 15.9% of patients had some shrinkage of their tumors.
- There were 17 complete responders, which equalled 6.3% of the patient population.

- 59% of the complete responders were still progression-free at seven years.

Thus, ten patients (out of 270) had a complete and durable response. So the cure rate in advanced melanoma was actually 3.7% of the treated patients.

Although 84.1% of the patients did not respond, most of them suffered from the toxicity of the treatment. Among the responders who had only a partial remission, the median duration was 5.9 months. Since this was not a randomized controlled trial, it is impossible to say how this outcome would have compared to some other treatment, such as chemotherapy, or even best supportive care.

According to medical historian Ilana Löwy's account:

> "Rosenberg and his collaborators affirmed that [IL-2] had produced spectacular regressions of otherwise incurable tumors in nearly half of their patients. The results of later clinical trials of IL-2 did not confirm all the initial claims made for it. The new therapy was less effective than Rosenberg had alleged.... The rate of therapeutic success... was significantly lower than the one reported in the 1985 article" in the *New England Journal of Medicine.*

In a retrospective review of IL-2, subtitled "Time for an Obituary?", Malcolm J. Moore, MD, Professor of Medicine and Pharmacology at Princess Margaret Hospital, Toronto, made some devastating remarks about the failure of IL-2 as a treatment for advanced kidney cancer. He pointed out how some of the remissions of cancer with IL-2 could have been spontaneous in nature, i.e., not due to any particular medical treatment:

> "In a study comparing gamma interferon [a different biological response modifier] with a matched placebo, the response rates were 4% and 7% to gamma interferon and placebo, respectively, and 1% of patients experienced a durable complete response rate."

The astonishing thing here is that placebo alone (a dummy injection) was associated with a 7% response rate in kidney cancer. So, logically, some of the highly positive effects seen after IL-2 treatment could have been due to a spontaneous remission of the patient's disease rather than the treatment itself. There were many subsequent attempts to improve on Rosenberg's original figures by combining IL-2 with other treatments, such as interferon or high dose chemotherapy. But, according to the 2019 edition of the DeVita-Hellman-Rosenberg cancer textbook, IL-2, "consistently failed to produce statistically significant benefit in overall survival in randomized phase III trials."

And according to the medical information service *UpToDate*:

> "High-dose interleukin-2 (IL-2) was the first immunotherapy approach to produce durable remissions in patients with advanced disease. However, these benefits were limited to a small fraction of patients, and treatment was associated with substantial toxicity."

A 2018 review of IL-2 pointed to the lack of valid studies that prove actual benefit in terms of overall survival:

> "However, the question that needs to be addressed includes the evaluation of survival benefits.... To answer this question, much larger clinical trials with extended follow-up period should be conducted."

In other words, 35 years after IL-2 was featured on the cover of *Newsweek* and Rosenberg appeared on national TV, no one could say that IL-2 really extended patients' overall survival. In fact, the latest 11th edition (2019) of the DeVita-Hellman-Rosenberg textbook concludes a lengthy discussion of the topic with this final judgment:

> "In the future, high-dose IL-2 will have little use."

## Endostatin and angiostatin

In the mid-1990s, Professor Judah Folkman, MD (1933-2008), of Boston Children's Hospital and Harvard Medical School, proposed two new drugs called angiostatin and endostatin to fight cancer. These were based on a brilliant and original idea, to prevent the formation of new blood vessels that tumors needed to feed themselves and eliminate waste material.

But in 1998 Dr. Folkman's work was prematurely publicized on the front page of the *New York Times* as a potential cure for cancer. The Nobel laureate James D. Watson, PhD, co-discoverer of the double helix structure of DNA, was quoted as saying, "Judah is going to cure cancer in two years."

Professor Watson also claimed:

> "Dr. Folkman would be remembered along with scientists like Charles Darwin as someone who permanently altered civilization."

The director of the NCI, Richard Klausner, MD, called Professor Folkman's work "the single most exciting thing on the horizon" for the treatment of cancer:

> "I am putting nothing on higher priority than getting this into clinical trials," Dr. Klausner said. The mouse studies are "remarkable and wonderful," he said, and "very compelling."

The reader can imagine the impact that these words, in America's so-called newspaper of record, had on millions of cancer patients around the world. Oncologists and many public figures, including Folkman himself, were besieged with frantic calls from patients demanding the miracle cure. To his credit, Dr. Folkman discounted all exaggerated claims and with characteristic good humor announced:

> "If you have cancer and you are a mouse, we can take good care of you."

In the end, angiostatin and endostatin were far less effective than hoped for. According to a 2016 summary:

> "The clinical benefit is typically modest, toxicity occurs, acquired resistance emerges, and the biomarker(s) that will predict which patients will respond…remains elusive."

Dr. Folkman's idea ultimately gave rise to a commonly used anticancer drug, Avastin. This represented a transition from cellular poisons to the intelligent targeting of cancer's molecular abnormalities. Some people also saw in this development an enormous opportunity for financial gain. Wall Street and the drug industry's involvement grew apace, until it finally came to dominate the field of oncology to an unprecedented degree.

## Chapter 6. Clinical trials: a sordid history

Clinical trials have a sordid history. Most people know about the gruesome Nazi concentration camp experiments, in which helpless victims were tortured or mutilated for the sake of "science." But the Nazis, while certainly the most extreme case, were not the only culprits. In the U.S., there was the infamous Tuskegee Project, in which African-American men were allowed to die from untreated syphilis, even after the cure, penicillin, had been discovered. This is a source of continuing distrust of clinical trials among African-Americans. During this same time, declassified records show there were 425 secret human radiation experiments conducted in the U.S. According to one 2017 account:

> "Between April 1945 and July 1947, eighteen subjects were injected with plutonium, six with uranium, five with polonium, and at least one with americium. The experiments were performed at Manhattan Project-affiliated hospitals in Rochester, New York; Oak Ridge, Tennessee; Chicago, Illinois; and San Francisco, California."

From 1946 to 1963, the U.S. military stationed more than 200,000 soldiers within sight of one or more nuclear bomb tests either in the Pacific or Nevada. Many of these soldiers, with their top officers' complicity, were thereby exposed to dangerous levels of ionizing radiation (the type that can cause cancer). Other examples:

- The Lawrence Berkeley Laboratory conducted 93 human radiation experiments on Bay Area residents starting in 1936. Incredibly, these were still going on in the 1980s.
- Between 1945 and 1949, 820 poor pregnant white women were given tracer doses of radioactive iron in experiments performed at Vanderbilt University, Nashville, Tennessee.
- In the 1950s, scientists fed 125 intellectually disabled children at the Walter E. Fernald State School in Waltham, Massachusetts, milk and cereal containing radioactive tracers, without their or their parents' knowledge or consent. According to an article in the *New York Times,*

> "Scientists from Harvard University and the Massachusetts Institute of Technology fed radioactive milk to a group of boys who had been led to believe that they were joining a 'science club.'"

As a result of such horrors, international treaties were signed on the proper treatment of patients in experimental situations. In the 1970s, this consolidated into the idea of informed consent. Patients' participation was supposed to be entirely voluntary and they were supposed to fully understand both the potential benefits as well as the risks of the procedure. Hospitals established Institutional Review Boards to review clinical trials from an ethical point of view and generally represent the interests of patients in this process.

According to a noted medical ethicist, Professor Robert J. Levine, MD, of Yale University, physicians are:

> "...ethically obligated to put the interests of the individual patient ahead of the interests of science and society,"

Oftentimes, however, the concept of informed consent is given mere lip service. Studies show, for instance, that often patients do not understand what they are signing. Only 52% of patients in one survey could name the drugs they were receiving. And a mere four out of 100 could name all the likely side effects of their treatment. Too often, informed consent is just a legal formality enacted between doctor and patient. Nurses have revealed that little attention is given to patients' views in this context, and still less work has explored the total experience of clinical trial participation from the patients' perspective.

According to Japanese doctors, informed consent should be a roundtable discussion of patients, families and physicians before fighting an incurable cancer. But it rarely is. The problem of human experimentation did not end with the implementation of informed consent. Abuses continue to happen. The FDA is supposed to monitor these situations, but is overwhelmed by the scale of the failure to obtain informed consent, the forgery of signatures on forms, and the failure to tell patients that a drug is experimental.

Here are some of the worst examples:

- In 1999, two-year-old Elyse MacEwen's parents allowed her to be enrolled in a clinical trial for a form of childhood cancer instead of getting the standard treatment of surgery plus chemotherapy. According to *U.S. News & World Report,* the parents were never informed of the conventional treatment and it was only after she finished her experimental therapy that they were asked to sign a consent form.

- The U.S. government suspended all government-funded research trials involving humans at Duke University Medical

Center, a top cancer hospital, because of lax safety oversight. Duke was barred from conducting such research for a year.

- The West Los Angeles Veterans Administration Healthcare Center was slapped with an unprecedented suspension order because of unsatisfactory safeguards for the hospital's human and animal research subjects. Days earlier, the NIH watchdog office had canceled the hospital's contract to perform human research.
- In 2000, the government suspended clinical trials at the University of Pennsylvania, after an 18-year-old patient died while undergoing experimental gene therapy.
- Also in 2000, researchers at St. Elizabeth's Medical Center in Boston failed to report the death of a patient in gene therapy experiments. Gene therapy might also have contributed to the growth of cancer in another patient, according to the FDA. The experiment was stopped, according to the *New York Times.*

Simply put, the U.S. government has sometimes done a poor job of monitoring abuses in clinical trials, while the major media, in general, has been uncritical of big medical interests. In 1,000 spot-checks the FDA found the following infractions:

- 213 researchers failed to obtain consent from subjects;
- 364 failed to stick to their approved research plan; and
- 140 did not report adverse reactions from test drugs.

According to a report in *U.S. News & World Report*, the National Institutes of Health (NIH) found that 50 institutions violated human subject protection laws in cancer trials alone. An internal audit found that, over a three-year period, one third of the 23,455 cases reviewed had noteworthy problems.

Despite intense pressure to get patients to join trials, the public remains skeptical about their usefulness and safety. Periodically, patient organizations, some financed by drug companies, have stepped up their efforts to recruit patients into clinical trials. They usually fail miserably.

According to a 2017 report from the Fred Hutchinson Cancer Research Center, Seattle:

> "In the end, only a small portion of adult cancer patients participate in trials, less than 5%, a rate that has remained fairly constant over decades."

In 2003, David F. Horrobin, MD, PhD, himself a founder of pharmaceutical companies, argued in *The Lancet* that enrolling cancer patients in large clinical trials in most cases was unethical. Dr. Horrobin, who himself died of cancer later that year, had been involved in biomedical research for decades. A dynamic figure in oncology, he taught at Oxford University and edited two biomedical journals. As he wrote in *The Lancet,*

> "I am thoroughly acquainted with the many important ethical and statistical issues that impinge on clinical trials."

Yet longstanding intellectual questions only became real to him when he himself was diagnosed with lymphoma. He wrote:

> "And so, I entered a universe parallel to the one in which I had lived for 30 years."

Suddenly, he was the patient with a terminal diagnosis and could now see everything from the other side.

But nothing indicates the cancer field's transition away from patient care towards profitability more than the disastrous high-dose chemotherapy fiasco of the 1980s and 1990s.

## Chapter 7. The high-dose chemo fiasco

**"Fifty years from now, we will look at this period with horror and say 'How could this have happened.'"**

*—Larry Norton, MD, Memorial Sloan-Kettering Cancer Center; President, American Society of Clinical Oncology, 1999*

In the early 1980s, top oncologists decided that it was time to radically increase the use of chemotherapy for breast cancer. Combination chemotherapy had been shown to be quite effective at preventing recurrences in earlier stage high-risk breast cancers. But the treatment of metastatic breast cancer remained an unsolved problem. So some ardent believers decided that, to quote a 1999 report in the *New York Times*,

> "If a little chemotherapy killed some of the cancerous cells in a woman's body, a lot might kill them all."

The use of high-dose chemotherapy for solid tumors of adults was based on the unproven theory that cancer drugs usually failed because they were not strong enough. Therefore, some doctors' idea was to administer enough of the toxic drugs to kill the patient, but then to bring her back from the brink of death with the reintroduction of her own preserved bone marrow. Technically, this procedure went by the ungainly name of "high-dose chemotherapy with autologous bone marrow transplant." This is usually called high-dose chemo. But the reader should remember that when this term is used in reference to breast cancer it refers to a painful and difficult treatment that began with the extraction of a quart or more of the patient's own bone marrow.

Up until that time, in stage IV breast cancers, even higher doses of chemo were not very effective. For example, the University of Toronto oncologist Ian Tannock, MD once compared two dose levels of a commonly used three-drug regimen in metastatic breast cancer. Patients who received the lower dose survived on average 12.8 months versus 15.6 months for those on the higher dose. But this 2.8 month benefit of increasing the dose, said Tannock, was of borderline significance. It probably could be accounted for by the rigorous inclusion and exclusion criteria for entrance into the trial.

The randomized controlled trial, the so-called jewel in the crown of clinical research, was first proposed by Sir Austin Bradford Hill in 1937. In 1962, it was mandated for all new FDA drug approvals.

But in the 1980s, many oncologists abandoned the gold standard of the randomized controlled trial based on transparently flawed calculations.

The decision to give this new treatment outside the system of clinical trials created one of the greatest scandals in American medical history. It wasted billions of dollars in health care dollars and led to the premature death of thousands of women, who had put their faith in their oncologists.

To be clear, this assault on the clinical trial system did not originate with any alternative medicine fringe group. It came from the mainstream community. In the course of the high dose chemo fiasco, four billion dollars flowed from desperate patients and their insurance companies to hospitals, the oncology profession and, ultimately, Big Pharma.

One could say the randomized controlled trial, which was so revered in theory, came into head-to-head conflict with free market capitalism. And capitalism won. Many oncologists and hospital administrators were involved in the program and sold false hope to gullible patients, with tragic results. And the FDA, the self-proclaimed guardian of public health, proved powerless to stop the high-dose chemo fiasco. American women by the thousands, encouraged by leading doctors, were directed away from ongoing clinical trials in favor of dubious treatments of limited efficacy. In the end they were fleeced of their money and their hope. Many of these doctors, it later emerged, were being financially compensated by a shadowy company that marketed the treatment *en masse* nationwide, before it went bust.

## High-level support

According to the *JNCI,* if high-dose chemo had been a new drug, the FDA would not have allowed it to be marketed before thorough testing. But all the drugs being used had already been approved. So high-dose chemo with bone marrow transplant was considered a procedure, not a drug, and procedures per se do not require FDA approval. So FDA did nothing. And that is how high-dose chemo evaded proper evaluation for about 15 years.

Emil Frei III, MD (1924-2013), first suggested the high-dose chemo procedure for women with advanced stage IV breast cancer. Frei was physician-in-chief of the Dana-Farber Cancer Institute in Boston, the hospital named after Sidney Farber, MD, who developed the first effective chemotherapy program.

From 1980 to 1981, Frei served as president of the American

Society of Clinical Oncology (ASCO), the highest honor that one's colleagues in the cancer field can bestow.

But in this promotional activity he was not alone. Soon, other past, present and future presidents of ASCO joined him in endorsing the high-dose approach to breast cancer. They included:

- James F. Holland, MD, of Mt. Sinai Medical School, president of ASCO (1976-1978)
- Vincent J. DeVita, MD, Yale University professor, former director of the National Cancer Institute, and president of ASCO (1978-1979)
- Gabriel N. Hortobagyi, MD, of the University of Texas M.D. Anderson Cancer Center, Houston, president of ASCO (1988-1989)
- George P. Canellos, MD, of Dana-Farber Cancer Center, president of ASCO (1993 to 1994)
- Karen Antman, MD, dean of Boston University Medical School, president of ASCO (1994 to 1995).

In December 1984, a young associate of Frei, William Peters, MD, PhD, of Duke University, moved from a small Phase I clinical trial to the next step, a somewhat larger Phase II trial. The treatment seemed to be doing well. But this was an illusion, a classic instance of what statisticians call selection bias. That was because only women who were healthier overall, or had already responded positively to the drugs in question, were eligible for the Phase II trial. This problem should have been obvious to otherwise accomplished scientists. But their enthusiasm overruled normal skepticism.

Mainly because of Dr. Peters, Duke became the national epicenter of high-dose chemo for breast cancer. Women would spend upwards of one month confined to a sterile room in the hospital. Because their immune systems had been wiped out, even a common cold encountered in the outside world could prove fatal.

Hospitals such as Duke generally charged between $80,000 and $100,000 per procedure (equal to $150,000 in 2020 dollars). This yielded a profit of between $20,000 and $40,000 per patient.

At the 1999 meeting of the American Society of Hematology, a Duke colleague of Dr. Peters, David A. Rizzieri, MD, claimed that high-dose chemo yielded a:

> "...40% complete remission rate among 425 women with metastatic breast cancer."

This sounded amazing to women who were otherwise given

a minuscule chance of success. He then analyzed survival among these alleged complete responders:

> "Among the subgroup of patients who responded, 16% were alive and still completely free of disease at the five-year mark (for an overall survival rate of 20%)."

This 20% figure reverberated throughout the media. But Rizzieri's claims were highly inflated. They were based on an obvious statistical flaw that was soon exposed in the *Journal of the National Cancer Institute (JNCI)*. In that article, Gabriel N. Hortobagyi, MD, once a high-dose chemo enthusiast, indicated his growing unease with the procedure. As he explained the statistical flaw:

> "If you have 100 patients and you have a treatment applicable to 20 of the 100, and 20% of those 20 are alive after 10 years, that's only a 4% absolute survival rate, not a 20% survival rate."

But most reporters at the time didn't want to hear caveats. Caveats don't sell newspapers. Instead, papers and airwaves were filled with accounts of heroic doctors who "hit the patients with all the anti-cancer drugs their systems could tolerate," who made "thrilling advances" and "major breakthroughs" that could render patients "cancer-clean."

Women with advanced breast cancer flocked to receive high-dose chemotherapy without final proof, according to the *JNCI*. With great difficulty, three U.S. randomized trials were eventually set up to test the concept, but there were few takers among the patients and these trials dragged on for years. Based on false hope, many were led to believe that high-dose chemo gave them a much better chance of living than any conventional treatment. So most patients refused to enter randomized controlled trials, where they might be consigned to the conventional treatment group, but instead demanded the supposed cure.

## Entrepreneurial oncology

In those days, there was a lot of money to be made from high-dose chemo, not just by the drug companies, but by hospitals, managed care groups, and oncologists running inpatient clinics as well. This led, in the 1980s and 1990s, to the new form of cancer care called entrepreneurial oncology. Essentially, this meant exploiting the business opportunities of cancer for a profit. Instead of a model of care based on relief of patients' suffering, it was based on the rapid enrichment of the doctor and hospital. This fit in perfectly with Ronald Reagan's greed is good philosophy.

Bone marrow transplantation, said Siddhartha Mukherjee, MD, in his Pulitzer prize winning book, *The Emperor of all Maladies* (2010), was "big business: big medicine, big money, big infrastructure, big risks." The authors of *False Hope,* the RAND Corporation report on high-dose chemo, agreed:

> "Oncology is big business.... Financial incentives drove both for-profit and not-for-profit cancer centers to promote the widespread use and rapid diffusion of the procedure."

Because of Reagan-era inspired cuts to Medicare, many hospitals were desperate for new profit centers. And giving high-dose chemo was highly profitable for American hospitals.

To be clear, this procedure could not be given at freestanding community oncology clinics. It could only be done in fully equipped, sterile, live-in hospitals, never on an outpatient basis. However, by the late 1980s, various cancer centers and hospitals in the United States had created transplant wards to administer high-dose chemo to women who sought it.

According to the *New York Times* (1999):

> "Private hospitals also joined in the fray. Some advertise heavily for patients and even pay for patients to travel there for the procedure.... But the academic medical centers...did not stand aside and let all the profits go elsewhere. By the early 1990s virtually every major medical center was offering bone marrow transplants for breast cancer patients and a growing number of community hospitals were offering them as well."

Some hospitals, such as Beth Israel Deaconess in Boston, had entire floors devoted to administering high-dose chemo with bone marrow transplantation:

> "At academic centers, bone marrow transplant programs quickly became 'the cash cow for the cancer service,' said William McGuire, a cancer specialist at Mercy Medical Center in Baltimore."

Even small hospitals took out big ads in newspapers to tout their programs. For example, in 1999, Mercy Health Partners of

Wilkes-Barre, Pennsylvania sponsored a newspaper advertorial called *House Calls.* In it, an oncology nurse advised patients to come to her hospital for high-dose chemo. The cancers treated included, of course, breast cancer, but also the equally unproven treatment of advanced ovarian cancer.

## Deaths from high-dose chemotherapy

The procedure was also quite dangerous. According to the *New York Times:*

> "Even though...pioneers at academic centers selected patients who were young and otherwise healthy, they could not save some from the terrible effects of the powerful anticancer drugs. Fifteen to 20% of the women in those early days died from the harsh drugs alone; others had permanent injuries, including hearing loss, nerve damage, and heart damage."

The total number of women who died is unknown, but in 1993 Dr. William Peters of Duke stated that therapy-related mortality was 12%. If we prorate that figure to the U.S. nationwide, it suggests that there were about 5,000 premature deaths caused by the procedure. Other estimates of the death toll go as high as 9,000.

What makes these figures difficult to comprehend is that the FDA acted vigorously when alternative practitioners seemingly endangered the public's health. For instance, laetrile (amygdalin) was a purported anticancer remedy made from cyanide-containing apricot kernels. When a single infant, Elizabeth Hankin, died in Buffalo, New York from the accidental ingestion of her father's laetrile pills, the FDA swung into action. It not only pilloried laetrile advocates, but put up warning posters in 36,000 U.S. post offices to alert the public to the alleged dangers of laetrile.

But when it came to high-dose chemo, the FDA sat on its hands. Could this be because laetrile emanated from so-called fringe practitioners espousing an unorthodox theory of cancer, while high-dose chemo came from the highest echelons of academic medicine?

## Role of the media

In 2003, the medical journalist Shannon Brownlee pointed to the role of the media in promoting the risky high-dose chemotherapy procedure. With refreshing candor, she acknowledged that there was scarcely a shred of evidence that high-dose chemo prolonged the life of any stage IV breast cancer patient over standard treatment. So why did so many patients think the opposite?

> "At least part of the treatment's popularity was due to the hundreds of articles and television segments that appeared in the 1990s.... I have looked at about 200 of them, and with a few notable exceptions, practically every story portrayed high-dose chemotherapy as an advanced breast cancer patient's only hope."

The mass media—including some medical reporters—and the oncology profession, were locked in a codependent relationship. The doctors and Big Pharma companies needed skilled writers to interpret science for the layperson and publicize new treatments. The writers needed cancer doctors for access to breaking news and for jobs and freelance assignments.

Many writers on the topic did include a warning that the procedure was technically unproven, since phase III clinical trials did not even begin until 1992. And some, to their credit, mentioned that it was risky. But, as Brownlee astutely noted in a *Washington Post* opinion piece:

> "The risk was part of the drama, and many breast cancer patients skipped right over the caveats about the lack of scientific evidence. The upshot was that we in the media helped sell a pricey, unproven, vile treatment to some of the most vulnerable readers imaginable."

## A split in oncology

The dispute over high-dose chemo split the world of oncology. Proponents included some of the biggest names in the field, as well as hospital directors, desperate patients, misguided activists, and compliant journalists. The insurance industry tried to deny coverage, but it was overwhelmed by a coalition of proponents. Ultimately, according to *Health Affairs* (2001):

> "Most health plans reluctantly agreed to cover the treatment in response to intensive political lobbying and the threat of litigation."

On the other side were government oncologists at the National

Cancer Institute and salaried academics, who were skeptical of what their more entrepreneurial colleagues were up to. These dissenters and their hospitals refused to profit by performing an untested and dangerous procedure. They insisted on rigorous clinical trials, although ironically, some of the centers that were participating in these trials were also offering high-dose chemo on a fee-for-service basis, thus undercutting their own scientists.

In 1996, Dr. Peters released the results of a clinical trial in which high-dose chemo appeared to extend survival. However, there were problems with this study. First, it was released as a brief Abstract at an ASCO meeting, and not as a proper peer-reviewed journal article that could be critiqued by scientists around the world. Second, it compared patients receiving high-dose chemo to others who were assigned to observation alone. It did not answer the key question, whether high-dose chemo was better than the standard chemotherapy of the time.

In the late 1990s, the results of a prospective, randomized trial of high-dose versus standard-dose chemo were published. As a result, the outlook went from guarded to bleak, to quote *Health Affairs*. The bottom line was summed up in a *New England Journal of Medicine* editorial:

> "This form of treatment for women with metastatic breast cancer has been proved to be ineffective and should be abandoned in favor of well-justified alternative approaches."

*Discover* magazine later asked a key question about this high-dose chemo fiasco:

> "How could so many oncologists ignore basic principles of science?"

In retrospect, we can see the reasons. For one thing, in the Reagan era, with so many cutbacks in funding of public institutions, American hospitals grew increasingly desperate for new sources of income:

> "The [high-dose chemo] treatment was a rare source of profit for hospitals…when they were being squeezed financially…. Many turned to Response Oncology, a company based in Memphis, Tennessee, that franchised bone marrow transplants. Company trainers would arrive at a hospital and, in two days, teach nurses and oncologists how to do the procedure. The company also helped

> hospitals build transplant wings and handle their insurance claims."

Response Oncology, trading on Wall Street, became a major force in pushing high-dose chemo to desperate patients. In 1998, it reported net revenue of $29.6 million. At one time, the company had more than 400 associated medical oncologists and a network of 28 wholly owned IMPACT centers, as well as 24 other centers across the country. In 2001, after high dose chemo collapsed, the company filed for chapter 11 protection; in 2002 it went out of business.

Under Response's business model, referring oncologists were each paid a fee for collecting data for studies involving different combinations and doses of approved chemotherapy drugs. And some studies were in fact done. But mainly Response Oncology was giving payments to doctors who recruited patients to take their treatment.

According to an online history of the company, the procedure was also used for a wide variety of other types of cancer. Some doctors became alarmed when these self-described entrepreneurial oncologists began to spread high-dose chemo to other types of cancer patients as well. To quote *Discover*:

> "Some began treating ovarian cancer with high-dose chemotherapy, too, although there was no evidence that it improved a patient's odds. Others subjected women with smaller, less-advanced breast tumors to high-dose chemo."

There were even proposals to use it in prostate cancer:

> "The doctors were silent until one pointed out that advanced prostate cancer rarely responds to chemotherapy, no matter how high the dose."

## The day of reckoning

The day of reckoning came in June 1999, 15 years after the saga had begun, when the results of four randomized clinical trials were presented at the annual meeting of the American Society of Clinical Oncology (ASCO) in Atlanta. Three major clinical trials were negative. But hard-core proponents clung to one small clinical trial. This was a positive study conducted by Werner R. Bezwoda, MD, a oncologist from Johannesburg, South Africa. Bezwoda was called "a magician known for curing late-stage breast cancer." In the face of the three negative American studies, he continued to make great claims for the procedure. He said that only 19 out of 75 advanced breast cancer patients receiving high-dose chemo had relapsed versus 52 out of 79 with conventional therapy.

As to mortality, Dr. Bezwoda claimed that, at the time of writing, just eight out of 75 high-dose chemo patients had died. But of the women who received conventional treatment, 28 of the 79 had died. That was 10.7% versus 35.4%, a three-fold difference.

To a growing number of skeptics, however, Bezwoda's numbers looked too good to be true, and they demanded further details. A team of American oncologists was dispatched to South Africa to examine the patient files, but they found a complete lack of follow-up and documentation. When confronted directly, Bezwoda could not verify his claims. In fact, it soon emerged that his work was fraudulent. In March 2001, he was formally dismissed from the University of Witwatersrand and drummed out of the profession.

Bezwoda certainly deserved severe criticism. But, that said, there followed a transparent attempt to shift the blame away from American shores and onto a single renegade foreigner. For example, Larry Norton, MD, ASCO's president-elect, was quoted as saying that the South African doctor had duped us all. This was as if many American oncologists had not initiated, promoted and profited from the fiasco, but had fallen victim to the South African "Wizard of Wit."

Dr. Bezwoda's clinical trial was characterized as "The Fraudulent Study That Killed Thousands of Breast Cancer Patients." This line reached the height of absurdity with the following statement by the ASCO leadership, as reported in the *Los Angeles Times:*

> "Dr. Werner Bezwoda has led thousands of women with breast cancer to undergo expensive, debilitating and often fatal bone marrow transplants."

But how could a single study from an obscure South African doctor have deceived hundreds of skilled, well-trained American oncologists for 15 years? Serious questions remained:

- What was the role of top American oncologists, including at least five presidents of ASCO, who championed high-dose chemo?
- What was the role of drug companies, which raked in hundreds of millions from the treatment?
- What was the responsibility of Response Oncology, with its 400 associated medical oncologists around the U.S.?

When asked why Dr. Bezwoda was allowed to present his claims at a huge plenary session of the ASCO meeting, John Durant, MD, the Society's executive vice president, had this to say:

> 'He misled us, he misled the public, he misled the people who are being treated. I am very, very distressed, and very angry."

Only a few reporters or historians dug deeper to reveal the roots of this tragedy in the greed of entrepreneurial oncology and Big Pharma.

Almost all of Dr. Bezwoda's patients were poor South African women.

## Chapter 8. Precision oncology

The current strategy for fighting cancer can be summed up in two words: precision oncology. This theory builds on 40 years of research into targeted therapies that are directed against particular genetic mutations in cancer.

In a sense, the first targeted drug was tamoxifen, since this worked on a particular subset of breast cancers, whose cells had receptors for the female hormone estrogen. Next came Herceptin in 1998. About 30% of breast cancers have an overexpression of the protein HER2. Herceptin acts like a small guided missile that target the receptors that fuel the growth of some breast tumors. It binds to HER2 and thereby slows down cell duplication.

In 2001, the FDA approved Gleevec, which was also designed to target a particular genetic mutation called the Philadelphia chromosome. Due in part to the use of Gleevec, the five-year survival rate for chronic myelogenous leukemia patients increased from 31% in 1993 to 59% in 2009.

On May 28, 2001, *Time* magazine featured Gleevec on its cover, with this headline:

> "There is new ammunition in the war against cancer.
> These are the bullets. Is this the breakthrough
> we've been waiting for?"

In a way, cancer treatment today is still inspired by those dramatic events of two decades ago. The underlying idea behind many new cancer drugs is still to identify a key mutation and then to create a drug that precisely targets it. Not surprisingly, Gleevec received extraordinary media coverage. As the *Fortune* editor, Clifton Leaf wrote in his book, *The Truth in Small Doses,* many oncologists not only hailed Gleevec as a genuine breakthrough, but saw it as a model for cancer therapy in the generation to come.

The current idea is to target the key mutations in a tumor, in order to wipe out these different genetic changes with a combination of drugs. This is more than some vague theory. It is in fact the official policy of the United States government.

### 21st Century Cures Act

In his 2015 State of the Union address, President Obama put the resources of the U.S. government behind this genetic approach to cancer. To the applause of almost the entire Congress, he announced the launch of a $215 million Precision Medicine Initiative, whose stated goal was to accelerate genetically-based medicine.

President Obama provided the rationale for this initiative:

> "Advances in precision medicine have already led to powerful new discoveries and several new treatments that are tailored to specific characteristics, such as a person's genetic makeup, or the genetic profile of an individual's tumor. This is helping transform the way we can treat diseases such as cancer.
>
> "Patients with breast, lung, and colorectal cancers, as well as melanomas and leukemias, for instance, routinely undergo molecular testing as part of patient care, enabling physicians to select treatments that improve chances of survival and reduce exposure to adverse effects."

President Obama implied that these new treatments would extend overall survival and reduce side effects. His announcement was followed on December 13, 2016 by swift passage of the 21st Century Cures Act. In a Congress notorious for party divisions, the vote in the Senate was almost unanimous: 94 to 5 (with one member not voting).

While this massive health reform law, as it was called, had many provisions, one of its main ones was this:

> "The approximately $6.8 billion bill will fund major federal initiatives like Vice President Joe Biden's Cancer Moonshot program and the Obama administration's Precision Medicine Initiative."

But, according to Sy Mukherjee of *Fortune* magazine, the bill's most ardent supporter was Big Pharma. In fact, according to *National Public Radio,* during the Congressional deliberations:

> "More than 1,300 lobbyists roamed the halls of Congress on the 21st Century Cures Act, and disclosure reports show most of them were working for pharmaceutical companies."

On the other hand, the bill was opposed by some consumer organizations, where it was seen as an end run around the FDA's once-rigorous clinical trial system. Only Bernie Sanders, the independent Senator from Vermont, and a few others, called the bill what it was, another giant Big Pharma deception:

> "At a time when Americans pay, by far, the highest prices in the world for prescription drugs, this bill provides absolutely no relief for soaring drug prices. The greed of the pharmaceutical industry has no limit, and this bill includes numerous corporate giveaways that will make drug companies even richer.... It's time for Congress to stand up to the world's biggest pharmaceutical companies, not give them more handouts."

In the end, though, the vast majority of both Democrats and Republicans aligned themselves with the wishes of the drug lobby and big corporate donors. Behind all the favorable publicity about precision medicine, the bill further weakened the FDA's once rigorous evaluation system and made it easier for companies to speed their high-priced medicines to market.

But where are these new cures supposed to come from? Instead of large and rigorous clinical trials, which might establish that a particular treatment conveys an increase in overall survival, there

Senator Bernard Sanders of Vermont has consistently opposed bills that promote Big Pharma's greed and corruption.
Photo by Gage Skidmore

are very small trials, subsections that involve just a few patients, providing hints from various combinations of new and unproven treatments.

There are several major flaws in this approach. Cancer is just a common name for over 100 different diseases. Thus, in an answer to the question, "What is cancer?" the American Cancer Society states:

> "There are many types of cancer. It's not just one disease. Cancer can start in the lungs, breast, colon, or even in the blood. Cancers are alike in some ways, but they are different in the ways they grow and spread."

Clinical trials are traditionally performed on a particular type and stage of cancer. In a randomized controlled trial, it usually takes about 300 patients with the same characteristics to yield a statistically meaningful result. As the genomic revolution progresses, however, the diagnostic categories narrow. Thus, it is common to direct the treatment under study to patients with a particular configuration of mutations or cell surface markers.

## Driver Mutations

According to a 2019 journal article:

> "A driver mutation is an alteration that gives a cancer cell a fundamental growth advantage for its neoplastic transformation [malignant growth]. It differs from passenger mutations in that these do not necessarily determine the development of the cancer."

Tumors having a single driver mutation are not common. According to a 2018 study in the *Proceedings of the National Academy of Sciences,* about 27% of tumors are linked to a specific driver mutation. But the remaining 73% have a more diffuse pattern of mutations, without any clear link between a single mutated gene and the tumor.

So in three-quarters of the cancers studied, there are multiple mutations, and not a solitary driver. And to complicate matters, there is a great deal of disagreement among scientists over what distinguishes driver from passenger mutations.

As the same NIH authors wrote:

> "Distinguishing driver mutations from passenger ones poses a formidable challenge.... The number of driver mutations required for the onset of cancer is...a fundamental question that remains a matter of debate."

Presumably, though, each and every driver mutation will need to be targeted by a drug that is specifically designed to correspond to that genetic variant or its product. The NIH authors compiled a list of 198 cancer genes. But even they say that this is on the low side, since recent studies have extended the list of cancer genes beyond those included in their own network. In a footnote, they make reference to an extended set of 369 known cancer genes. So we may be talking about several hundred driver mutations requiring drugs for their treatment. And the list continues to grow.

A review of COSMIC, a database of cancer mutations maintained by the Wellcome Trust in Cambridge, U.K., is sobering. In *Science* magazine they explained the following:

> "The rates of different mutational processes vary among tumors and cancer types. Though numbers vary widely, most cancers carry 1,000 to 20,000 somatic point mutations and a few to hundreds of insertions, deletions, and rearrangements."

## Next Gen Sequencing

Starting in 2011, with the rise of relatively inexpensive next generation sequencing, it became possible to decipher the entire genome of an individual's cancer. But this proved to be a mixed blessing, since it revealed a picture of almost unimaginable complexity.

To quote from a 2012 article at *Bloomberg News*:

> "When analyzed at the molecular level, a cancer that has traditionally been viewed as a single disease commonly fragments into many different subtypes, each possibly requiring a different treatment."

According to Vanesa Martinez, PhD, of the Technological University of Dublin (2018):

> "Cancer could…be thousands of different diseases. What's more, cancer could be thousands of different diseases within the same person. Welcome to the cancer ecosystem."

Sir Michael Stratton, head of the Cancer Genome Project, Cambridge, U.K., added:

> "Approximately 100,000 somatic mutations from cancer genomes have been reported in the quarter of a century since the first somatic mutation was

> found.... Over the next few years several hundred million more will be revealed by large-scale, complete sequencing of cancer genomes."

To quote the NCI article on the genetics of cancer:

> "Each person's cancer has a unique combination of genetic alterations. Some of these changes may be the result of cancer, rather than the cause. As the cancer continues to grow, additional changes will occur. Even within the same tumor, cancer cells may have different genetic changes."

The implications of this for drug companies is staggering. The cost of developing a new drug is currently estimated at between $648 million and $2.7 billion per drug. That cost, plus the company's profit margin, is usually spread out over a large number of patients. For previous blockbuster drugs, the right patients are numerous and easily identifiable. So, in the past, a new cancer drug could reach a fairly large portion of the patient population. For example, the HER2 mutation, which was the molecular target of Roche's drug, Herceptin, affects about 25% of breast cancer cases. Since one year of treatment witih Herceptin costs $70,000 per patient, there is a potential market of billions of dollars. And in fact, Herceptin has largely fulfilled its potential: it was Roche's top-selling drug in 2018, posting annual sales of almost $7 billion worldwide.

But, as drugs become increasingly focused on relatively rare mutations, the size of the market necessarily shrinks. For example, Xalkori targets a mutation that only affects 4% to 5% of non-small cell lung cancer patients. And the 2018 revenue from that drug was, predictably, only one-twelfth that of Herceptin, or about $500 million per year.

Each time scientists more precisely target a tumor's unique set of mutations, the market for that particular configuration shrinks even further. New medicines may be increasingly precise. But drug companies also find it increasingly difficult to come up with enough paying customers to make up for the ever escalating cost of development. Hence, their frantic demand that the government shoulder almost all the expenses of creating new cancer drugs.

## The wrong targets

In 2019 it was shown that there was a fatal flaw in some of the targeted drugs. Some targeted anticancer drugs never actually interact with their intended targets. According to a groundbreaking paper in *Science Translational Medicine,* drug developers have been directing targeted agents at irrelevant molecular targets.

The proposed mechanism of action was incorrect, is how the paper's senior author, Jason M. Sheltzer, PhD, of Cold Spring Harbor Laboratories, New York, succinctly summarized this astonishing finding. Sheltzer is a winner of the Presidential Early Career Award for Scientists and Engineering. He and other young scientists used a revolutionary genome editing tool called CRISPR, which is more precise, faster and cheaper than the older method.

Removing the drug's molecular target with CRISPR should have deactivated the drug in question. But, instead, the drug continued to kill cancer cells at the same rate as before. As Dr. Sheltzer told *Science,* "the cancer cells did not care whatsoever" that their supposedly essential target was now gone. As the paper put it:

> "The proteins ostensibly targeted by these drugs are nonessential for cancer cell proliferation. Moreover, the efficacy of each drug that we tested was unaffected by the loss of its putative target."

The Cold Spring researchers CRISPR-ed a total of ten targeted drugs in succession, seven of which were already in clinical trials. In each and every case, knocking out the DNA of the supposed target made no difference to the effectiveness of the drug. As veteran science writer Sharon Begley wrote at STAT News:

> "More than 180 previous studies had identified [those targets] as essential in various forms of cancer.... But in DNA-knockout after DNA-knockout...the cancer cells kept on [growing] despite the lack of an 'essential' protein. It was like a car from which the carburetor had been stolen speeding down the highway unfazed."

The researchers showed, in the words of a *Science* commentary, that the drugs thwart cancer by interacting with different molecules than intended. What got Dr. Sheltzer thinking about this topic was the fact that 93% of targeted drugs fail in clinical trials and never make it to market. A detailed analysis from Massachusetts Institute of Technology (MIT) scientists, in the journal *Biostatistics* (2019), showed that, on average, new cancer drugs have an astonishingly low 3.4% success rate of obtaining FDA approval. The MIT authors called that success rate dismal.

Sheltzer's CRISPR findings have the potential to upset the prevailing dogma of oncology, which is called the somatic mutation theory. According to this theory, cancer begins with a genetic change in a single cell that passes it on to its progeny, thereby generating a clone of malignant cells. Dr. David L. Vaux's article "In Defense of the Somatic Mutation Theory," claims:

> "...the strongest validation of the Somatic Mutation Theory comes from the successful treatment of certain malignancies with drugs that directly target the product of the mutant gene."

That being the case, disputing the link between the targeted agent and its supposed target not only undermines that particular drug, but questions the entire theory behind their usage.

## The case of Xalkori

One of the drugs that treats a genetically defined type of lung cancer is Pfizer's Xalkori. Xalkori's clinical trial history illustrates many of the problems that are associated with this new class of precision cancer drugs. Xalkori is directed at the five percent or so of non-small cell lung cancer patients whose cells have what is called an ALK mutation. In medical jargon, they are ALK-positive. In 2011, FDA approved Xalkori to treat this subset of lung cancer patients.

In fact, the FDA advisory board was so excited by the trial results that it approved Xalkori five weeks ahead of schedule. According to Mace Rothenberg, MD, the former Vanderbilt oncology professor who became Pfizer's vice president for cancer in 2008:

> "Xalkori represents a new chapter in personalized medicine for lung cancer, enabling physicians to prescribe the right treatment for the right patient."

## Xalkori clinical trial

FDA's approval was based on two clinical trials. The larger of these was conducted at the famous Massachusetts General Hospital in Boston. "Mass General" is among the oldest and most celebrated hospitals in America. It is the largest teaching hospital of Harvard Medical School. Mass General physicians are frequently faculty members at Harvard Medical School and their papers are often published in the *New England Journal of Medicine.* It is rated number two on the *U.S. News* Best Hospitals Honor Roll.

For the Xalkori trial, Mass General doctors screened 1,500 patients with advanced lung cancer and ultimately recruited 136 whose cells were ALK-positive.

These patients were younger non-smokers with adenocarcinomas, as opposed to other cancer cell types. This automatically predicted a longer-than-average survival. So the Mass General doctors were dealing with a population likely to respond well to treatment. The doctors established many reasons to exclude patients from their trial.

One of these was if they had "any concurrent or uncontrolled illness." This is a common requirement in clinical trials, but it excludes a goodly portion of the patient population. That is because, in the real world, 6 in 10 American adults have a chronic disease and 4 in 10 have two or more. On that basis, about half the population could have been excluded from the trial.

In the end, 57% of the patients in the Mass General trial had an objective response to Xalkori. An objective response means a shrinkage of measurable tumors.

In actuality, only one patient out of the 136 trial participants had a complete response. The rest had partial responses, which are defined as a 30% or greater decrease in the measurable cancer burden.

We do not know what impact, if any, these partial tumor shrinkages had on the length of the patients' overall survival or their quality of life. Since this was not a randomized trial, there was no way of knowing what percentage of patients would have had the same, or better, outcomes had they been given a more standard treatment, or no treatment at all.

## Mild side effects?

But what really stood out, and convinced many people of Xalkori's excellence, was this statement in the paper's Abstract:

> "[Xalkori] resulted in grade 1 or 2 (mild) gastrointestinal side effects."

A grade 1 side effect is mild and transient; grade 2 is moderate; grade 3 is severe; grade 4 is life-threatening; and grade 5 is fatal. In giving its approval, the FDA noted many potential side effects, including double vision and lung inflammation, which it said could be life-threatening.

But in the paper's Abstract, the Mass General authors reported no serious, much less life-threatening, adverse events. To a world weary of the side effects of toxic chemotherapy, the mildness of the new targeted agents such as Xalkori was welcome news indeed. Or, as five oncologists wrote shortly thereafter:

> "Xalkori is relatively non-toxic. It is a triumph for a targeted therapy."

Another prominent oncologist told the Associated Press that Xalkori and similar drugs:

> "...are far superior to chemotherapy and...in many cases cause...tumors to melt away with few side effects."

On the basis of such claims, with public anticipation at a high pitch, Pfizer, whose Chief Executive Officer made $27.9 million in 2018, priced the little red pill at $17,000 per month, or $211,000 per year. It was in part because of the Massachusetts General clinical trial that Xalkori was so quickly approved, and sales boomed. In 2017 Xalkori earned Pfizer $594 million. And, according to *Forbes:*

> "Xalkori could potentially generate $1 billion in annual sales...."

In granting accelerated approval, the FDA ignored one simple fact: Pfizer had not proven that the drug actually extended overall survival or improved the quality of life of the patients involved.

## Along came ALEX

Then, six years after publication of the Mass General trial, conflicting data emerged. This was a study named ALEX, a more rigorous randomized controlled trial, one of whose arms was administration of the drug Xalkori. The purpose of the ALEX trial was to compare Xalkori to a competing drug from Roche called Alecensa.

The ALEX authors employed the same dose of Xalkori as the Mass General scientists. They concluded that Alecensa was more effective than Xalkori. (The trial was sponsored by Roche.) But let us keep our eye on what ALEX revealed about Xalkori.

During a follow-up of 17.6 months, disease progression or death occurred in 68% of the Xalkori-treated patients. In addition, by that point, there was central nervous system progression, such as brain metastases, in 45% of the Xalkori patients. But most striking of all was the dramatically different picture of the drug's side effects in the ALEX trial. The Mass General authors had stated that Xalkori resulted in grade 1 or 2 (mild) gastrointestinal side effects. In the full paper, they broke down these side effects by grade. While mild grade 1 side effects were common, they reported only five instances of moderate grade 2 side effects, and no instances of serious to severe grades 3 or 4. But in the 2017 ALEX trial, there were adverse events of some kind in 97% of the Xalkori patients. In addition, there were serious side effects in half the patients. The most common were nausea (48%), diarrhea (45%) and vomiting (38%). And these adverse reactions were actually fatal (grade 5) in 7 patients, which was 5% of the total. Yet it was in part some of the Mass General doctors' claims about mild side effects of Xalkori that had preceded FDA's rapid approval of the drug, and of media reports of a new non-toxic wonder drug.

There were many links between Pfizer and the doctors performing the Mass General study:

- Pfizer paid for the study at Mass General. This is a common practice and such trials often earn considerable money for hospitals.
- The study was designed jointly by representatives of Pfizer and the investigators.
- Data were collected from the academic sites and analyzed by representatives of Pfizer.
- Two of the paper's authors were Pfizer employees, four were its paid consultants or advisors, two owned Pfizer stock, and two more were recipients of research funding and honoraria, a form of cash payment.

Xalkori was swiftly recommended for approval by the FDA's powerful Oncology Drug Advisory Committee (ODAC). Its members at that time included noted medical oncologist Deborah K. Armstrong, MD, of Johns Hopkins University. Dr. Armstrong has disclosed performing contracted research for five drug companies, including Pfizer. According to Open Payments, her personal payments from Big Pharma for the years 2013-2018 came to about $19,000, while her associated research funding was about $470,000.

At the present time, three of the most influential members of ODAC are also Pfizer consultants. They include Alice T. Shaw, MD, who was one of the key authors of the Mass General paper on Xalkori. According to Open Payments, Dr. Shaw's associated research funding from drug companies came to about $9.5 million, of which $4 million came from Pfizer.

When it came time for publication, the Mass General authors

drew a portrait of Xalkori as both highly effective and without serious toxicity. This was followed by its publication in the *New England Journal of Medicine* and swift approval by the FDA. This rapid approval was worth many millions of dollars in sales to Pfizer.

One wonders, however, if the FDA would have been quite so quick to approve Xalkori had the Mass General paper concluded that, instead of a few mild GI effects, 50% of the Xalkori-treated patients would have serious-to-severe side effects. Or that 5% of them would actually die from the treatment itself, as happened in the later ALEX trial.

## Testing everyone

The precondition for precision oncology is to test the cancer patient population to identify targetable mutations. This can be done, but for a cost. One representative testing firm is Foundation Medicine, a division of Roche. At this writing, their charge for sequencing 324 cancer-related mutations is $5,800 per patient, of which Medicare reimburses $3,000. Since there are about 1.8 million new cancer cases in the U.S. each year, the annual price tag for sequencing every new cancer patient's DNA at this rate would come to over $10 billion. As things stand, Medicare or private insurance would pay for about half of that. But Americans without very good supplemental insurance would collectively be on the line for billions in new charges.

Americans collectively would have to spend on genetic analysis an amount greater than the annual budgets of the National Cancer Institute, the American Cancer Society, and half a dozen other cancer organizations combined. This is good news for companies such as Foundation Medicine and Roche, but not so good for the average consumer. It would be impossible for most Americans, especially the multitude living paycheck to paycheck, to come up with an extra $3,000 to perform this sort of testing.

## Providing the drugs

How much would it cost to develop all the new targeted drugs necessary to implement this strategy? Estimates vary greatly. Profs. Prasad and Mailankody estimate $648 million per drug. A high-end estimate from the Tufts Center for the Study of Drug Development is $2.7 billion to develop each new drug. Using the conservative $648 million figure, the cost of developing 160 new drugs (for just half of the most prominent mutations) would be over $100 billion.

That is more than the entire worldwide cancer drug market, which in 2017 came to $97.4 billion. As new mutations emerged, new drugs would have to be quickly developed.

Clearly, such new charges are beyond the reach of any country, including the United States. A strategy of fighting cancer in this way is not feasible, even for the wealthiest people in the richest country in the world.

In 2012, Dr. Leonard Saltz and two Memorial Sloan-Kettering Cancer Center colleagues, Drs. Peter Bach and Robert E. Wittes, led a brief rebellion against this state of affairs. They announced in a *New York Times* article that they were refusing to prescribe a new drug, Zaltrap, to their patients. That was because Zaltrap was no more effective than a previously approved drug, but twice as expensive. They pointed out that FDA was legally forbidden from taking price into consideration of approval, which in the case of Zaltrap was $11,000 per month. The three MSKCC authors wrote on behalf of their hospital:

> "Ignoring the cost of care, though, is no longer tenable. Soaring spending has presented the medical community with a new obligation. When choosing treatments for a patient, we have to consider the financial strains they may cause alongside the benefits they might deliver."

## Avastin and brain cancer

As we have shown in the case of Xalkori, one of the key features of precision medicine is the use of genetic markers to predict who will respond to a particular treatment, and who will not. But this process is far trickier than the average person realizes. For one thing, sometimes there is no rhyme or reason to why a particular person responds to a drug, while others do not. Take the case of Avastin. In early trials of the drug in the aggressive type of brain cancer known as glioblastoma multiforme, Avastin increased progression-free survival. But when it was subjected to a full-scale randomized trial, it did not extend the crucial overall survival of the treatment group.

As sometimes happens with cancer drugs, though, it appeared to have extended survival of a few patients, but it was impossible to predict who would respond. As the editor of *Fortune* magazine, Clifton Leaf, who is himself a cancer survivor, wrote in a 2013 *New York Times* op-ed:

> "Even after some 400 completed clinical trials in various cancers, it's not clear why Avastin works (or doesn't work) in any single patient. 'Despite looking at hundreds of potential predictive biomarkers, we do not currently have a way to predict who is most likely to respond to Avastin and who is not,' says a spokesperson for Genentech, a division of the Swiss pharmaceutical giant Roche, which makes the drug."

Precision oncology is all about prescribing the right medicine for the right patient. But it is simplistic to think that one can simply match up a genetic marker with a drug and reliably make cancers regress or patients live longer. That will not stop oncologists from continuing to test this idea, or desperate patients from volunteering for this sort of trial. Precision oncology has already been tested several times, and will be tested in the future. Indeed, precision oncology is more than just a theory. It is therefore vital that we pay close attention to the results that have been achieved so far.

## I-SPY trial

The I-SPY trial is an ongoing test of precision oncology as applied to breast cancer. I-SPY is a phase 2 trial in high risk breast cancer patients. It uses a unique trial design combining numerous small trials to evaluate new treatments. These are added to standard chemotherapy in various kinds of breast cancer.

Clinicaltrials.gov presently lists four cancer trials under the heading I-SPY. One of these has been completed, two are active but not recruiting, and one is currently recruiting patients. None has yet posted results there. So it is difficult to say that anything has been achieved so far to indicate that this approach increases patients' overall survival.

One of the drugs being tested in I-SPY is ganetespib, a product of Synta Pharmaceutical Co. The goal of the ganetespib trial was to see if it increased overall survival when added to conventional treatment. In the treatment of lung cancer, according to a 2017 report to the American Society of Clinical Oncology annual meeting, the overall response rate of ganetespib and the standard chemotherapy drug Taxotere was 13.7%, compared to 16% with Taxotere alone. What this means is that adding the targeted agent ganetespib to chemo slightly *lowered* the response rate. More importantly, the median overall survival was 10.9 months in the combination arm and 10.5 months in the Taxotere arm. This represented a difference of 12 days, which was not statistically significant.

The median progression-free survival with Taxotere alone was 4.3 months versus 4.2 months in the combination arm, a non-significant difference of 3 days. As a result of this failure, the small company that owned ganetespib went into a tailspin and plunged into penny-stock territory, until it was bought out by a large biotech company.

## The SHIVA trial

The French SHIVA trial was published in 2015 in *Lancet Oncology.* Oncologists enrolled 741 patients at eight hospitals. All of these patients had identifiable and targetable mutations. The authors:

> "...only included patients for whom a molecular alteration was identified within one of three molecular pathways...which could be matched to one of ten regimens of molecularly targeted agents...."

Half of the patients received standard chemo, while the other half received drugs designed to target their particular tumor's individual mutations.

The main endpoint was progression-free survival. In the group that got the targeted agent the progression-free survival was 2.3 months versus 2.0 months in the chemo group. This equalled a gain of nine days and was not statistically significant. But at the same time there were the same or more severe to life-threatening side effects in the precision medicine group than in the chemo group:

> "...43% of 100 patients treated with a molecularly targeted agent and 35% of 91 patients treated with cytotoxic chemotherapy had grade 3-4 adverse events."

Not long ago, scientists were enthusing about how precision medicine would minimize harmful side effects and guarantee a more successful result. These results come up far short of that.

## NCI-MATCH trial

NCI-MATCH is actually a large number of small clinical trials under a single umbrella. Each one of these small trials consists at most of 35 patients who share a single mutated gene in their tumors. But there was bad news in store for proponents of precision

medicine. The largest study of this concept was announced at the annual meeting of ASCO in 2015. This was, and is, the National Cancer Institute's Molecular Analysis for Therapy Choice trial, or NCI-MATCH for short. This trial is taking place at an extraordinary 1,173 separate medical sites across the U.S.
According to NCI officials, this trial:

> "...would probably cost $30 million to $40 million for the first stages of NCI-MATCH and...the budget could expand by 15% to 20% as more drugs are added to the list of agents tested."

The goal of this giant convoluted trial is to determine whether targeted therapies for specific gene mutations will lead to objective responses, according to an article in *JAMA Oncology.*

Both established drugs and new investigational items are included in this ongoing trial. Results from various arms of the trial were first presented at the 2017 meeting of the Society for Immunotherapy of Cancer, the 2018 annual meeting of the American Society of Clinical Oncology, and again at their 2019 meeting.

This ongoing trial is unlike most previous clinical trials. It encompasses 40 separate substudies, or specific treatment arms. Each substudy is designed to ultimately include 35 patients apiece, whose tumors have a specific genetic alteration. But what is unique is that each substudy will be defined purely by its characteristic mutations. Each group will include various tumor types, stages and anatomical locations, which is the more traditional way of grouping patients in a clinical trial.

As of 2018, 6,000 patients had their tumors analyzed for genetic mutations and were ready to participate in one or another arm of the NCI-MATCH trial, again depending on their tumor's key mutations, and not its anatomical location in the breast, lung, colon, etc. The primary endpoint of NCI-MATCH is the objective response rate. This is the tumor shrinkage rate, and not a measure of actual patient benefit. So further studies would be needed to confirm the results of these small, preliminary trials.

## The first results

At the 2018 ASCO meeting, scientists reported on the first three substudies, or treatment arms. Each was designed to have at least 35 patients, which is small for a phase II trial. Being a small phase II trial, no meaningful results could be generated about survival. The patients in this subset had tumors with one of three genetic mutations. Each patient was treated with an established drug that was known to target one or another of these specific mutations.

In the first substudy, the authors reported that nobody had a complete response, but 3 out of 37 patients (8.1%) had a partial response to the drug that targeted their particular mutation. An additional 43% had what was considered stable disease. The median duration of stabilization was 4.6 months. In a commentary in *Lancet Oncology* on this small trial, called "Is Precision Medicine an Oxymoron," two oncologists warned:

> "This finding [on stabilization] should be interpreted with caution because these were nonrandomized trials with patients with widely disparate prior therapy."

The second NCI-MATCH study concerned patients whose tumors were positive for a certain receptor and were therefore treated with a different experimental drug.

Two out of 41 patients (5%) had some tumor shrinkage but 39 out of the original 49 patients developed side effects from the treatment, half of which were severe or life-threatening:

> "Common adverse events were fatigue, anorexia, dry mouth, nausea/vomiting, diarrhea, constipation, mouth sores [oral mucositis], anemia and liver function test abnormality."

It is likely that 5% partial responses in a highly targeted drug population would never have passed muster in any previous trial.

Finally, in the third NCI-MATCH trial, 65 patients, all of whom had tumors with the same mutation, were given an experimental drug taselisib, developed by Roche. The mutation in question occurs in about 15% to 30% of breast, endometrial, and colon cancer patients. But the 65 patients in this small trial spanned 45 separate tumor locations or types. This trial achieved an objective response rate of *zero*. The scientists claimed that 27% of these patients had a progression-free survival of six or more months. But just two patients remained on the study at the one year mark:

> "The most common toxicities were fatigue (38%), diarrhea (38%) and nausea (34%), all predominately grade 1-2, with 2% of [patients] requiring dose reductions, and 11% discontinuing taselisib because of toxicity."

Incidentally, this was the drug whose over-promotion led to the downfall of Dr. José Baselga at Memorial Sloan-Kettering Cancer Center. After these dismal results, Roche pulled the plug, not just on taselisib but on a whole class of similar drugs, because of what the company called the "poor survival edge and harsh side effects for breast cancer."

So the results of the first three NCI-MATCH small trials were dismal. Despite this, here is how NCI reported these results in 2018:

> "The NCI-MATCH trial, the largest precision medicine trial of its kind, has achieved a milestone with the release of results from several treatment arms, or substudies, of the trial. NCI-MATCH precision medicine clinical trial...strengthens the path forward for targeted cancer therapies."

## The 2019 ASCO meeting

Further results from the NCI-MATCH trial were presented at the 2019 ASCO annual meeting. But because of the previous poor results, mainstream science journalists seem to have lost interest in the topic, perhaps awaiting a more newsworthy outcome. There were a few reports on Arm H of the trial. In this particular subgroup, patients received a combination of two targeted drugs. The primary goal was the response rate, in other words, tumor shrinkages. Secondary goals were progression-free survival and overall survival.

Over a two-year period, a total of 33 patients were evaluated. The overall response rate was 33.3%. In other words, one third of the patients had a shrinkage of their tumors by 30% or more. The median duration of this response was 12 months. As with the other small trials, this trial included patients with many distinct tumor types—17 to be exact. The median progression-free survival was 11.4 months and the median overall survival was 28.8 months.

Meanwhile, frequent side effects included fatigue, a low neutrophil blood count, a low level of sodium or phosphorus in the blood, and urinary tract infections. There was one case of life-threatening sepsis caused by the body's extreme response to an infection. But, according to the authors, this drug combination showed promising activity, warranting further investigations.

A few writers even claimed that these results proved that the precision medicine approach was effective in rare cancers. But since this was not a randomized trial, one cannot say whether these results were better, the same, or worse than with other treatments. It is true that the trial met its primary outcome, which was a

33% response rate. But that seems an arbitrary number, and does not prove that these patients fared any better than patients receiving a different treatment pathway.

## Lighting the NCI-MATCH

Many people consider precision medicine to be the future of cancer treatment. Enabling physicians to prescribe the right medicine for the right patient, as Dr. Mace Rothenberg put it, is a very attractive idea. But, in practice, it faces innumerable obstacles. COSMIC contains a list of many kinds of mutations that can allegedly cause cancer. These include a dozen different categories. Under the heading of somatic mutations alone, there are presently 536, listed from A to Z. And the number keeps increasing as new ones are discovered and added to the catalogue.

We can leave it to cancer geneticists to explore and explain the complexities of genetic mutations in cancer. But for the layperson the takeaway message seems pretty simple: most cancers are very, very complex at the genetic level. So controlling them at that level would take many more drugs than currently exist. Even if they did successfully attack each and every mutation in a cancer, which is difficult to do, the tumor might quickly revive, as Professor James D. Watson suggested in 2009:

> "Given the inherent genetic instability of most cancer cells, the use of drugs acting against single drivers [mutations] would all too soon lead to the emergence of genetic variants driven by increasingly destructive second, if not third, drivers."

Paradoxically, the rush towards precision medicine is also undermining the clinical trials system. The more precisely one identifies and targets a patient's mutations, the more difficult it becomes to assemble a large group whose tumors have an identical genetic signature. Finding another patient with the same exact mutations would be extremely lucky. But how are they going to find 100, 200 or more patients with an identical cancer genome? Because that is what one needs for an effective clinical trial.

## Why doesn't precision medicine work better?

At a time of general enthusiasm for targeted drugs, Professor Watson's warning was all but ignored. A few years later he was joined in his criticisms by another expert in genetics, Sir Michael R. Stratton,

MD. Stratton was the founder of the Cancer Genome Project at Cambridge University, U.K., and the author of 270 PubMed articles on the topic of cancer. As late as 2009, Professor Stratton reaffirmed his belief that "all cancers arise as a result of changes that have occurred in the DNA sequence of the genomes of cancer cells." He wrote about the bright future of precision medicine:

> "We are moving into an era in which it will be possible to obtain the complete DNA sequence of large numbers of cancer genomes. These studies will provide us with a detailed and comprehensive perspective on how individual cancers have developed."

To further that goal, by 2012, Professor Stratton and his Cambridge colleagues had successfully analyzed the genetic profile of 100 human breast cancer samples. They then compared these to the genome of normal cells. Their goal was to identify the specific mutations that were causing each woman's cancer, thereby setting the stage for her cure.

But what they found was profoundly upsetting. Most breast cancers did not have one, or even a few, abnormal genes, as they had expected. There were in fact dozens of them. And many of these were considered driver mutations, which presumably confer a selective growth advantage and thus promote cancer's development.

Multiple mutations increase the tumor's ability to survive and reproduce itself. In addition, many cells have additional passenger mutations, which are of uncertain significance, but might also confer a survival advantage to the cancer. Among these 100 analyzed tumors, Professor Stratton and 75 Cambridge colleagues found driver mutations in at least 40 cancer genes and 73 different combinations of mutated cancer genes.

These results, they wrote, highlight the substantial genetic diversity underlying this common disease. In other words, cancer cells were not stable entities with one or two driver mutations, which could be effectively targeted.

They were more like a crazy quilt of genetic mutations. In sum, the Cambridge researchers found "a panorama of mutated cancer genes and mutational processes in breast cancer." They added that it yielded "a sobering perspective on the complexity and diversity of the disease."

## Need for 40 drugs?

The belief of the previous decade was now yielding to a daunting reality. Since there are up to 40 mutations in breast cancer, as the Cambridge researchers found, clinicians would need up to 40 drugs to counter them. But even that would not necessarily solve the problem, since Professor Stratton's group also found 73 combinations of cancer genes in breast cancer. Might not these combinations require yet other drugs? And, as Professor Watson suggested years earlier, as soon as one blocks a particular mutation, new genetic variants may emerge, for which no drugs yet exist.

Boston scientists once flippantly compared the problem to the arcade game Whack-a-Mole. In that game, as soon as you hammer down one cartoonish mole, another one emerges from its hiding place. Their example was the use of targeted therapies against a mutation in lung cancer.

These drugs cause dramatic initial responses, they said, but resistance to such drugs emerges within one to two years of continued monotherapy. These findings undercut the basic premise of the U.S. government's costly precision medicine initiative in regard to cancer.

## Chapter 9. Immune checkpoint inhibitors

*With Tibor Bakacs, MD, PhD, DSc — see Acknowledgments*

Originally, immunity was thought of as the ability of an organism to resist the attack of harmful microbes and parasites. This task is carried out by various specialized white blood cells that constitute the human immune system. The great Australian Nobel Prize laureate (1960) Sir Frank Macfarlane Burnet first suggested that the original role of the immune system was the surveillance of the body for the presence of cancer cells. This became known as the immune surveillance theory of cancer. This theory has undergone important modifications over the years. To quote an Italian oncologist:

> "Immunosuppressed patients have a high incidence of tumors. However, many patients develop cancer even in the presence of an apparently normal immune system. This indicates that tumor cells are able to escape immune surveillance."

One of the ways cancer cells do this is through activation of immune checkpoints. The *NCI Cancer Dictionary* defines these as:

> "...proteins made by some types of immune system cells, such as T cells, and some cancer cells that help keep immune responses in check and can keep T cells from killing cancer cells."

Conversely, immune checkpoint inhibitors break the link between a cancer cell and an immune cell, by interfering with certain key proteins. When these proteins are blocked, it releases the brakes on the immune system and T cells are able to kill cancer cells better. Some immune checkpoint inhibitors are used to treat cancer.

The immune system is normally in a delicate balance between tolerating normal tissues ("self") and attacking foreign entities ("non-self"). If this balance is disturbed, an autoimmune reaction may occur. The *NCI Cancer Dictionary* defines an autoimmune reaction as follows:

> "A condition in which the body's immune system mistakes its own healthy tissues as foreign and attacks them. Most autoimmune conditions cause inflammation that can affect many parts of the body."

To avoid damaging bystander tissues in an immune response, there are feedback loops that provide a kind of emergency brake on the immune system. Since the late 1990s, these emergency brakes have been referred to as immune checkpoints. They are checkpoints in the sense that they can stop an overactive immune response from proceeding and damaging the host. Up until 2010 there were a total of 22 articles in the world literature on the topic. But after the first immune checkpoint drug, Yervoy, was approved by the FDA in 2011 there came a flood. There are at this writing almost 5,000 such articles, and they are increasing at a rate of over five per calendar day.

## How immune checkpoint drugs ignited a revolution

Following the success of vaccines against infectious diseases, there was a tacit assumption around the world that immunization would someday protect us against cancer as well. But cancer is not generally caused by an infectious process. So creating vaccines against cancer turned out to be no simple matter. Most of the cancer vaccines that one reads about are not really aimed at preventing cancer but are treatments that attempt to stimulate the immune system to attack established tumors. Occasionally this has worked; more often it has not. Thus, for a long time, the field of cancer immunotherapy seemed unable to fulfill the great hopes once placed in it. In fact, it began to lose credibility. The general mood of many scientists was summed up by a University of Washington immunologist in 2005:

> "Despite nearly 50 years of intense investigation, attempts to use the immune reaction as a tool against cancer have...met with only moderate success. What is the realistic prospect that the next 50 years will see an improvement in this dismal state of affairs? Many investigators, myself included, have a large vested interest in the field of cancer immunology and will be reluctant to entertain any discouraging viewpoint, but the actual facts are, I believe, discouraging."

It is hard to remember that not even a decade has gone by since scientists discovered a drug that could manipulate the immune system in such a way as to bring about major responses in some advanced cancers. This revolution was initiated by James P. Allison, PhD, then at the University of California, Berkeley, and Tasuku Honjo, MD, of Tokyo, Japan. For this epochal accomplishment they shared the 2018 Nobel Prize in physiology and medicine.

A special 2018 issue of *Science* titled "The Cancer Immunotherapy Revolution" reviewed the newly approved immunotherapies that manipulate components of the immune system to attack tumors. According to the Cancer Research Institute, there are over 2000 immuno-oncology agents under development, of which more than 900 have reached the clinical trial stage. Meanwhile, success stories of terminal cancer patients defying the odds and achieving complete remissions are accumulating.

## Major safety issues

The use of immune checkpoint inhibitors (ICI) has also created major safety issues. Originally, it was hoped that checkpoint blockades would selectively target the interaction between immune cells and cancer cells, thus leaving normal tissues alone. However, these drugs often compromise the immune system's tolerance of healthy tissues. As a result, a new category of drug side effects has been established. This was the immune-related adverse event (irAE for short). This reaction was first named about a decade ago, but is now the subject of thousands of PubMed-indexed papers.

In 2016, the *New York Times* broke the news that the immune system, unleashed by cancer therapies, can attack organs.

> "As their use grows, doctors are finding that they pose serious risks that stem from the very thing that makes them effective. An unleashed immune system can attack healthy, vital organs: notably the bowel, liver and lungs, but also the kidneys, adrenal and pituitary glands, the pancreas and, in rare cases, the heart."

According to a 2016 European review, irAEs affect up to 90% of patients treated with Yervoy, and in 70% of those treated with Opdivo, Keytruda or similar drugs. In fact, in some trials, irAE incidence may reach up to 96% of patients.

Side effects are traditionally scored according to their severity from grade I to grade V (which is death from the treatment). According to the European review, irAEs mainly affect the skin and the gastrointestinal tract. William Murphy, MD, and Annie Mirsoian, PhD, of the University of California, Davis, have said that not enough researchers have investigated the risks of the new therapies:

> "The widespread application of immunotherapy has been limited by the induction of dose-limiting, and oftentimes life-threatening, immune-related adverse reaction events…ranging from mild, requiring dose and scheduling adjustments, to life-threatening. Immune checkpoint blockade therapies…can adversely result in autoimmunity."

In 2017, Yale immunologist Kevan Herold, PhD, told an immunology meeting that patients receiving immune checkpoint drugs were in fact human experiments of the autoimmune process. In a *Science* article titled "Powerful new cancer drugs are saving lives, but can also ignite diabetes or other autoimmune conditions," science writer Jennifer Couzin-Frankel states:

> "Diabetes isn't the only condition triggered by the [immunotherapy] drugs. In Tennessee, a man and a woman in their 60s, both in clinical trials combining two checkpoint inhibitors for advanced melanoma, died of immune attacks on their heart. Other patients have come down with colitis, which occurs when the immune system targets the gut."

The Nobel Prize committee, while giving its highest honor to Professors Allison and Honjo, also emphasized the crucial need to better understand these adverse events:

> "Similar to other cancer therapies, adverse side effects are seen, which can be serious and even life threatening. They are caused by an overactive immune response leading to autoimmune reactions, but are usually manageable. Intense continuing research is focused on elucidating the mechanisms of action, with the aim of improving therapies and reducing side effects."

Some believe that the extent of irAEs has been systematically understated in the scientific literature. In a 2018 article in *JAMA Oncology,* eight melanoma experts from Memorial Sloan-Kettering Cancer Center reported on their experience in treating melanoma with two immune checkpoint drugs, Yervoy and Opdivo. They explained why and how adverse events were systematically understated:

> "Our extensive experience using combination checkpoint blockade led us to believe the adverse

> events reported in clinical trials did not capture the full extent of the clinically relevant toxic effects. Trials uniformly emphasize...grade 3 to 4 adverse events even though grade 2 events are often serious. Also, trials often miss late toxic effects and do not capture emergency department visits unless they result in admission."

In our opinion, a therapeutic paradigm shift will be required to fully understand what is going on. Autoimmunity is emerging as the nemesis of immunotherapy. Several years ago Dr. Bakacs and I proposed an alternative explanation of these autoimmune side effects. In a paper that we co-authored with Jitendra Mehrishi, PhD, FRCPath, then of the University of Cambridge, U.K., we pointed out that, in this new treatment, the side effects caused by the patients' own white blood cells were very similar to the chronic graft-versus-host-disease reaction, which is often seen after bone marrow transplantation.

We theorized that Yervoy induced a graft-versus-malignancy effect, which wiped out metastatic melanoma in a minority of patients, but also caused an autoimmune reaction in the majority. This is quite contrary to the conventional view that Yervoy works by interfering with a specific link between cancer and the immune cell.

In our view, it is counterproductive to put the genie back in the bottle through the use of immunosuppressive treatments, such as steroids. The use of steroid drugs will probably undo the beneficial effects of the treatment. To quote an extensive review from the Gustave Roussy cancer center in Villejuif, France:

> "Although steroids can be used to treat these irAEs, the associated immunosuppression may compromise the antitumour response."

Instead, in our view, one should harness the autoimmune forces against cancer. One could dramatically lower the dose of the immune checkpoint drugs and actually add other immune stimulating treatments, such as heat therapy and medicinal mushrooms. But this of course would greatly reduce the cost of this treatment, which is the opposite of what Big Pharma is trying to do.

The toxicity of Yervoy was demonstrated by the first big clinical trial. This reported 14 deaths related to the use of this new drug, of which seven were associated with irAEs. However, when my colleagues and I tried to alert the scientific community to the danger that lurked within this new drug, and proposed an alternative explanation for its mechanism of action, our paper was repeatedly rejected by the top journals.

An editor of the *New England Journal of Medicine* wrote us:

> "I am sorry to inform you that your submission… has not been accepted for publication in the *Journal*. It was evaluated by members of our editorial staff. After considering its focus, content, and interest, we made the editorial decision not to consider your submission further. We are informing you of this promptly so that you can submit it elsewhere."

Following that, the same article was rejected by eight other leading journals, six of whose editors did not bother to provide a scientific reason for the rejection. They also refused to submit it for peer review. One *JAMA* editor who sent it for peer review wrote us:

> "Sorry to say, but we would not be interested in publishing a paper on this topic at this time in *JAMA*. Best of luck publishing your paper in another good journal."

*The Lancet* editor wrote:

> "Though we enjoyed reading your piece, we regret that we will be unable to offer publication. This is not to say that we do not appreciate the interest of the topic, of course—the pressure on general journal space means that we are often forced to make difficult decisions."

Finally, the paper was published in the peer-reviewed medical journal, *Immunobiology*. This journal was established in 1908 and is published by Elsevier, which also publishes *The Lancet*. But it has an impact factor (a standard measure of a journal's influence) of 3.2, compared to the *Lancet's* massive 59.1. So publication in a high-impact journal would have brought about 20 times as much attention as the paper actually received. Now, of course, there is almost universal recognition of the dangers, as well as the benefits, of immune checkpoint drugs such as Yervoy. But at the time, the topic was seen as too hot to handle by most of the scientific journals, although none of them came out and said as much.

## The problem of me-too drugs

It may sound as if there is a huge amount of creative thinking going on in the drug industry around the topic of immunotherapy. But that is an illusion. What has actually happened is the creation of a plethora of "me-too" drugs. These are lookalike compounds that seek to reinvent the wheel. They are merely attempts to reduplicate the commercial success of the first entries in the marketplace.

Take one such drug, Keytruda. According to *Forbes,*

> "Keytruda sales have grown from $55 million in 2014 to $7.2 billion in 2018. This represents an overall growth of 130 times, and an average annual growth of 334%."

The effect on Merck has been extraordinary. The company had been rapidly declining because of the lapses of key patents and competition from generic manufacturers. It had an overall annual growth that averaged a mere 0.1%. Then along came Keytruda, with its average annual growth rate of 334%. It quite simply rescued the company. The owners of patented drugs very similar to Keytruda hope to seize a portion of the market for themselves. Even a fraction of $7.2 billion is still a lot of money.

This trend was on full display at an FDA-led seminar at the 2019 meeting of the American Association of Cancer Research. The seminar concerned the leading kind of immune checkpoint. There are currently six drugs approved to target this checkpoint. Many of the proponents and developers of new and established checkpoint drugs came together for an extraordinary session at that seminar. The meeting was chaired by the FDA Oncology Center of Excellence director Richard Pazdur, MD, who has been called the closest thing America currently has to a cancer czar. He also understands cancer from the inside out, having lost his wife to ovarian cancer in 2015. According to *Barrons:*

> "Pazdur began the session by asking the drug developers if their checkpoint inhibitors were all really the same drug."

Probably there is no more relevant question about the current state of cancer drug development than this. The drug developers hedged, but they couldn't hide what was going on. According to an official of AstraZeneca, which markets the checkpoint drug Imfinzi:

> "The majority of these agents…appear at least from a safety and efficacy perspective to be relatively similar."

What else is there to a drug other than safety and efficacy? Well, for one thing, the price. These new drugs are all about dividing up market share or getting a bonanza by selling out for millions or even billions of dollars to a Big Pharma giant. According to a representative of Genentech, which developed the approved immune checkpoint inhibitor Tecentriq:

> "Although there are some differences, probably the end effect is more similar than different."

Some scientists quibbled with this characterization, but Pazdur came back at them forcefully:

> "Do we just have too many of these same drugs here?"

In other words, the FDA is obliged to evaluate hundreds of very similar drugs, but the upshot will not be any substantially new drugs, but just a host of nearly identical items. This is a waste of FDA's time and resources. And in the end the consumer gets almost nothing in return.

Capitalism is often lauded as the source of daring innovators who take huge risks and therefore deserve huge rewards. But what was on display at the AACR Seminar was a riot of unnecessary and unproductive competition among companies vying for a slice of the marketplace. There is money to be made by having a patented molecule gain approval for even a tiny segment of the cancer market. Once a drug is approved, it can also be used off-label by any oncologist, without getting further FDA approval.

Another strategy for a start-up company is to develop a new drug that then attracts the attention of Big Pharma. According to a Credit Suisse report, Bristol-Myers Squibb, Merck, Pfizer and Eli Lilly are all on a buying spree. Total biopharma deals reached over $114 billion in 2018. And the report predicts that Big Pharma will become even more acquisitive, as (to quote an investor's newsletter):

> "Big Pharma's 'giant maw' continues to scoop up small...players in the drug marketplace."

But, as you wade through the details on these business arrangements, remember where the whole idea of checkpoint inhibitors came from. It didn't come from Big Pharma. It was developed in an academic, governmental and nonprofit setting. In his formative years, James Allison was a professor at the University of California, Berkeley. As the Nobel Prize announcement put it:

> "Allison and co-workers performed a first experiment at the end of 1994, and in their

> excitement it was immediately repeated over the Christmas break. The results were spectacular. Mice with cancer had been cured by treatment with antibodies that inhibit the brake and unlock antitumor T-cell activity. Despite little interest from the pharmaceutical industry, Allison continued his intense efforts to develop the strategy into a therapy for humans."

Notice the phrase "little interest from the pharmaceutical industry." Contrary to the Reagan era myth that capitalism is the only engine of progress, and that innovation is intrinsic to the free enterprise system, the discovery of immune checkpoint inhibitors was entirely made by salaried employees at a public university supported by National Institutes of Health grants. In fact, Professor Allison still works as a salaried employee of a public institution, namely, the University of Texas M.D. Anderson Cancer Center.

But U.S. government agencies are not allowed to produce, much less market finished commercial drugs. So researchers must find a for-profit company to produce and market a drug that, under other circumstances, NCI itself would be fully capable of carrying through to completion. At a certain point, Professor Allison had to sell his ideas in the marketplace. In other words, he had to find a buyer for what became Yervoy.

Dr. Allison was luckier than many others, for he managed to attract the attention of a small biotech company, Medarex, which was a commercial spinoff of the Dartmouth College immunology department. Professor Allison's anti-CTLA-4 drug was initially called MDX-010. They then commercially interested the Pharma giant Bristol-Myers Squibb.

Nor did the drug industry even initiate the human studies. This was done in a 2003 clinical trial at the National Cancer Institute, under the direction of a government researcher. Incidentally, according to Open Payments, Dr. Allison's payments from Big Pharma in 2018 were a mere pittance. He received a total of $405.73, all in the form of food and drink, including a $23.42 meal from Pfizer. This is what a true scientist's balance sheet looks like.

## High doses mean high profits

The toxicity of immune checkpoint inhibitors is now an established fact. Even the first small clinical trial of Yervoy showed that the drug could be effective, with two complete and one partial response in

14 patients, but that it had serious side effects in almost all the patients. Grades 3 and 4 (severe or life-threatening) toxicity occurred in 9 of the first 14 patients. These effects included inflammation of the colon, skin and liver. What is now forgotten is that the trial was designed to sign up 21 patients, but NCI stopped recruitment because of this high rate of serious side effects.

Why then don't Bristol-Myers Squibb, Merck and the other manufacturers of such drugs recommend lowering the dose? There is evidence that low doses are as effective as high doses. The reason is financial. These drugs are sold *by the milligram,* and are among the most expensive substances on the face of the earth. For example, Yervoy by weight is almost 3,000 times as expensive as 24 karat gold. If it is possible to get a comparable therapeutic results at a fraction of the dose, Big Pharma stands to lose a great deal of money.

Manipulating the price of these drugs is a highway to phenomenal profits. No one has done more to expose this than Peter B. Bach, MD, Director of the Center for Health Policy and Outcomes, and Leonard B. Saltz, MD, head of the colorectal section of Memorial Sloan-Kettering Cancer Center. In 2017, they wrote an outstanding article on this topic, "Raising the dose and raising the cost: The case of pembrolizumab [Keytruda] in lung cancer," for the *Journal of the National Cancer Institute.*

Part of the answer to the toxicity of ICIs is to aim for the minimum effective dose. Too often, however, oncologists go in the opposite direction and seek the maximum tolerated dose. This means giving as much as possible without killing the patient. Since cancer treatments tend to be toxic, there is a huge difference in terms of toxicity between these competing two approaches. But would a low dose really be as effective as the typical high dose, with all its attendant toxicity? This may seem counterintuitive, but the answer is yes.

## The Shiraj Sen analysis

One of the most significant findings regarding the dosing schedule of immune checkpoint drugs was presented at the 2018 annual meeting of the American Society of Clinical Oncology. It was titled "Impact of immune checkpoint inhibitor dose on toxicity, response rate, and survival." The first author was Shiraj Sen, MD, PhD, a fellow at the M.D. Anderson Cancer Center, Houston. The senior author was Vivek Subbiah, MD, an associate professor in M.D. Anderson's Investigational Cancer Therapeutics department.

The authors analyzed data from patients who were treated in early-phase clinical trials at M.D. Anderson. (See Table 2 on next page.) They classified these patients into four groups in relation to the supposed maximum tolerated dose of the drug:

1. The low-dose group received less than one-third of the maximum tolerated dose of immune checkpoint drugs.
2. The medium-dose group got between one-third and two-thirds of the maximum tolerated dose.
3. The high-dose group received between two-thirds and 100% of the maximum tolerated dose.
4. The fourth very high dose group received more than 100% of the maximum tolerated dose.

The patients had many different kinds of cancer, such as renal cell, melanoma, sarcoma, etc. But the four groups were compared for such things as their immune-related side effects, as well as overall survival, progression-free survival, overall response rate, and the disease control rate.

There were five times as many cases of immune-related adverse events from the lowest to the highest dose. But there was barely any effect on such crucial things as overall survival as one increased the dose from less than a third to more than the maximum tolerated dose. As three other scientists recently put it:

> "Maximum tolerated dose...has proven challenging for checkpoint inhibitors...because there is no clear dose-response relationship, and the identification of a maximum tolerated dose may not be a realistic objective."

In fact, most drug researchers have been unable to identify a traditional maximum tolerated dose for most immune checkpoint inhibitors. This held true in studies of Yervoy, Keytruda, Opdivo and several other immune checkpoint inhibitors. Here is how seven M.D. Anderson doctors put it:

> "We identify no improvement in progression-free survival, overall survival, or disease control rate with escalating doses of immune checkpoint inhibitors administered in phase I trials .... Lower doses may reduce toxicity and cost without compromising disease control or survival."

**TABLE 2. EFFECT OF FOUR DOSE LEVELS ON RESPONSE TO ICIs**

| | Low Dose | Medium Dose | High Dose | Very High Dose |
|---|---|---|---|---|
| Progression-free survival | 2.76 months | 2.76 months | 2.46 months | 3.68 months |
| Overall survival | 6.18 months | 17.05 months | 5.16 months | 7.49 months |
| Overall response rate | 0% | 6% | 6% | 12% |
| Disease control rate | 62% | 71% | 41% | 81% |
| irAE side effect rate | 6% | 10% | 17% | 29% |

In addition, Keytruda, when given at doses of two milligrams versus ten milligrams (per kilogram of body weight, once every three weeks) showed an identical response rate in the two groups. It is hard to think of any conventional type of cancer drug where you could cut the dose five-fold and still get identical results.

## The dose-response relationship

Modern drug development began with the formulation of the dose-response relationship. The Renaissance medical pioneer, Paracelsus, who is considered the "father of toxicology," expressed the idea this way:

> "All things are poison, and nothing is without poison, the dosage alone makes it so a thing is not a poison."

Theophrastus von Hohenheim,
a.k.a. Paracelsus 1493-1541

In general, effects (and side effects) are expected to escalate as the dose increases. Throughout medicine, we see many examples of the dose-response relationship. In cancer, this pertains especially to chemotherapy drugs. According to Emil Frei, MD, in a classic paper on the topic, when a cancer drug is very effective, the dose-response curve is steep, which is considered a good thing:

> "A dose-response curve is generally evident in sensitive tumors, such as leukemias, lymphomas, testicular cancer and small cell lung cancer."

The FDA, says a leading cancer textbook, is "quite explicit in the centrality of the dose-response relationship of any agent for any purpose." In fact, the FDA's *Guidance for Industry* states as follows:

> "Exposure-response information is at the heart of any determination of the safety and effectiveness of drugs. That is, a drug can be determined to be safe and effective only when the relationship of beneficial and adverse effects to a defined exposure is known."

However, in the past 20 years, the dose-response relationship has been called into question. As the classic Holland-Frei cancer textbook puts it:

> "Dose is a significant determinant and antitumor activity and toxicology for the established 'classical' chemotherapeutic agents. With the introduction of

> the so-called targeted agents, however, there is not the same unequivocal evidence for a dose-response effect with these agents."

This unexpected development in oncology, which began with the targeted drugs and accelerated with the immune checkpoint inhibitors, undercuts the idea that more is better when it comes to anticancer drugs. In fact, it opened the door to the idea that small doses might be quite as good as the large doses.

In a rational world, much of the effort around these drugs would be devoted to finding the minimum effective dose for each and every patient, even if that cuts into the profits of Big Pharma. But this is hardly ever done. The idea of using low doses of immune checkpoint inhibitors has barely penetrated the world of clinical trials. This is in comparison to hundreds of clinical trials underway with typical high-dose immune checkpoint inhibitors.

## Renner analysis

A 2019 *Journal of Global Oncology* paper by three Chilean oncologists built on the findings of Shiraj Sen in his previous M.D. Anderson analysis. These oncologists stated:

> "There is a large amount of data showing that checkpoint inhibitors have significant activity at doses much lower than those currently approved. We review the evidence for reduced drug dosing as a strategy to increase the number of patients who can be treated and what would be needed to further validate this approach."

Looking at two of the most popular immune checkpoint drugs, Opdivo and Keytruda, the authors concluded:

> "Both drugs have shown similar response rates in a wide range of doses, some of them much lower than currently approved schedules."

As the Chilean oncologists suggest, the idea of using a high or very high dose is derived from 60 years of prior experience with cell-killing chemotherapy. By contrast, the distinguishing characteristic of immune checkpoint drugs is that they do not directly kill cancer cells. They help free up a blocked immune system, which then does the actual killing. But apparently one does not need much of these drugs in order to get a therapeutic effect. This is an extremely important concept, which has been hard to get across to the majority of cancer researchers, especially those trained in the era when chemotherapy was king.

"Yelling" at a tumor with the maximum tolerated dose is often no more effective than giving a fraction of that dose.

Renner also reported:

> "Less than 5% of the population has coverage for…immune checkpoint inhibitors in Peru and less than 10% in Chile, the richest country in the region."

And Chile and Peru are hardly the worst off. In fact, over 100 countries in the world are poorer, with a per capita Gross Domestic Product less than that of Chile. In 2013, Duke University scientists coined a term to describe the economic burden of drugs such as these: financial toxicity. Some patients are running up huge debts, or even going bankrupt, to pay for potentially life-saving medications. Financial toxicity refers to the extreme cost of these agents seen from the point of view of the average patient.

## Shin Hye Yoo study

Another study, published around the same time, from the Korean National University Hospital in Seoul, reached identical conclusions:

> "This study evaluated the efficacy of low-dose Opdivo as an alternative to the financial toxicity of standard-dose Opdivo in the treatment of non-small cell lung cancer."

The authors compared a low dose of Opdivo versus a standard dose. A low dose was one-twelfth to one-twentieth the standard dose of the others. You might expect those who got a tiny dose to do worse than those approved dose. But they reported:

> "The objective response rate was 13.8% in the standard-dose group and 16.7% in the low-dose group. Dosing of Opdivo…did not significantly affect progression-free survival or overall survival. Low-dose Opdivo can be effective…and is worth considering as an alternative option…."

The authors state, "It is unlikely the pharmaceutical industry will be interested in such a subject." Why unlikely? Because Big Pharma would make a fraction of its current profits if doctors adopted lower dose regimens.

The Korean scientists therefore suggest:

> "Independent governmental institutions, universities, or collaborative groups would have to take on this challenge, with the potential help of oncology nongovernmental organizations."

That's a great idea, provided one can find institutions that are truly independent of Big Pharma. But the systematic corruption of the field of oncology by Big Pharma money makes that solution rather complicated.

## Villejuif study

Finally, we will mention a 10-page analysis of the question of dose from six authors at the Institut Gustave Roussy in Villejuif, France, one of the most prestigious cancer centers in Europe. While their 2016 discussion is highly technical, the authors arrive at the same conclusion as other authors:

> "Higher doses of these immune checkpoint agents do not result in higher objective response rates. On the other hand, ICI drugs have no clear correlation between dose, efficacy and toxicities."

"No correlation between dose and efficacy." These are profoundly disturbing—and yet exciting—words. Clearly something very unusual is going on with these drugs. In fact, tumor responses and side effects are equivalent whether one gives a tiny one milligram of drug per kilogram of body weight, or twenty times that. It is hard to understand these facts in conventional terms. But it is precisely such counterintuitive findings that often lead to new paradigms in science.

## Changing the dosage

As we have shown, small changes to a drug's dosing schedule can have a major impact on the company's bottom line. For instance, the most common form of lung cancer is non-small cell lung cancer. In the immune treatment of non-small cell lung cancer, Merck first gained approval for personalized dosing based on the patient's weight. But soon afterwards, Merck pushed for a fixed dosing schedule of 200 milligrams once every three weeks for all patients.

Such a simple change might seem trivial. But in 2017, in the *Journal of the National Cancer Institute,* Daniel A. Goldstein, MD calculated the increased costs that are generated by this one small-seeming change. In the U.S., for just one drug for one type of cancer, the cost using *personalized* dosing used to be $2.6 billion. But under a *fixed* dosing program, this rose to $3.4 billion. Returning to personalized dosing would yield a 24.0% annual savings of over $825 million. Those extra $825 million could go a long way towards reducing the burden on cancer patients. Instead, it goes into the coffers of Big Pharma, where it helps pays for the $20 million per person salaries of chief executive officers.

In the Chilean study, there was another shocking chart. It shows that when one gives Bristol-Myers Squibb's drug Opdivo at the lowest dose, the yearly cost per patient was $4,922. That's not cheap, but the co-pay would be around $1,000 for many people in the U.S. However, at the high dose that Bristol-Myers Squibb insists upon, the cost comes to $147,663. The copay on the highest dose would then be almost $30,000. That's more than the lifetime savings of 60% of all American families.

By insisting on the high dose, Bristol-Myers Squibb, Merck and their collaborators are brazenly bankrupting people with cancer. And as of 2015, 71% of the world's population was living on less than U.S. $10 a day. One way of addressing this problem would be to prescribe a much lower dose of these drugs. According to Alex Renner:

> "Both Keytruda and Opdivo have significant efficacy at much lower doses than those approved by regulatory agencies, because their therapeutic window is much broader than traditional chemotherapy."

Like most big corporations, Merck claims that its core purpose is to benefit humanity. According to its homepage:

> "Our core values are driven by a desire to improve life, achieve scientific excellence, operate with the highest standards of integrity, expand access to our products and employ a diverse workforce that values collaboration."

The degree to which the public buys this line is indicated in a 2019 Gallup poll showing that Big Pharma had sunk to the very bottom of 25 U.S. industries in terms of public approval. Big Pharma has a positive public rating of 27% versus 58% who hold a totally negative opinion. A drastic reduction in both the dose and price of the immune checkpoint drugs would go a lot further in winning the public's confidence than any number of fine statements.

### The big vial trick

Another trick that drug companies use to boost sales is to make drugs available only in oversized vials. The patients, whose dose is based on their body weight, will usually not need the exact amount in a super-sized vial, and much of it goes to waste. The other half of this maneuver is to forbid pharmacists from sharing the same vial between patients.

Peter Bach, MD and Leonard Saltz, MD, of MSKCC exposed this trick in a 2016 paper. This clever stratagem leads to "large volumes of wastage of cancer drugs in the United States." Keytruda was initially approved in the U.S. in 2014, when it was sold in 50 milligram vials. But a year later, Merck introduced 100 mg vials and stopped the distribution of 50 milligram vials. And 100 mg remains the only size of Keytruda vials available. According to Peter Bach, MD, writing in the *British Medical Journal*, this is a ploy to sell an excess of these precious drugs:

> "These drugs must be either administered or discarded once open, and because patients' body sizes are unlikely to match the amount of drug included in the vial, there is nearly always some left over. The leftover drug still has to be paid for, even when discarded, making it possible for drug companies to artificially increase the amount of drug they sell per treated patient by increasing the amount in each single dose vial relative to the typically required dose."

This seemingly trivial factor results in the excess sale of billions of dollars in drugs. And it is not just immune checkpoint drugs. At the *British Medical Journal* website, there is a listing of 20 different anticancer agents showing the estimated total cost of leftover drugs, from Abraxane to Yervoy. The total wastage comes to well over a billion dollars per year. Here are some representative amounts of health care money overcharged to cancer patients:

- Velcade ................ $308.7 million
- Avastin ................ $284.5 million
- Rituxan ................ $253.9 million
- Kyprolis ................ $231.4 million
- Keytruda ................ $197.9 million

- Neupogen.............$106.0 million
- Opdivo .................$ 68.9 million
- Yervoy .................$ 46.5 million

Most of this waste could be saved simply by providing the drug in smaller vials, while allowing pharmacists to share a single vial among several patients. But FDA cooperates with Big Pharma in preventing this from happening. The ingenuity of Big Pharma is limitless when it comes to stealing the public's money.

### The rise of a rare disease

The immune checkpoint inhibitors have gained a reputation for causing a number of rare and difficult conditions. An example is hypophysitis, which is an inflammation of the pituitary gland. This can cause direct effects of headache and vision problems (such as lost, blurred, or double vision). But according to the California Center for Pituitary Disorders, it can also indirectly cause several other conditions, including adrenal insufficiency, hypothyroidism, hypogonadism, and diabetes. Symptoms can include one or more of the following:

- Polyuria (excessive urination)
- Polydipsia (excessive thirst)
- Decreased libido (loss of sexual desire)
- Erectile dysfunction
- Weight loss
- Galactorrhea (milky nipple discharge)
- Amenorrhea (missed menstrual periods)
- Hyponatremia (decrease in blood sodium)
- Fatigue

Any or all of these appearing in a person who has received ICIs is a cause of concern. But they are also so common as to leave some former patients in a state of perpetual anxiety.

Before the introduction of ICIs, hypophysitis was exceedingly rare. In fact, only about 100 cases were ever reported in the world medical literature. But in 2014, pituitary inflammation was described as a common adverse event of Yervoy, which had been introduced just three years earlier. A 2016 paper from Massachusetts General

Hospital stated that the condition occurs in a significant minority of patients who receive immune checkpoint inhibitor drugs.

And this was only one of the unusual conditions and diseases that are triggered by these immune checkpoint inhibitors, especially at the higher doses promoted by drug companies and their agents.

Some other possible hormonal side effects of ICIs include inflammatory arthritis, which can progress from mild pain with inflammation to severe pain associated with signs of inflammation or joint swelling and irreversible joint damage.

And, with that, we are only one-third of the way through the ASCO report on possible side effects of the checkpoint drugs. What is noteworthy is the similarity of these numerous side effects to autoimmune reactions, which can also strike almost anywhere in the body.

According to the *NCI Cancer Dictionary,* in regard to autoimmunity:

> "Common signs and symptoms include fatigue, fever, muscle aches, joint pain and swelling, skin problems, abdominal pain, digestion problems, and swollen glands. The symptoms often come and go and can be mild or severe."

This is nearly identical to the common side effects from ICIs, which may also include fatigue, fever, muscle aches, joint pain and swelling, colitis, and so forth, all of which have been amply described in the scientific literature.

On page 50 of the ASCO report there is an extraordinary statement. The authors reproduce a wallet card, created by the Oncology Nursing Society (ONS), which details symptoms to watch for in patients with a history of immunotherapy. Patients are supposed to carry this card to give to healthcare providers in case of a sudden onset or flare up of symptoms.

The card states that common side effects "may present as rash, diarrhea, abdominal pain, cough, fatigue, headaches, vision changes, etc." We wanted to reproduce this card in this book, but were denied permission by a representative of the Oncology Nursing Society (ONS).

In an email, we were told that their Society:

> "...does not allow permission to reprint the wallet card in publications other than those published by ONS and ASCO."

Readers of the card are warned that "minor changes in how a patient is feeling may indicate early signs of an adverse event [AE], and patients may not attribute the change to their cancer treatment." So patients are asked to carry these cards in order to alert medical staff about their newly unpredictable immune systems.

In 60 densely packed pages, ASCO's only explanation of the mechanism of action of these side effects is the following sentence:

> "The principal mechanism of the encountered toxicity is inflammatory and the principal management is immunosuppression with corticosteroids."

There is no explanation of why a drug that is chemically defined and aimed at a single protein on T cells (a type of immune cell) should cause this witches' brew of side effects. Nor do they make any connection between triggering systemic inflammation and the actual mode of action of the drug itself. And the best these 29 carefully chosen experts can recommend is to use immune-suppressive steroid drugs for patients treated with immune-enhancing drugs like Yervoy, Opdivo and Keytruda. And in fact steroid use is believed to diminish the desirable effects of these drugs.

It also skirts the fundamental issue of the mechanism of action here. We are well aware of the conventional explanation of how these drugs supposedly work. But just after the Hodi clinical trial paper was published in 2011, Tibor Bakacs, our coauthor Jitendra Mehrishi, PhD, then of Cambridge University, and I were struck by the similarity between Yervoy's side effect profile and the TGN1412 Catastrophe.

This was a clinical trial in London in which a similar drug, called TGN1412, precipitated a cytokine storm leading to life-threatening multiple organ failure in six healthy human volunteers. TGN1412 was also known as theralizumab. It was an immune modulating drug developed by a German professor, which was withdrawn from development after it induced severe inflammatory reactions in its first-in-human study in London in March 2006. Like Yervoy, it too seemed safe based on preclinical findings. But according to a 2010 report on the catastrophe titled "From Discovery to Disaster":

> "After the very first infusion of a dose 500 times smaller than that found safe in animal studies, all six human volunteers faced life-threatening conditions involving multiorgan failure for which they were moved to the intensive care unit."

So in 2012, while the scientific world was entranced by the elegant theory of Yervoy being active through its effect on the CTLA-4 molecule, we put forward the theory that at least part of the drug's mechanism of action was a generalized unleashing of the immune system. In our view, these weren't exactly side effects, but were probably part of the treatment effects. Because the immune system goes everywhere in the body, this unleashing could naturally affect every organ of the body. We therefore were not surprised to see such widespread negative effects all over the body. In fact, we expected them.

We now know that many targeted drugs do not work by acting on their supposed targets at all. Using the new CRISPR gene editing technology, scientists at Cold Spring Harbor and elsewhere have shown that at least ten targeted drugs work even when their supposed targets are deleted with surgical precision from the cells. This has thrown the field of targeted therapy into confusion.

At the time, Yervoy was thought to target only T lymphocytes that were specifically engaged with the tumor. However, our interpretation of the clinical trials is that the beneficial effects of Yervoy are due more to a generalized unleashing of all T cells, resulting in their immune intolerance of both cancer and healthy tissues. This was because the molecular target of Yervoy, the CTLA-4 receptor, is expressed not only on the tumor-specific T cells, but also on practically all other T cells.

We also suspected that the dose recommended by the manufacturer was far too high, and that much lower doses would probably be just as effective. Otherwise, one risked the kind of reactions that occurred in the TGN1412 catastrophe.

What we saw with Yervoy was in fact very similar to a so-called graft versus host disease (GVHD) following foreign bone marrow transplantation. Part of GVHD is a graft versus malignancy (GVM) reaction. In a GVM, the immune system turns its fury against the tumor in a way similar to how it will reject a foreign organ transplant (unless of course the patient is immunosuppressed with steroids or other drugs).

We followed this paper with a call for using a much lower dose of these same drugs. We speculated that low doses would have comparable results to the higher dose currently in use. This has been fully borne out by subsequent developments, including studies at the University of Texas M.D. Anderson Cancer Center, Professor Allison's home institution. Their paper concluded with these words:

> "Lower doses may reduce toxicity and cost without compromising disease control or survival."

Establishing the mechanism of action of a new entity is an important part of rational drug development. So raising questions about the mechanism undercuts the argument for approval. However, we believe that it is inevitable that the mechanism of action of many targeted drugs will be reexamined and revised. This will probably extend to the immune checkpoint inhibitors as well.

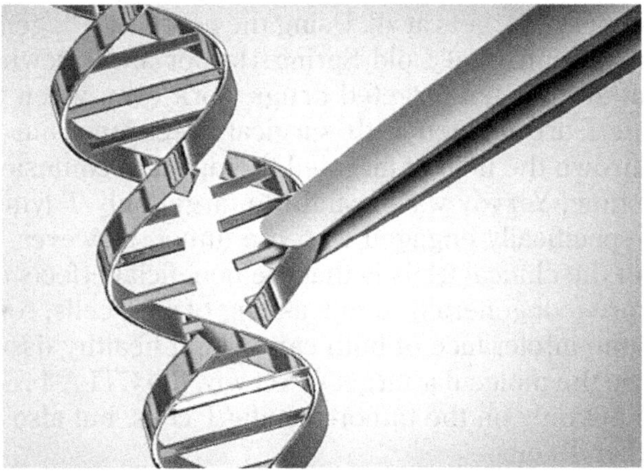

CRISPR gene editing technology is revolutionizing the field of targeted therapy.

## Chapter 10. Oncology's report card

**"Human kind cannot bear very much reality."**

—*T.S. Eliot,* The Four Quartets

There is another reason that the FDA and Big Pharma collude to approve drugs based on surrogate endpoints, and that is because most cancer drugs simply do not work very well. In fact, a totally honest appraisal would put a serious dent in the cancer drug marketplace. Many people would be upset, and Wall Street would suffer a decline.

The truth is that despite FDA's compliance with the needs of the industry, most cancer drugs still fail during the course of clinical trials. According to the Tufts Center for the Study of Drug Development, as of 2016, only 11.8% of drugs that entered clinical testing were approved. When it comes to so-called 'targeted' therapies, the success rate is even worse. To quote *Science* (2019):

> "Ninety-seven percent of drug-indication pairs that are tested in clinical trials in oncology never advance to receive U.S. Food and Drug Administration approval."

So that's a success rate of about 3%. But the truth may be even worse, for according to the 2019 article in *JAMA Oncology,* cited above, the majority of approvals are based on surrogate endpoints, not an increase in actual overall survival.

What is the actual benefit to patients? We know the answer to that as well, at least as it concerns phase II clinical trials. In 2015 some critical observers of modern oncology summarized the overall situation this way:

> "Many therapies for patients with cancer have a modest effect on survival that is often in the range of several months or less. It may be that the relatively small gains observed with therapy are a result of a subgroup of patients who respond well, while other patients gain no benefit or may even be harmed by the therapy."

What did the critical observers mean by referring to a subgroup analysis? Often a clinical trial of a patient population arrives at a negative result. The study's sponsors may have divided the overall group into various subgroups. If they did this often enough, they are likely eventually to discover a smaller segment of the trial population that appears to benefit. According to a 2005 article in *The Lancet:*

> "By testing enough subgroups, a false-positive result will probably emerge by chance alone. Investigators might undertake many analyses but only report the significant effects, distorting the medical literature."

So who were the critical observers who in 2015 penned the bold critique of oncology? They weren't exactly radical outsiders. In fact, they were some of the most famous figures in oncology, including:

- John Mendelsohn, MD, President of the University of Texas M.D. Anderson Cancer Center, Houston;
- Richard L. Schilsky, MD, Senior Vice President and Chief Medical Officer of ASCO; and
- Professor Alexander Eggermont, MD, Professor of Oncology, General Director of the Institut Gustave Roussy in Villejuif, France, and president of the European Academy of Cancer Sciences.

Their article, published in ASCO's flagship, the *Journal of Clinical Oncology,* presented a powerful argument for a new personalized approach to cancer treatment. But in order to clear the way for this approach, the distinguished authors delivered a devastating blow to conventional oncology, the type of treatment that most of the world's cancer patients receive every day.

Their paper came in the form of a meta-analysis, a study of other studies. The authors reviewed 570 phase II single-agent studies involving over 30,000 patients that were published between 2010 and 2012. They then looked at the response rates, progression-free survival and overall survival. Again, their claim was that personalized medicine would deliver better results. But when it came to non-personalized cancer treatments, the results in numerous phase II trials were shocking:

1. The median overall response rate (tumor shrinkages) was 10.5%.
2. The median progression-free survival was 2.7 months.
3. The median overall survival was 8.9 months.

Almost nothing that oncologists did would budge cancer's stubborn bottom line. As to the crucial question of the median overall survival, none of the usual variables affected survival. In other words, it mattered little if the patients in question were:

- Chemotherapy newcomers, or were returning for further treatment.
- Receiving cytotoxic chemotherapy or more targeted agents.
- Treated in a randomized or nonrandomized trial.
- Were included in a large or a small trial.
- Had their results published in a high or low impact journal.
- Receiving an oral or injectable drug.
- Were administered an FDA-approved or non-approved agent.
- Were in a single center trial or one where multiple centers were involved.

In each and every one of these cases, the median overall survival did not rise above 10 months. (The one exception was leukemia, where patients did live a few months longer than those who had solid tumors.)

So there's the unvarnished bottom line about cancer treatment. Its top leaders had spoken and given conventional oncology a report card. To be generous, in our view, it got a "D minus."

But there was worse news. Even using the most advanced techniques, at some of the world's finest hospitals, some patients were still dying from the treatment itself. In these carefully controlled clinical trials, with billions of dollars riding on the outcome, the drug-related death rate on average was 2.3%. The authors suggested the obvious, that this was "perhaps because of the known adverse effects often accompanying the administration of cytotoxic agents."

## Section II: Three Complementary Treatments

**"The current scientific understanding of cancer is seriously flawed and in need of a new objective re-appraisal."**

*—Edward J. Calabrese, PhD, University of Massachusetts, Amherst (2019)*

This book is mainly about the relationship of Big Pharma to the oncology profession. However, there is another aspect to this question that has not been dealt with. That is the emergence of a new kind of cancer treatment called complementary oncology. This means the integration of what is proven reasonably safe and effective in conventional oncology with non-conventional methods that extend the boundaries of the current paradigm.

Complementary oncology is a phrase that Professor Josef Beuth, MD, of the University of Cologne, and I used as the title of our book, *Complementary Oncology: Adjunctive Methods in the Treatment of Cancer* (2005). As an explanation we stated:

> "Complementary methods have played an important role in...treatments, showing benefits such as a higher quality of life, reduced instance and severity of the side effects of standard therapy, and a general improvement of the patient's immunological state."

The discussion of Big Pharma, and its relationship to oncology, raises a number of unanswered questions about its relationship to complementary oncology.

### A grand conspiracy?

Many people subscribe to what might be called the "Grand Conspiracy Theory" of alternative medicine. This is the belief that Big Pharma consciously and methodically suppresses complementary and alternative treatments in order to eliminate competition and thereby secure future profits.

I can see why people might believe this. Looking at the abysmal record of Big Pharma in so many areas, is it inconceivable that they might do such a thing? Think for instance of Big Pharma's nefarious role in America's opioid epidemic. This has all the earmarks of a conspiracy. According to a U.S. government website:

> "In the late 1990s, pharmaceutical companies reassured the medical community that patients would not become addicted to opioid pain relievers and healthcare providers began to prescribe them at greater rates."

The net result, said the U.S. Department of Health and Human Services, was that in 2016 alone,

> "Opioid overdoses accounted for more than 42,000 deaths... more than any previous year on record. An estimated 40% of opioid overdose deaths involved a prescription opioid."

According to a 2017 commentary in the *New England Journal of Medicine,* "the opioid epidemic has claimed more than 300,000 lives in the United States since 2000 and could claim another half million over the next decade."

Why bring this up in a book about cancer? Because it speaks to the amoral behavior of the drug industry's leaders. Despite all the honeyed words of public relations specialists, they have proven time and time again that they are only interested in increasing their profits, even at the cost of human lives. That is the takeaway lesson from the opioid catastrophe, which was created and perpetuated by Big Pharma executives.

And so I do not think one should reject out of hand the possibility that there might be a conscious direction to the campaign against natural, low-cost, unpatentable or generic medications. However, that said, I have never seen convincing proof of a coordinated strategy against alternative cancer treatment on the part of Big Pharma.

The author G. Edward Griffin is a master of conspiracy theories. Long before he wrote a widely circulated work on the Federal Reserve, he wrote *World Without Cancer.* In this, he alleges "a malicious conspiracy hiding behind the smiling mask of humanitarianism," and a "conscious direction behind the opposition to laetrile," which was the most popular alternative cancer treatment of the 1970s.

In my first book, *The Cancer Industry* (1980), I wrote in response:

> "A conspiracy theory must take into account the fact that the leaders of the cancer establishment themselves die of cancer. Many prominent cancer scientists, administrators, and politicians have died of the disease, as have many wealthy people asso-

> ciated with the establishment, including members of the Rockefeller family. Did someone fail to tell them about the suppressed cure?"

But then, in 1980 I offered an alternative explanation:

> "The suppression of unorthodox methods—and the promotion of the orthodox approach—takes place mainly at an objective, unconscious level. It is an outgrowth of underlying economic and social trends rather than of conscious design.... On the other hand, representatives of the far right [Griffin had been a spokesperson for the John Birch Society, ed.] may prefer a simple conspiracy theory since this targets only a few 'malicious' people and spares the system itself from any fundamental criticism.
>
> "Yet the evidence points to the fact that it is the system itself, rather than any particular clique of individuals, which is really to blame for failure to make progress against the cancer problem. In particular, the fact that cancer management is itself a big business means that it must function according to the rules of profit-oriented institutions."

In the intervening years, many individuals have tried to identify some central point from which Big Pharma directs its supposed war on alternative treatments. But no one has yet succeeded in this, nor are they likely to. Obsessing over this is also a waste of time and energy that should go into fighting—and changing—the way that new cancer drugs are developed. I offer a feasible program for doing exactly this, below.

That does not mean, however, that some extremely promising alternative approaches have not been tragically neglected. In order to round out the picture of how Big Pharma's domination has hurt the public, I shall now discuss three treatment approaches that have been undermined and ignored by standard oncology. Each deserves serious consideration.

## Chapter 1. Metabolic therapy

A typical human cell is like a small fluid-filled sac. Within that sac is a nucleus and a jelly-like substance called cytoplasm. And within that cytoplasm can be found a dozen or so other parts of the cell called organelles. Most prominent are several hundred little power plants called mitochondria. These occupy up to 25 percent of the volume of the cytoplasm.

According to one college biology text:

> "These organelles were first observed by light microscopists in the late 1800s, where they appeared to be somewhat worm-shaped structures that seemed to be moving around in the cell. Some early observers suggested that they might be bacteria living inside host cells, but these hypotheses remained unknown or rejected in most scientific communities."

In many ways, mitochondria are peculiar. Most scientists now accept the once-heretical idea of "symbiogenesis," which is that mitochondria originated as independent one-celled organisms. About 1.45 billion years ago they fused with our distant cellular ancestors. At that time, oxygen was starting to build up in the atmosphere. This posed a danger to most early cells. But mitochondria to the rescue! They take in toxic oxygen, generate energy, and expel harmless carbon dioxide.

According to biologist Lynn Margulis, PhD, the early cells and the mitochondria joined in a permanent symbiotic relationship, a marriage that continues to this day.

The mitochondria are special in that they have retained their own DNA for at least 1.45 billion years. No other cell parts do that. Their DNA is not twisted into a double helix, but has a ring-like structure, and is inherited through the maternal line. Before the early cells married the mitochondria, they could only generate energy through an inefficient process called glycolysis, or fermentation. But after partnering with mitochondria, they could produce as much as 19 times as much energy from a molecule of glucose.

How does this relate to cancer? In 1924, a German researcher named Otto H. Warburg, MD, PhD, showed that cancer cells differ fundamentally in their metabolism from normal cells. Normal cells have hundreds of helpful mitochondria that produce lots of energy from relatively little glucose. This process is called the Krebs cycle, named for Otto Warburg's most famous student and biographer,

Hans Krebs, MD.

Because of the failure of about half of their mitochondria, cancer cells must turn to the wasteful process of fermentation to produce energy. In part, cancer cells have reverted to an ancestral method of fermentation. This process demands a greater amount of glucose to produce energy. But unlike bacteria, they do this even when oxygen is present. Otto Warburg called this phenomenon aerobic glycolysis. Some people call it the Warburg Effect, in his honor.

Cancer cells tend to have high energy needs, and many grow quickly, invade neighboring tissue, combat and manipulate the immune system, and metastasize to distant sites. In other words, their energy demands go up, just as their energy efficiency goes down. How do they survive? There's only one solution to this dilemma: increase access to the fuel supply. Their main fuel is glucose (the kind of sugar that circulates in blood) and they need lots of that to produce an equivalent amount of energy as a normal cell. This explains why cancer cells are greedy for glucose. And as if that weren't enough, according to scientists at the University of Colorado, they even sometimes rob normal cells of their glucose rations. For example,

> "Leukemia cells create a diabetic-like condition that reduces glucose going to normal cells, and as a consequence, there is more glucose available for the leukemia cells. Literally, they are stealing glucose from normal cells to drive growth of the tumor."

Discovering the fact that cancer cells ferment to produce energy through aerobic glycolysis was epochal. It was arguably the most important finding concerning cancer in the period between the two World Wars. Warburg earned a solo Nobel Prize in 1931 for his many discoveries. He was seriously considered for a second Nobel Prize on four other occasions. In fact, this model of cancer's metabolism was popular well into the 1940s.

1983 German stamp
honoring the centenary of
Otto Warburg's birth

But after World War II, Warburg's theories fell out of favor. The reasons for this were mainly scientific, but were mixed with some personal issues. Scientists, most notably the American Sidney Weinhouse, MD, showed that *some* tumors did not actually overconsume glucose. On a personal level many people disliked or even despised Warburg. Although he came from one of Germany's wealthiest Jewish families, the Nazis declared him an "Honorary Aryan," and he was thus able to continue working in Berlin throughout that disastrous period. While other Jewish scientists were being hunted and killed, Warburg went about his business, unmolested and protected by top Nazis, who thought he knew the cure for cancer. He lived on a spacious estate outside Berlin and began every day by riding one of his prized gray Hanoverian mares.

Warburg died in Berlin in August 1970, his ideas largely discredited. But then a strange thing happened. Around the dawn of the new millennium, Warburg's ideas started to become popular again. As late as 1998 there were zero articles about the Warburg Effect in PubMed. Now they appear at a rate of about 300 per year. As a 2009 article in *Science* explained:

> "There is renewed attention to Otto Warburg's observation in 1924 that cancer cells metabolize glucose in a manner that is distinct from that of cells in normal tissues.... Warburg found that unlike most normal tissues, cancer cells tend to 'ferment' glucose into lactate [lactic acid] even in the presence of sufficient oxygen...."

Warburg's return to scientific relevance was paralleled by the rise of the positron emission tomography (PET) scan as a diagnostic tool in cancer. The most commonly used contrast agent in a PET scan is called FDG. This is a combination of a radioactive tracer with an artificial form of glucose. Cancer cells take up this glucose-like molecule, whose presence is then pinpointed by a special scanner that detects radioactivity. In other words, the PET scan is predicated on the existence of the Warburg Effect.

Selling PET devices has become an annual two billion dollar business worldwide. The first scientific paper on PET scanning was published in 1983. Now such papers appear at a rate of 2,000 per year. The success of the PET scan reminded researchers of the centrality of the Warburg Effect to the metabolism of the cancer cell.

As recognition of this indisputable fact, Profs. Douglas Hanahan and Robert A. Weinberg, in a 2011 revision of their classic paper on the hallmarks of cancer, added the "reprogramming of metabolism" as an essential characteristic of malignant cells. As "The Fundamentals of Cancer Metabolism" in *Science Advances* put it:

> "The field is based on the principle that metabolic activities are altered in cancer cells relative to normal cells, and that these alterations support the acquisition and maintenance of malignant properties. Because some altered metabolic features are observed quite generally across many types of cancer cells, reprogrammed metabolism is considered a hallmark of cancer."

Does this mean that science as a whole has come over to Warburg's view that cancer is fundamentally a metabolic disease? Hardly. For example, Hanahan and Weinberg adhere to the belief that genetic mutations are primary and that mutations in the nucleus then cause metabolism to go haywire.

But in 2012, Boston College Professor Thomas Seyfried published a landmark book, *Cancer As A Metabolic Disease.* He updated Warburg's thesis with many facts showing that cancer is fundamentally a disease of metabolism: the genetic changes observed in cancer, he said, are a secondary result of disordered metabolism. Seyfried's book was the most determined assault on the standard somatic mutation theory of cancer in many years.

One of the most robust arguments *against* the metabolic view has been the success of targeted anticancer agents. In an essay, "In Defense of the Somatic Mutation Theory of Cancer" (2011), Professor David L. Vaux, PhD, of Melbourne, Australia wrote:

> "The strongest validation comes from the successful treatment of certain malignancies with drugs that directly target the product of the mutant gene."

Exhibit A was the first very successful small molecule oral drug, Gleevec. This drug is used to treat chronic myelogenous leukemia, gastrointestinal stromal tumors (GIST), and some other diseases whose cells exhibit the Philadelphia chromosome. The theory behind Gleevec, and similar drugs, is that certain molecules can become mutated, which leaves the cell in an "on" position. This causes unregulated growth, which is a key characteristic of cancer. Gleevec, to all appearances, inhibits this defective molecule, thereby toggling the "on" switch to an "off" position, stopping the cancer.

But it is now a proven fact that Gleevec also converts cancer cells' mitochondria from reliance on the Warburg Effect back to a normal cell's respiration. Four years after the drug's initial approval, in 2004, German researchers showed that Gleevec affects the manner in which cancer cells process glucose. They stated that Gleevec reverses the Warburg effect by changing its mode of energy generation from fermentation to normal respiration. This results, they wrote, in decreased glucose uptake.

In 2019, these results were confirmed at the National Research Council in Naples, Italy. The Italian authors noted:

> "A significant reduction of glucose consumption and lactate secretion [both signs of fermentation] along with an increase of intracellular ATP [energy] levels was observed in response to Gleevec."

At Memorial Sloan-Kettering, 15 scientists, headed by Ronald P. DeMatteo, studied the effect of Gleevec on cancer cells of patients with gastrointestinal stromal tumors, or GIST. This is a disease in which Gleevec also shines. DeMatteo found that Gleevec works on the metabolic level in GIST. It decreases the amount of glucose taken up by cancer cells, reduces the amount of fermentation, and increases the activity of the mitochondria:

> "Gleevec therapy decreased glucose uptake and downstream glycolytic activity [fermentation] in GIST…by approximately half and upregulated [normal] mitochondrial enzymes and improved mitochondrial respiratory capacity."

All of this shows that Gleevec, whatever else it does, is a powerful metabolic agent.

## Attacking mitochondria

There are clear indications that cytotoxic chemotherapy and many targeted drugs attack the mitochondria. For example, Adriamycin, Herceptin and Sutent all can cause heart damage due to their impact on the mitochondria inside normal heart muscle cells. At least six other cancer drugs are known to damage the mitochondria of normal muscle cells, leading to weakness and fatigue in patients. These six are among the most common and useful anticancer drugs. They have little in common except their effect on mitochondria: Platinol, Taxol, Trisenox, Novantrone, Avastin, and Nexavar.

There is also evidence that nearly all the beneficial effects of chemotherapy and targeted agents come about through their action on cancer cells' mitochondria. In 2013, the oncologist Anthony Letai, MD, PhD, and colleagues at the Dana-Farber Cancer Institute, Boston, published an article with the provocative title, "Mitochondria: Gatekeepers of Response to Chemotherapy." In it, they wrote:

> "A longstanding question among not only patients but also the oncologists that are treating them is 'Why does chemotherapy work?'.... The mechanisms behind successful treatment of cancers are poorly understood."

Probing the mechanism of cancer drug activity, the scientists found:

> "Regardless of whether they are considered 'cytotoxic' or 'targeted,' most chemotherapies function by inducing a form of irreversible programmed cell death called apoptosis."

Other scientists pointed out the centrality of apoptosis to cancer:

> "...because ultimately all chemotherapies are believed to result directly or indirectly in induction of apoptosis."

But the key thing is that apoptosis begins as an attack by chemotherapy or targeted agents on the outer membrane of a cancer cell's mitochondria. The Dana-Farber authors consider this attack a "critical event during apoptosis." As a result, after this attack has occurred, the "mitochondria are progressively impaired in their ability to generate ATP [energy] and cannot maintain cellular survival...."

In fact, a drug's attack on the mitochondria's membrane is considered the "point of no return" for cancer cells. Findings like these have begun to shift attention away from the nucleus and towards the mitochondria—and metabolism, in general—as the central player in the question of cancer and its destruction.

Yet according to the somatic mutation theory (SMT), a mutation in the nucleus must come first; and then as a result of that DNA mutation, cells develop an altered metabolism. But according to the Dana-Farber researchers, the primary effect of both chemo and targeted agents is on the mitochondria and is *not* based on any interaction with the genes in the nucleus.

In fact, Professor DeMatteo seems to be able to restore normal metabolism with Gleevec and thus, in effect, to convert those cells from cancerous to normal. This raises the prospect that cancer may not need to be killed, but can be reprogrammed—or redifferentiated—back to normalcy.

In *Cancer as a Metabolic Disease*, as well as in his 178 PubMed listed papers on the topic, Professor Thomas Seyfried has pressed the case that cancer is defined by its abnormal metabolism. Disordered genes are secondary effects of that primary cause. Seyfried has stated that the "evidence against the central genetic dogma of oncology is now overwhelming." He claims that respiratory insufficiency at the level of the cell is the real source of mutations in the genome. Those who want to fully explore this fascinating, and fateful, question, should read Seyfried's book on this topic.

Professor Seyfried has raised the following key points in support of the metabolic theory:

1. Tumors have been found that have no somatic mutations.

2. "Normal tissues have been found to harbor mutations in known cancer genes and hotspots."

3. Cancer is very rare in chimpanzees, despite the fact that they have about 99% the same genome as humans.

4. Mitochondria transferred from normal cells to cancer cells can turn the cancer normal. But mitochondria from tumor cells can make normal cells malignant.

5. No tumor has yet been found that has completely normal mitochondria.

Whatever the role of genetics ultimately proves to be, the metabolic theory yields a simpler and less expensive approach to the cancer puzzle. It is simple because, ultimately, it has a single target, which is defective cellular metabolism centered in the mitochondria.

Broadly speaking, the metabolic approach includes two main components. The first of these is dietary manipulation. As a general rule, Seyfried advocates that patients follow a reduced calorie and ketogenic diet. As for medications, there is ongoing research, both laboratory and clinical, on the use of repurposed generic drugs for impacting metabolism. One such repurposed drug is metformin, a widely used oral medication for type 2 diabetes on the World Health Organization's list of essential medications. PubMed lists 4,500 studies on metformin and cancer, which appear at a rate of 500 per year. The NCI currently lists 14 clinical trials underway on metformin and cancer. Some of these studies state that the mechanism of action of metformin is metabolic:

> "Metformin may stop the growth of tumor cells by disrupting the energy source within [cancer] cells."

Other repurposed drugs include statins, aspirin, the antibiotic doxycycline, and the deworming agent mebendazole. Big Pharma and its defenders could not be happy with this shift. That is because repurposed drugs are generally out-of-patent and can therefore be manufactured by generic drugmakers, potentially at a low cost. For example, metformin currently sells for around four dollars per bottle for 60 (500 mg) tablets, or eight cents per pill. The probable retail cost would be under $100 per year. This is a far cry from the $475,000 per infusion price tag of Novartis's new therapy, Kymriah.

As we have shown, the targeted drug Gleevec also works as a metabolic agent, reprogramming cells to a normal metabolism. One wonders how many other so-called targeted agents work in exactly the same way. Young scientists at Cold Spring Harbor, armed with the new CRISPR gene editing tool, are poised to uncover the actual mechanism of many cancer drugs. This may turn out to be abnormal metabolism.

William Kaelin, MD, a professor of medicine at Harvard University, said in reference to the CRISPR findings:

> "I hope people will really wake up to the need to be much more rigorous."

As scientists become much more rigorous, they may find themselves increasingly in conflict with the central dogma of cancer, the somatic mutation theory, which insists that in each and every case cancer is a genetic disease. A reorientation towards the primacy of cancer metabolism could set the stage for a true revolution in oncology.

## Chapter 2. The Kleef protocol

In light of the potential side effects and other limitations of cancer immunotherapy, the best protocol would be one that includes cytokines (such as IL-2) and immune checkpoint drugs (such as Yervoy and Opdivo), but in the smallest effective dose.

These drugs would then be supplemented, as the need arose, with other treatments to boost the immune system, such as hyperthermia or medicinal mushrooms. It might even include low doses of chemotherapy, because of their anti-angiogenic and immune-modulating properties. It would also pay special attention (as research at M.D. Anderson Cancer Center suggested) to the lymphocyte count and the diversity of the gut microbiome, which impact the likelihood of a response to immunotherapy.

Tibor Bakacs, MD, PhD, DSc, and I, along with several co-authors, have been writing about the potential danger of checkpoint inhibitors since 2012. We warned of the potentially catastrophic consequences of unleashing the immune system against normal bodily tissues, as high-dose treatment can do. This did not win us any friends in the cancer establishment.

Then, in 2014, the Israeli immunotherapist Shimon Slavin, MD, Tibor Bakacs and I published a paper in *Pharmacological Research*, advocating treatment with lower-than-typical doses of immune checkpoint drugs in cancer. Soon afterwards, a protocol based around that idea was devised by the director of an independent cancer clinic in Vienna, Austria, Ralf Kleef, MD.

Kleef had served a two-year postdoctoral fellowship at the Cancer Research Institute and Sloan-Kettering Institute, working with Helen Coley Nauts and Lloyd J. Old, MD. In 1997, we worked together in the Practice Outcomes Monitoring and Evaluation System, a joint project of the National Cancer Institute and the NIH Office of Alternative Medicine. Later, Kleef worked as a postdoctoral investigator under Wayne Jonas, MD, director of the OAM. In 2001, Kleef and Jonas co-authored a landmark paper on the use of Coley's toxins, fever therapy and hyperthermia in cancer.

Kleef's use of lower doses of immune checkpoint inhibitors has been groundbreaking. Through a series of meeting presentations, abstracts and peer-reviewed articles, he has established proof of principle of what he calls a dose-adapted immune checkpoint therapy. Kleef uses two approved immune checkpoint drugs, Yervoy and Opdivo, which together form an FDA approved combination for melanoma. But he used these drugs in an off-label way, both in terms of the dosage and in the types of cancer to be treated.

The two immune checkpoints drugs are accompanied by other treatments that stimulate the immune system, such as interleukin-2 and regional and whole-body hyperthermia, the latter according to the method of Joan M. Bull, MD, of the University of Texas Medical School, Houston.

Kleef's proof of principle was the case of a 50-year-old woman who had been heavily pre-treated for triple negative breast cancer. She had far advanced lung metastases and severe shortness of breath, and had exhausted all conventional treatment when she came to him. In June 2015, Kleef treated her with low doses of Opdivo and Yervoy.

Kleef's patient experienced a complete remission of her extensive lung metastases and all cancer-related symptoms, with only transient and weak autoimmune symptoms. She remained alive for 27 months after the start of treatment. Although individual cases like this cannot be generalized to larger patient populations, it is also obvious that a triple negative breast cancer patient with such far advanced lung metastasis has an extremely low chance of extended survival.

Kleef presented this case at the Third Immunotherapy of Cancer Conference in Munich, Germany in 2016. Later, it formed the basis of a 2018 article in the peer-reviewed journal, *Integrative Cancer Therapies*. Since the treatment of that triple negative breast cancer patient, over 111 stage IV patients, suffering from a variety of cancer types, have been treated with a similar dose-adapted immune checkpoint blockade. A retrospective analysis was presented at the 8th Annual Meeting of the Oncology Association of Naturopathic Physicians in San Diego, CA, in 2019. In this presentation, the overall response rate in consecutively treated patients was 48%, with an objective response of 33%.

- 17 patients had a complete remission
- 20 patients achieved major partial remission
- 16 patients had stable disease
- 58 patients had progressive disease

This was very good considering the late stages of most of these patients, and the variety of tumor types under treatment. The median follow-up period was 22 months (3 to 47 months). The safety of Kleef's therapy was demonstrated by its side effect profile, which was superior to standard-dose treatment:

- Grade I side effects were observed in 21% of patients

- Grade II in 14% of patients
- Grade III in 7% of patients
- Grade IV in 2% of patients

With better patient selection, preservation of the immune and gastrointestinal systems, and appropriate doses of immune checkpoint inhibitors, this treatment might fulfill the promise of Carl H. June, MD, of the University of Pennsylvania, that the present moment is only "the tip of the iceberg" of effective immunotherapy of cancer.

It is important to note that Dr. Kleef's protocol consists entirely of FDA and EMA approved treatments. Therefore, his promising early results can now be either confirmed or refuted through prospective, controlled clinical trials. All that is required is the collective will to do so, and the funding to carry out the necessary trials.

In this context, it is useful to recall the words of a former director of the U.S. National Cancer Institute, Richard Klausner, MD:

> "As I go around the country, I talk about the tragedy of cancer to remind people that the tragedy is not our inability to prevent the inevitable or to do the impossible; tragedy is when a person, a group or a society fails to achieve the possible."

Kleef clinic in Vienna, Austria

## Chapter 3. Coley's toxins

William B. Coley, MD (1862-1936) showed, in the course of a 40-year career, that the injection of a mixture of two bacterial byproducts (popularly called "Coley's toxins") could have a profound effect on the progression of cancer.

For six decades after his death in 1936, his daughter, Helen Coley Nauts (1907-2001), systematically tracked down and published the outcome of all known cases of cancer treated with Coley's toxins—more than a thousand individuals. A surprising number of these had long remissions, which were often tantamount to a cure of the disease. Mrs. Nauts also identified the factors that greatly increased the likelihood of a favorable outcome. This represents a valuable intellectual heritage of over 100 years, a heritage that is now in danger of being totally lost through neglect.

The results of Coley's toxins when properly used have astonished most of the observers who looked at them without prejudice. Of course, today Coley is given lip service almost everywhere

William B. Coley, MD
1862-1936

as the "Father of Cancer Immunotherapy." But at the same time almost no mainstream author has an inkling of what was actually accomplished with this remarkable treatment.

In 18 detailed monographs, and numerous papers, Mrs. Nauts and her medical coauthors compiled a record of Coley toxin's successes—as well as its failures—over a period of 110 years from 1891 to her death in 2001. It would require a book of its own to fully explain the scope of this project. But I will briefly summarize the results in soft tissue sarcoma (STS), as analyzed in Mrs. Nauts' Monograph #16 (published in 1975).

Soft tissue sarcomas are relatively rare tumors of connective tissues, muscles, and veins. Beyond surgery for the earlier stages, these tumors are still very difficult to treat. There were 186 cases included in Mrs. Nauts' book on soft tissue sarcomas. For each case there was a microscopic confirmation of the diagnosis, usually by Memorial Hospital's skilled pathologists under the direction of James Ewing, MD. Of these, 49 patients were judged to have operable tumors, while 137 were deemed inoperable. The main endpoint was five-year survival, which was and remains a standard measure of treatment success.

The brilliance of Mrs. Nauts was her ability to extract from thousands of her father's letters, articles, and other documents, a clear understanding of what factors led to the greatest likelihood of success with his treatment. This is something that Coley himself, in the course of a very busy career as a surgeon, never managed to do.

To keep this discussion within bounds, I shall focus only on the inoperable cases (understanding that the operable cases generally fared even better).

1. Type of toxin: The best results were achieved with the toxins produced for Coley by Bertram H. Buxton, MD (1852-1934), a Cornell University Professor of Experimental Pathology, and Martha Tracy, MD (1876-1942), a graduate and future Dean of the Women's Medical College of Philadelphia, who was then doing post-doctoral work at Cornell. In 1912, Buxton returned to England and Tracy took over production. Modern-day preparations of Coley's toxins have generally been based on the formula designated Tracy XI. The five-year survival with Tracy's formula reached 67%. All formulations other than those of Buxton and Tracy were inferior and some commercial preparations (such as that of Parke-Davis) were actually inert.

2. Stage of disease: There was a 50% 5-year survival among the primary inoperable cases, as well as the recurrent inoperable ones and those with cachexia or a poor general condition. Mrs. Nauts emphasized that the toxins only provided palliation in terminal or end-stage disease.

3. Duration of therapy: The rate of response and survival went up dramatically as the duration of the treatment increased.
    - Those who took the treatment for one week had no five-year survival.
    - Those who took it for two weeks had 14% five-year survival.

- Those who took it for two months had a 42% chance of five-year survival.
- Those who took it for four months had 48% five-year survival.
- Those who took it for six months experienced 80% five-year survival. Patients also needed to take the treatment as often as they could tolerate it, which in practice meant either every day or every other day.

4. Reaction Elicited: Among the inoperable soft tissue sarcoma patients who developed little or no fever or chills, there was only a 20% chance of 5-year survival. But among those who routinely developed a fever of 102° to 104° F, and chills, there was a 60% 5-year survival.

Coley noted as early as the 1890s that results with sarcoma were better than with more common types of cancer. But it is incorrect to state that Coley's toxins were *only* effective as a treatment of sarcoma. There were in fact significant results in many common forms of cancer, including breast and colon, which are the subjects of some of Mrs. Nauts other monographs.

There is an extraordinary chart in her contribution to a 1982 book, *Bacteria and Cancer,* in which Mrs. Nauts summarized the 5-year survival of 437 inoperable cancer patients after fever therapy alone. Mrs. Nauts gave the fraction of cases "cured," and to which I have added the percentages:

- Giant cell tumors 15/19 = 78.9%
- Uterine sarcoma 8/11 = 72.7%
- Cervical carcinoma 2/3 = 66.7%
- Hodgkin lymphoma 10/15 = 66.7%
- Ovarian carcinoma 10/15 = 66.7%
- Breast cancer 13/20 = 65%
- Malignant melanoma 10/17 = 58.8%
- Soft tissue sarcoma 78/138 = 56.5%
- Non-Hodgkin lymphoma 42/86 = 48.8%
- Colon cancer 5/11 = 45.5%
- Kidney cancer 3/7 = 42.9%
- Testicular cancer 14/43 = 32.6%
- Ewing sarcoma 11/52 = 21.2%

Total 221/437 = 50.6%

Some people might think that these results, while valid a century ago, are no longer possible today. But there is a contemporary analysis of the effects of Coley's toxins in stage IV cancer. This was a cohort of patients who were treated with the MBVax company's Coley's fluid, as reported in Donald H. MacAdam's very informative book *The Reinvention of Coley's Toxins* (2018). The MBVax vaccine was created for MacAdam's company by Stephen Hoption Cann, PhD, of the University of British Columbia, based on the historic Tracey XI formula. The overall objective response rate (the total of complete and partial responses) using MBVax's Coley's fluid was 71%. There were 18 patients with verifiable stage IV cancer who experienced a complete response, which was 21% of the total number traced. One of these was René Chee, PhD, a biologist with degrees from Stanford University and the University of California, San Diego. Dr. Chee was diagnosed with a rare and aggressive cancer in 2008. In 2016 she and her husband Edward, a fellow Stanford graduate, wrote a book, *Curing Cancer With Immunotherapy,* about her successful use of Coley's fluid.

### Not-so-benign neglect

One of the oddest things about modern oncology is that virtually everyone acknowledges Coley's pioneering role in immunotherapy, yet almost nobody practices his kind of treatment. How can this be? First of all, the organization that Mrs. Nauts founded in 1953, the Cancer Research Institute, now only pays lip service to her historic role, but does not publicize her immense contribution.

In the 1970s, Mrs. Nauts ran the Cancer Research Institute out of her New York City apartment. Today, the organization takes in over $35 million per year in donations and has net assets of over $50 million. In 2017 its director received a compensation package of $464,756. Six other employees were earning between $150,000 to $350,000. An article at their website states, without any basis in fact, that Coley's toxins are far inferior to modern day methods of immunotherapy. In answer to the question of why Coley's toxins are not being used today, this is what they say:

> "A final hurdle—and perhaps the most pertinent one today—is the fact that cancer immunology has progressed so far in the past few years that other approaches have far eclipsed Coley's toxins."

How can one say this, when there are no proper clinical trials by which to make such a comparison? Meanwhile, the Cancer Research Institute has not made Mrs. Nauts' groundbreaking monographs available. These are in serious danger of disappearing, since only a few copies still exist in libraries around the world, and some of these are relegated to warehouses. A widespread dissemination of Nauts' work would show that modern drugs have *not* far eclipsed Coley's results.

A clear-cut and detailed affirmation of the validity of the historical results, with online and print republication of Mrs. Nauts's monographs, might precipitate sweeping changes in the treatment of cancer worldwide. In fact, a recognition of what Coley's toxins actually achieved might create a crisis for the business of oncology, since the cost of Coley's treatment would be about 1/50th that of conventional approaches.

One beneficial outcome might be the formation of a Coley Cancer Center, which would research questions related to the mechanism of action of the toxins, foster the development of the most effective versions of the vaccine, and treat people with the best possible integrative approaches. Creating such a center might be a good thing to do with $50 million in assets.

But one cannot, at this point, simply introduce these toxins into general practice, without getting FDA approval and training doctors and other healthcare providers to fully understanding that in cancer, fever can and should be used as a beneficial part of the treatment.

It is crucial to educate the professionals who serve on institutional review boards. The minimal results reported with Coley's toxins at Nordwest Hospital in Frankfurt showed that, without such an understanding, institutional review boards will never approve a full-scale fever treatment.

Under pressure from the hospital's board, the doctors involved in this trial were forced to give anti-fever drugs such as acetaminophen (Tylenol) to bring down the fevers that were the main anticancer component of the treatment!

The toxins were then given only twice a week for two weeks, a dose level that Nauts showed in abundant detail was unlikely to bring about any long-term remissions.

Coley showed that fever is part of the natural defense against cancer and other diseases. But at the present time, the trend regarding fever is not a good one. There are over 65,000 references to fever *reducing* (antipyretic) drugs in PubMed versus a mere 36 references to "fever therapy" for cancer.

A properly designed Coley Cancer Center would have a staff that fully understood the positive role that fevers perform in this treatment. It would have an institutional review board that included the world experts on this type of therapy. Coley patients could safely achieve a fever every day or every other day for a period of four to six months. Best of all it would be a modern version of an old-fashioned sanitarium, which could comfortably house cancer patients, with well trained medical staff on call for consultations and evaluations. Under such conditions, the world could finally realize the true potential of Coley's revolutionary treatment.

From 1965 to 1975
William B. Coley's methods
were on this blacklist published
by the American Cancer Society.

# Section III: Scientific Research Methods

## Chapter 1. What is an effective treatment?

**"The best interest of the patient is the only interest to be considered."**

*—William J. Mayo, MD, co-founder of the Mayo Clinic*

Patients are given drugs based on claims of beneficial activity. But few people investigate what researchers actually mean when they call a cancer drug effective. Scientists who conduct clinical trials use a flexible definition. Different studies declare a drug effective based on similar sounding, but different, criteria. Patients, who are in a vulnerable position, may not stop to ask exactly what is being promised by advocates of an aggressive treatment.

Very few treatments are proven to deliver any actual benefit to cancer patients. That is because they are based on dubious measurements, or what scientists call surrogate endpoints.

The *NCI Cancer Dictionary* defines a surrogate endpoint this way:

> "In clinical trials, [it is] an indicator or sign used in place of another to tell if a treatment works. Surrogate endpoints include a shrinking tumor or lower biomarker levels. They may be used instead of stronger indicators, such as longer survival or improved quality of life, because the results of the trial can be measured sooner."

The use of surrogate endpoints may increase the speed and efficiency of getting new drugs to market. But many experts warn that these surrogate endpoints have little or nothing to do with actual patient benefit. A review in *JAMA Internal Medicine* concluded:

> "Most studies of surrogate endpoints in oncology find low correlations with survival.... The evidence supporting the use of surrogate endpoints in oncology is limited."

From the beginning, shrinking tumors was not a major goal in itself, but simply a convenient tool for tracking a drug's contribution to the real goal, which is increased overall survival with a good quality of life. The DeVita textbook strongly affirms that:

> "A key principle in drug development is that the benefit sought in oncology is first and foremost increased overall survival."

The decision to measure tumor shrinkages was only made "to reduce error and not because it represented a value that conferred benefit." Even the National Cancer Institute website states:

> "Surrogate endpoints are not always true indicators or signs of how well a treatment works."

But oncology as a whole often ignores this crucial point. For most kinds of cancer there are in fact no reliable surrogate endpoints in any clinical trial. Surrogate endpoints are thus not a sufficient basis for the FDA to approve a new drug. They are not true indicators of how well a treatment works, but are in fact unreliable substitutes that allow drug companies to gain rapid approval of unproven remedies.

A commentary in *JAMA Internal Medicine* exposed the misuse of surrogate endpoints as a barometer of the success of new drugs:

> "The most important commonality across these measures is their lack of patient centeredness: the inability to reliably correlate these surrogates with outcomes that patients care about."

In other words, surrogates do not generally measure things that bring real benefit to cancer patients—increased overall survival with a reasonable quality of life. The problem was well summarized by oncologists at the Sunnybrook Health Sciences Center in Toronto:

> "Measuring overall survival as an endpoint in clinical trials requires large patient numbers and increased length of follow-up, thus potentially delaying the approval of new agents."

However, they reiterated what so many have said before, but which cannot be said often enough:

> "Overall survival offers the greatest clinical gain, provided that quality of life is not compromised. As an endpoint, overall survival is easily measured, unambiguous, objective, felt to be clinically significant, and unaffected by the timing of assessment."

Shrinking a tumor, which is what oncologists mean by a response, does not automatically provide any survival benefit to patients. As a measure of actual value, it is of little use. It does not correlate well with increased survival.

On this point we are in agreement with the American Cancer Society:

> "The goals of treatment are to 'cure' the cancer, if possible; prolong survival; and provide the highest possible quality of life during and after treatment."

That is absolutely correct. Prolonging survival means helping people live months or years longer than they would have without the treatment in question. If a drug does not do that, it is ineffective from the patient's point of view.

But in recent years—and this is crucial—the FDA has caved in to Big Pharma on this fundamental point. Since 1992, they have given accelerated approval to drugs based on dubious markers of alleged benefit. Why have they lowered their standards in this way? To quote *MedPageToday:*

> "The FDA does not make decisions in a vacuum—it is under constant pressure from politicians, pharmaceutical companies, and advocacy groups to speed up the drug approval process."

In drug development, every month counts. According to John Abraham, PhD, of King's College, London:

> "Indeed, speed of regulatory review is now the primary quantitative performance indicator for the agency."

It is not only cheaper to do smaller phase II trials, but such trials are much quicker to perform. Since, with a patented agent the clock is ticking on the company's exclusive control, every month added to a drug's shelf life can mean tens or hundreds of millions of dollars in increased sales. A phase II trial generally takes about two years, while a phase III trial can take up to five. So, naturally, companies, and Big Pharma in general, are always trying to shorten the testing period by weakening the FDA's requirements of proof.

An insightful website, healthnewsreview.org, which stopped regular publication in 2018 for lack of financial support, reported this point very accurately:

> "The use of weak surrogate-based evidence has flooded the market with expensive duds.... That's especially concerning in cancer: drugs are frequently approved on the basis of uncertain markers such as 'progression free survival,' which

> is the amount of time between treatment and worsening of symptoms."

A very important *JAMA Oncology* study of new drugs approved from 2009 to 2013 showed the result of this weakening:

- Only 30% of the FDA's cancer drug approvals were based on an actual increase in overall survival.
- 35% were based on the surrogate progression-free survival.
- Another 35% were based on the surrogate objective response rate.
- No approvals were based on maintaining or improving quality of life.

A 2019 analysis by the *Wall Street Journal* was headlined "Fast-Track Drug Approval, Designed for Emergencies, Is Now Routine." It showed that the problem is only getting worse:

> "The U.S. Food and Drug Administration approved a record 43 new drugs last year through fast-track programs that skip or shorten major steps other drugs must pass, or 73% of total new drugs. That compares with 10 expedited drugs, or 38% of the total, approved 10 years ago."

It is often claimed that the FDA lowered its standards in order to speed effective new drugs to market. This was the takeaway message from the HIV/AIDS pandemic. But fewer than half of the cancer drugs it approves actually extend survival, even by as little as one month. The other approvals merely promote the bottom line of Big Pharma, while providing an illusion of effectiveness to patients and doctors.

Patients, swayed by television, online and newspaper reports, may clamor for the fast approval of a new "miracle drug" they have heard about. But patients as a group do not benefit from having weak or useless items added to the medical drug supply. This proliferation of new drugs also makes an oncologist's job more difficult. Once upon a time, oncologists had to thoroughly understand a few dozen drugs and how to use them. According to one oncologist:

> "In a 60-year period, between 1940 and 2000, the FDA approved 72 drugs to treat cancer. But that number more than doubled over the next decade. In 2018 alone, the FDA approved 19 cancer-related drugs."

The National Cancer Institute website now lists 555 cancer drugs, each with its own panoply of side effects. Cytotoxic chemotherapy, targeted agents, immune checkpoint inhibitors, each of these alone, and in combination, creates situations that are difficult to comprehend, much less control. The proliferation of drugs makes life more confusing for all concerned, and reduces the possibility of choosing the most promising path. And the drugs keep coming—relentless economic growth being a Wall Street imperative—with 45 new oncology approvals in 2019 alone.

The FDA is under enormous pressure to keep the industry thriving through a steady stream of new approvals. This is more of an economic than a medical imperative. According to the University of Toronto economists Myron J. Gordon and Jeffrey S. Rosenthal, capitalist firms operating in a competitive market are subject to a growth imperative. By this they mean that without constant growth, bankruptcy is practically certain in the long run. So there is relentless economic pressure—whose source is ultimately Wall Street investors—to come up with a steady stream of new drugs and indications—to fulfill the competitive needs of drug companies.

In response to this pressure, in recent decades the FDA has introduced various back door ways for companies to gain a new drug approval. None of these ways requires rigorous proof of actual benefit to patients. In fact, they were explicitly formulated to grant approval *without* such proof.

The FDA can now speed up the approval of an unproven drug by using any of the following programs:

1. Accelerated Approval
2. Priority Review
3. Breakthrough Therapy Designation
4. Orphan Drug Designation
5. Fast Track Designation
6. Regenerative Medicine Advanced Therapy

Sometimes a drug receives two or three special approvals at once. This happened in 2018 with the drug Vitrakvi. According to an FDA media release:

> "The FDA granted this application Priority Review and Breakthrough Therapy designation. Vitrakvi also received Orphan Drug designation, which provides incentives to assist and encourage the development of drugs for rare diseases."

This trend is essential for Big Pharma and Wall Street. The profitability of a new drug is based on the company's exploitation of its patents. A patent excludes anyone else from marketing that agent for 20 years. It is a legal monopoly. During that time, according to current U.S. law, one can charge patients whatever the market will bear. The biggest purchaser of drugs, Health and Human Services, was precluded by the reactionary *Medicare Modernization Act of 2003*, from negotiating prices. And that is the essence of how new drugs have become so astronomically expensive in the U.S.

Since it usually it takes from eight to ten years to complete the development of a new compound, there is a limited window of time during which a drug can be made profitable. After 20 years, a drug generally loses patent protection and becomes generic. According to a legal information website:

> "It's estimated that once a generic drug hits the market after a patent expiration, name brand sales drop by 80 percent."

So every month that the company can shave off the drug approval process, through accelerated approval, is worth a small fortune. To be clear, a big drug company's motive for shortening the FDA's once-rigorous testing process is not humanitarian. It is entirely profit-driven. They say they are speeding effective new drugs to market to benefit suffering humanity. But how can anyone know that a new drug is effective, before there is proof of increased overall survival?

Or, as *ProPublica* put it in 2018:

> "As patients (or their insurers) shell out tens or hundreds of thousands of dollars for unproven drugs, manufacturers reap a windfall. For them, expedited approval can mean not only sped-up sales but also...FDA incentives worth hundreds of millions of dollars."

## Danger of accelerated approval

A similar situation is found in the wake of the FDA's accelerated approval process. Since December 11, 1992, the FDA has frequently granted accelerated approval to a drug "on the basis of studies that predict — rather than establish — clinical benefit," to quote Matthew Herder, writing at statnews.com (2019). Herder succinctly summarizes the risks associated with this set-up:

> "In theory, such risk is temporary: all accelerated approvals require post-market trials to confirm the effectiveness of the drug after approval. The trouble lies in getting those post-market studies done, and done well. Most are completed within four years, but delays are common. In the meantime, patients are exposed to unforeseen safety risks or, in some cases, forego other care options while taking new drugs that ultimately do not serve their intended purposes. In addition, when these studies are finally completed, they often fail to yield clinically meaningful information."

Some Big Pharma firms don't want to risk billions of dollars in potential sales on the chance that they might uncover new side effects, or that an FDA commissioner might pull an ineffective drug from the market. This only happened once, as we describe below.

According to an exposé by the investigative team at ProPublica:

> "While the FDA expedited drug approvals, it's content to wait a decade or more for the post-marketing studies that manufacturers agree to do. Plus, since the drug is already on the market, the manufacturer no longer has a financial incentive to study its impact—and stands to lose money if the results are negative. Of post-marketing studies agreed to by manufacturers in 2009 and 2010, 20% had not started five years later, and another 25% were still ongoing."

In other words, Big Pharma drags its feet on almost half of these post-marketing studies, because they do not want any negative studies to appear while they still have a functioning patent.

## Buying a voucher

One of the more bizarre aspects of the drug approval process is that companies can buy and sell FDA Priority Review vouchers. This has nothing to do with the intrinsic merit of the drug in question, but is purely a financial transaction. Thus, in 2018, the British-Swedish giant AstraZeneca (AZ) paid $95 million to a smaller drug company, Sobi, for the right to have one of AZ's new drugs given an expedited review. They planned to use it on any of ten drugs under development. According to an industry website:

> "Using the voucher, AstraZeneca will be able to shave four months off the FDA regulatory review of one drug, enabling it to race through the process in six months. AstraZeneca is yet to disclose which drugs it will use the voucher on...."

In 1992, under the terms of the Prescription Drug User Act (PADUA), the FDA agreed to a two-tier approval system. According to the agency's website:

> "A Priority Review designation means FDA's goal is to take action on an application within 6 months (compared to 10 months under standard review)."

Initially, Priority Review was touted as a way of speeding up the development of promising drugs. According to the FDA:

> "A Priority Review designation will direct overall attention and resources to the evaluation of applications for drugs that, if approved, would be significant improvements in the safety or effectiveness of the treatment, diagnosis, or prevention of serious conditions when compared to standard applications."

But a thriving market has now developed in buying and selling shortcuts to the FDA review process:

> "In November [2018] Eli Lilly bought a voucher for...$80 million, [and] in March [2019] Biohaven Pharmaceutical paid a little more, $105 million, for another voucher. While the first voucher sold for $67 million, the value of the assets quickly spiraled, culminating in AbbVie paying $350 million for one."

This practice resembles the indulgences that rich people bought from the Catholic Church in medieval Europe as "a way to reduce the amount of punishment one had to undergo for sins." It was this sale of indulgences that motivated Martin Luther, in 1517, to nail his "95 Theses" to the door of the Castle Church in Wittenberg, Germany. This was the beginning of the Reformation in Europe. The parallel seems obvious and the resistance, when it comes, may eventually be as revolutionary.

## What is survival?

We all think we know what survival means—staying alive. But if you delve into the medical literature you discover confusion about this simple word, at least when applied to cancer. That is because, in oncology, the word survival is used in many different ways.

According to the *NCI Cancer Dictionary,* there are a dozen types of survival:

1. Cause-specific survival
2. Disease-free survival
3. Disease-specific survival
4. Event-free survival
5. Five-year survival
6. Mean survival
7. Median overall survival
8. Metastasis-free survival
9. Overall survival
10. Progression-free survival
11. Relapse-free survival
12. Relative survival

By far, the most important of these is the median overall survival. This represents how long people on average actually live following the start of their treatment. Overall survival is straightforward, meaning:

> "...the length of time from the start of treatment for a disease, such as cancer, that patients diagnosed with the disease are still alive."

That in fact corresponds to the general dictionary definition of the word "survival":

> "The state or fact of continuing to live or exist, typically in spite of an accident, ordeal, or difficult circumstances."

And according to a 2013 medical journal article:

> "Overall survival...traditionally represents the most clinically relevant and convincing endpoint in clinical trial design...."

From the point of view of statistical analysis, overall survival is also the most precise measurement of the effect of a treatment for a life-threatening disease such as cancer. That is because, to quote the same 2013 article,

> "It can be assessed with 100% accuracy both for its occurrence and timing."

But usually when drug developers and medical reporters talk about survival they mean something else: progression-free survival. Progression-free survival is a much more ambiguous term. FDA defines it as:

> "The time from randomization until objective tumor progression or death, whichever occurs first."

As Mary Chris Jaklevic wrote at HealthNewsReview.org:

> "Most new cancer treatments haven't been proven to help patients live longer or feel better. Instead they delay the growth of tumors, which may be faster to measure but doesn't necessarily indicate a tangible benefit for patients."

Progression-free survival is often what medical writers mean by increased survival. This is utterly confusing and misleading to the average reader. Thus, as the same reporter explained:

- The headline in the U.K.'s *Telegraph* about the drug Lynparza reads as follows: "Revolution in prostate cancer care as off-label breast cancer drug doubles survival."
- A story in the *Miami Herald* claimed that the drug veliparib could help at least 30 percent more patients and have wide-ranging implications in the treatment of ovarian cancer.
- The website *Healthline* called the approval of the drug Tecentriq big news with a substantial survival benefit for people with triple-negative breast cancer.

In each and every case, the revolutionary, wide-ranging big news, as these papers called it, concerned an increase in progression-free survival, and not actual overall survival. In fact, the phrase progression-free survival is so misleading, that in 2019 Vincent Rajkumar, MD, of the Mayo Clinic very reasonably called for it to be renamed "progression-free *duration,*" to remove the implication that it had anything to do with the patient's actual survival. As Dr. Rajkumar wrote:

> "Terms are useless if they convey a wrong meaning. No matter what the intent and rationale are, the

> word PFS [progression-free survival] is being misused. Patients are increasingly getting data directly from the media and the internet. So it is time to replace misleading terms."

There are other reasons to reject the use of progression-free survival as a surrogate endpoint. Progression-free survival generally represents an estimated length of time, during which the disease has seemingly not progressed or grown in volume or extent. But establishing the exact date that a progression began is next to impossible. And determining whether cancer has progressed at all is in part subjective.

We first learned this from a 1976 study from the Mayo Clinic's Charles Moertel, MD and James A. Hanley, PhD, in which 16 experienced oncologists were asked to measure whether a tumor had grown by 25%. In that case, they couldn't agree with each other 25% of the time.

Progression-free survival is not a common sense concept. As stated, it is defined as the length of time from random assignment in a clinical trial to disease progression, or death from any cause. It can also mean that the patients in question survived longer before doctors detected a tumor worsening. It does NOT mean that the patients actually survived even one day longer than they would have without treatment.

To summarize: overall survival and progression-free survival, despite sharing the word survival, are very different animals. An increase in overall survival represents a real benefit, at least to patients in a defined group. It is a definite thing, an unambiguous endpoint measure, which gives precise accuracy for the time of the event, to quote the FDA. It means that, on average, these patients lived longer, and had a greater chance of being kept alive compared to those who did not receive the treatment.

In a devastating study of progression-free survival in *JAMA Internal Medicine* in 2018, two dozen researchers from Canada, Japan, Poland and Egypt, confirmed what many smaller studies of the topic had already concluded. To quote a summary from the industry website, *CenterWatch:*

> "Progression-free survival is too unpredictable and inconsistent to serve as a viable surrogate for overall survival."

How sobering that, after 40 years of largely futile striving to find a quicker and cheaper way to approve drugs, there was no better endpoint of a study than overall survival. This *JAMA Internal*

*Medicine* report examined 38 randomized clinical trials involving 14,000 patients, spanning 12 different types of cancer. The average difference in progression-free survival between the intervention and the control arms was a mere 1.9 months.

To quote an analysis of this landmark study by the science journalist, James Miessler:

> "There are only two possible reasons to use progression-free survival as an endpoint in oncology—the belief that it's a valid surrogate endpoint for overall survival and the assumption that patients who live longer without disease progression—even without longer survival—will experience a higher quality of life."

In other words, some people argue that progression-free survival is desirable in itself because it automatically leads to an improvement in one's health-related quality of life. Supposedly, the patient in question will experience relief from continuous worry about the progression of the disease. This may seem like a commonsensical benefit, but it turns out to be not necessarily true. Again, to quote Miessler:

> "Progression-free survival's association with improved health-related quality of life is far from self-evident...because health-related quality of life is likely to be impaired by adverse events resulting from the treatments responsible for prolonged progression-free survival."

In stage IV cancer, the side effects of chemotherapy may destroy any relief from disease progression that the patient might have otherwise enjoyed. Yet, for the last few decades FDA has often granted accelerated approval based on progression-free survival or one of the other surrogate endpoints. At its website, FDA explains why:

> "In 1992, FDA instituted the accelerated approval regulations. These regulations allowed drugs for serious conditions that filled an unmet medical need to be approved based on a surrogate endpoint. Using a surrogate endpoint enabled FDA to approve these drugs faster."

Accelerated approval was a compromise between the need for rigorous proof of effectiveness (FDA's standard for 25 years) and growing demands for more rapid entry of drugs into the marketplace. Accelerated approval was supposed to be provisional. The company was allowed to market its drug for a while, making hundreds of millions of dollars in the process, but was still required to perform randomized controlled trials to prove that it had an impact on overall survival.

Despite its inferiority as an endpoint, there are economic reasons why promoters of new cancer treatments favor progression-free survival in clinical trials. According to an official U.S. 2013 Agency for Healthcare Research and Quality (AHRQ) report:

> "In comparison to overall survival, the gold standard for cancer drug evaluation, progression-free survival can be evaluated using shorter, smaller and less costly studies."

But progression-free survival introduces an opportunity for biases in favor of approval. To quote the AHRQ report:

> "Progression-free survival's use as a primary endpoint, however, can be challenging, as it is subject to a wide range of potential biases, and its use as a surrogate for overall survival has been demonstrated only for certain disease and treatment scenarios."

## A hypothetical situation

Here is an example of how one could extend progression-free survival without actually helping the patient live a day longer. In this hypothetical situation, Patient A enters a clinical trial and starts treatment on Experimental Drug X. Let us say that he is scheduled to be examined by his doctors every three months. At his first three-month evaluation, he has no apparent increase in the size of his tumors. He is thus declared to be experiencing progression-free survival. At his six-month evaluation, however, his doctors see that the disease is in fact progressing. Patient A then dies on the one-year anniversary of beginning his new drug treatment. But FDA rules mandate that progression-free survival is to be measured by the time progression is first detected. Since this was first noticed on the six-month anniversary of the start of treatment, patient A is entered into the record books as having had six months of progression-free survival.

By contrast, Patient B is diagnosed with the exact same type and stage of disease as Patient A. She entered the same clinical trial as patient A, but she received drug Y, which is an old standard treatment, instead of experimental drug X (like patient A). Unfortunately, her disease progressed steadily over the following year. Like patient A, she died exactly one year after starting treatment. Thus she experienced *no* progression-free survival.

When it came time to write up the results, the investigators accurately reported that "patient A gained six months of progression-free survival from drug X," whereas patient B had no such increase. They therefore concluded that drug X was superior to drug Y. Based on such results, they might even have achieved their goal, which was accelerated FDA approval for drug X.

But, here are two points to consider:

- Experimental drug X did not provide any *actual benefit* to patient A or others like him. He did not live a day longer than patient B, since they both died exactly one year after they entered the clinical trial. So what exactly was the benefit to patient A of achieving this increased "progression-free survival," if it did not extend his life?
- The definition of progression is subjective. It can be based on prejudice or human error. In fact, in the Moertel study, oncologists, shown the same scans twice in a "blind" fashion, did not even agree with *themselves* 19% of the time.

In fact, FDA's *Guidance for Industry* on this topic contains the extraordinary statement that "there are no standard regulatory criteria for defining progression." The FDA grants approval based on progression-free survival, but cannot provide a standard definition of what progression even means!

## Objective response rates

Another surrogate endpoint is the objective response rate. Measuring the response of a tumor to a particular drug can be an important consideration in a new drug's approval. An objective response can be either a complete or a partial response.

A response is the shrinkage of a tumor. In the days when scientists thought about cancer simplistically, the size of a tumor seemed of overwhelming importance. Many people still assume that shrinking tumors is in fact the goal of therapy. It may seem odd to learn that shrinking a tumor is, formally, a surrogate marker. Unless the tumor is pressing on a nerve, or otherwise interfering with a vital organ, it may not be important to reduce its size.

A comprehensive review of the relationship of objective

responses and overall survival by Vinay Prasad, MD, found little correlation between the two. While tumor shrinkage is a commonly used surrogate measurement in cancer trials, it often has a low correlation with longer life expectancy. Mikkael Sekeres, MD, director of the leukemia program at the Cleveland Clinic, has explained:

> "I would say to a patient, this drug may be more likely to shrink a tumor either partially or even completely, but that may in fact be a pyrrhic victory if it doesn't help you live better or longer."

Sekeres voted against approving the cancer drug Folotyn at an FDA advisory panel meeting in 2009. But his side was out-voted ten to four. Three years later, the European Medicines Agency rejected the same drug because it had not been proven to actually help patients. To this day, Folotyn's FDA-mandated label contains this caveat:

> "This indication is based on overall response rate. Clinical benefit such as improvement in...overall survival has not been demonstrated."

And, indeed, a search of PubMed (10 years after its approval) reveals no randomized controlled trials of the drug. Based on this surrogate endpoint, though, the manufacturer, Allos Therapeutics, rolled out the drug for a certain type of lymphoma. The treatment's cost: $30,000 per month. And Folotyn is far from unique. A 2016 analysis in *Lancet Oncology* concluded:

> "A retrospective study of U.S. Food and Drug Administration approvals of cancer drugs found a high percentage are based on surrogate endpoints— progression-free survival or tumor response—with no published analysis of the surrogate's correlation with survival."

One odd fact about using the response rate as a surrogate is how weak these responses have to be to gain new drug approval. A 2019 report in *JAMA Internal Medicine* showed that of 85 cancer drugs approved on the basis of the percentage of patients whose tumors shrank beyond an arbitrary threshold, not many such shrinkages were necessary to gain approval.

The median response rate measures the percentage of patients whose tumors shrank by a specified amount. On average, just 41% of patients had such shrinkages. And in 16% of cases, the FDA approved a drug simply because it shrank tumors in fewer than 20%

of the patients. The authors concluded:

> "Many cancer drugs are approved on the basis of low or modest response rates, typically in single-arm studies."

Let's put that another way. If you told your doctor that you wanted a 50-50 chance that a drug would shrink tumors to a significant degree, how many of these 85 FDA-approved drugs would deliver that? The short answer is: none.

## The Naci analysis

Huseyin Naci, PhD, MPH, of the London School of Economics, has been actively studying and criticizing the drug approval process. In a 2017 article in the *Milbank Quarterly,* Naci focused on 37 new drugs that had received FDA's accelerated approval between 2000 and 2013. He showed that only one third of the studies leading to approval were actually randomized controlled trials. And many of these were irrelevant. In scientific terms, they were outside the therapeutic areas for which the agents received their initial accelerated approval. Professor Naci's conclusions were as follows:

> "Most clinical studies including these agents are small and nonrandomized, and about a third are conducted in unapproved areas.... Most randomized trials including these therapeutic agents are not designed to directly evaluate their clinical benefits...."

But now access to the database that Naci used to make this analysis is itself under attack. One impact of President Trump's pro-business agenda emerged in late 2019 when the FDA proposed new rules that would severely curtail the ability of independent researchers such as Naci to search the documents upon which FDA decisions are made. This is the so-called gray literature, which consists of unpublished data, such as that found in white papers, reports, and government documents, according to the medical journalist, Christina Bennett, MS.

Independent researchers, such as Marian McDonagh, PharmD, associate director of the evidence-based practice center, Oregon Health and Science University, used gray data to provide a window into the FDA's pro-industry bias. This was how Professor Naci was able to prove that half of the randomized control trials that led to approvals between 2014 and 2016 had a high risk of bias.

But in June 2019, the FDA announced plans to remove the gray documents from the Drugs@FDA website and to replace them with so-called integrated reviews of the data. These integrated reviews will hide and obscure the actual facts. This effort was part of the Orwellian-sounding New Drugs Regulatory Program Modernization. Under this "modernization," studies such as those of McDonagh and Naci would be impossible to perform. This is yet another example of how various administrations have watered down FDA's standards to make it a rubber stamp for the drug industry.

## The Haslam review

In 2019, Alyson Haslam and others showed in the *European Journal of Cancer* a weak association at best between progression-free survival and actual patient benefit. They concluded:

> "Most surrogates in oncology had low or modest correlation with overall survival, which suggests that caution should be used when making conclusions based on surrogate markers."

In fact, in at least one instance, a drug which increased progression-free survival led to a *decrease* in overall survival. This was the phase III Bellini trial, reported in the *ASCO Post* in June 2019. The addition of the drug venetoclax to standard drugs appeared to hasten the deaths of patients with multiple myeloma. The combination including venetoclax had a progression-free survival that was nearly double that of the more traditional group (22.4 months vs. 11.4 months). However, and it's a big however, the overall survival was not improved:

> "Median overall survival was not reached in either arm but favored the [standard] group."

To quote an editorial in the *British Medical Journal:*

> "In the recent Bellini trial, patients with multiple myeloma who received venetoclax had *shorter survival* than those who received a control treatment (even though venetoclax appeared more effective than the control on the basis of commonly-used surrogate endpoints like progression-free survival and response rate)."

## EMA's approvals

Big drug companies are multinational and many of the same problems of drug testing exist outside the U.S. Let's take a look at the Western world's other large drug regulator, the European Medicines Agency. A 2017 study in the *British Medical Journal* drew equally devastating conclusions about the regulatory environment in Europe:

> "Most drugs entered the European market without evidence of benefit on survival or quality of life. At a minimum of 3.3 years after market entry, there was still no conclusive evidence that these drugs either extended or improved life for most cancer indications. When there were survival gains over existing treatment options or placebo, they were often marginal."

At the time of approval, only 35% of new cancer drugs in Europe increased median overall survival. Only half (51%) of the EU-approved cancer drugs actually benefited cancer patients in any way. Almost every patient was exposed to the toxicity of these agents. But perhaps the most shocking finding of all was that, even when a drug did extend survival, that benefit was very small:

> "The magnitude of the benefit on overall survival ranged from 1.0 to 5.8 months (median 2.7 months)."

So even the "good drugs," by which we mean those that actually did extend survival, only did so by on average fewer than three months. In some cases, cancer drugs have been approved in the EU based on a one-month increase in survival. According to *Reuters:*

> "There's not much evidence to show that most new cancer drugs approved in Europe in recent years can help patients live longer or improve their quality of life...."

A 2019 follow-up study in the *British Medical Journal* showed that the problem is getting worse. The authors, based in the U.K., Canada and the U.S., looked at randomized controlled trials used to gain European approval for cancer drugs. During the years 2014 to 2016, the European Medicines Agency approved 32 new cancer medicines based on 54 studies. Of these 54 clinical trials, only 39 were randomized controlled trials that were available for analysis.

And of those 39, only 26% actually measured overall survival as a primary endpoint. The remaining 74% used surrogate endpoints, which are unproven to predict whether or not the patients will live longer. But even more startling was their finding that about half of the studies were at "high risk of bias." This was especially so when drug researchers used surrogate endpoints like progression-free survival and response rates, rather than measuring the real benefit of actual survival.

Huseyin Naci, PhD, the *British Medical Journal* study's first author, told STAT news:

> "We hope that patients will be advocates for more robust research and will demand better evidence that supports regulatory approvals of cancer drugs."

One must also question the ethics of performing clinical trials on terminally ill patients, with all the likely adverse events, and a survival advantage that averages less than three months.

The former European Medicines Agency building at Canary Wharf, London, United Kingdom. Because of Brexit, in 2019 the EMA moved to Amsterdam.

## Chapter 2. The takeover

Daniel S. Greenberg, founding editor of *Science & Government Report,* spent decades exposing "the penetration of pharmaceutical industry money into academic medical research." In his 2001 book, *Science, Money, and Politics: Political Triumph and Ethical Erosion,* this veteran journalist gave an overall assessment of the takeover of medicine by Big Pharma:

> "If their ethical senses were outraged by these events, the major institutions of science successfully concealed their distress from public view. Comfortable within the scientific ghetto, deft at raising public expectations and thereby stimulating generous support, the politicians of science are not comfortable with the seamy underside of their glittering enterprise. But they are not moved to do anything effective about it."

Today, the process is complete, as drug companies control, from start to finish, the evaluation and approval of new cancer drugs. By doing so, they are able to generate tens of billions of dollars in sales, one of the most profitable legal businesses in the world. In a very real sense, a million individuals' scourge has become a profitable market for Big Pharma. One could even say that, to a certain degree, Wall Street depends on this illness for its own prosperity, since cancer is crucial to the fate of several large drug companies, and pharmaceuticals are an important part of the stock market. Johnson & Johnson, Merck and Pfizer, are part of the 30-company Dow Jones Index, and all of them are dependent on cancer drug sales for their profitability.

Here are five key elements to Big Pharma's control of the drug approval process:

1. Big Pharma firms have a huge network of what former *New England Journal of Medicine* editor Marcia Angell, MD, called "hired hands." These are doctors at major universities and drug testing centers who accept drug company money.

2. Big Pharma spends billions on advertising and public relations, dominating once-independent journals and shaping media coverage of their products.

3. It has captured the Food and Drug Administration by exploiting the revolving door of employment.

4. They design, perform, analyze and ghost write the decisive papers on their drugs.

5. They employ an army of over 1,400 lobbyists to bribe, cajole and pressure Congress into doing their bidding. They have rarely been known not to get their way.

No surprise, then, that doctors who perform clinical trials, many of whom are taking money from pharmaceutical companies, are more likely to strongly endorsed the benefit of the experimental arm, consisting of patients getting the new drug under study.

Not everyone in oncology is corrupt. But the growing influence of Big Pharma over many of the leading figures in oncology has serious consequences. Between 1975 and 2004, the proportion of studies in which the authors declared a new drug to be safe and effective in a clinical trial increased from 31% to 49%. During this time, drugs were not conspicuously more effective. Instead, oncologists were more compliant. The end result has been an explosion of expensive new anti-cancer agents, most of which are of unproven value to cancer patients, but which generate enormous profits.

Meanwhile, the cost of cancer treatment has increased from five hundred dollars per patient a few decades ago to hundreds of thousands of dollars today. In 1975, the chemotherapy drug Adriamycin was called very expensive because it cost $400 to $500 for a full eight to ten course treatment. Today, in some cases, a course of a treatment for a single patient can top one million dollars.

To be clear, when we talk about the undermining of oncology, we are not just talking about a few epic cases of research fraud. Those are rare instances in which an individual fabricates, falsifies, or plagiarizes data. They often make headlines. What we are saying is that Big Pharma, with an army of financially interested collaborators, has created a culture in which drugs are given an aura of benefit where none actually exists.

This is among the biggest problems in cancer treatment today. Big Pharma's cancer drugs, by and large, are expensive, toxic and have not been proven to work. But, through skillful advertising, much of the public believes the opposite. Even many oncologists buy into this illusion. And many cancer patients are clueless on the crucial question of the actual effects of the drugs they are given. According to a 2012 article in the *New England Journal of Medicine:*

> "Chemotherapy for metastatic lung or colorectal cancer can prolong life by weeks or months and… is not curative. But overall, 69% of patients with lung cancer and 81% of those with colorectal cancer

> did not...understand...that chemotherapy was not at all likely to cure their cancer."

Thanks to a constant barrage of misleading advertising, the public is misinformed about the true effectiveness of standard drugs, and therefore discouraged from seeking alternatives. One major issue, of course, is the indefensible cost of new drugs. Would-be reformers, including top leaders of major political parties, complain about this situation. And it is intolerable. But a bigger issue, which they never discuss, is how few of these drugs are actually effective.

## Chapter 3. Advertising and propaganda

According to a 2018 report on the drug industry by the nonprofit group Oxfam:

> "These corporations deploy massive influencing operations to rig the rules in their favor and give their damaging behavior a veneer of legitimacy."

One of the more insidious aspects of their "massive influencing operations" is flooding the airwaves, internet and print media with direct-to-consumer pharmaceutical advertising (DTCPA).

In the U.S., DTCPA has become "the most prominent type of health communication that the public encounters." Think about that: the drug industry's clever but misleading ads have become the main source of health information. This was a result of the so-called Reagan Revolution. According to a history of drug advertising:

> "In 1982, after the Reagan administration appointed a new commissioner to the FDA, it rescinded... regulation in favor of a plan under which pharmaceutical companies would voluntarily disseminate information on prescription drugs to consumers."

What few Americans know is that direct-to-consumer drug advertising is banned in almost every other country on earth. Only in the U.S. and New Zealand are companies allowed to make product claims directly to patients. Most countries consider this an assault on consumers at their most vulnerable, such as when they are dealing with cancer. It is entirely forbidden by the European Union, "which has repeatedly cited concerns over companies' ability to provide unbiased information about their products."

The average American TV viewer watches nine drug ads each and every day, totaling 16 hours of these ads per year. A 2018 study from Yale University found that companies frequently ignore already weak regulations, and TV networks (reaping advertising dollars) have no problem with this:

> "Few broadcast direct-to-consumer ads were fully compliant with FDA guidelines. The overall quality of information provided in ads was low, and suggestions of off-label promotion were common...."

Medical researchers around the world have issued warnings about the corrupting influence of drug company ads on the public's consciousness:

> "More stringent scrutiny and issue of warning letters or blacklisting of...pharmaceutical companies are mandatory." (India)

> "Achieving a fair balance of benefit versus risk information is a major problem with regard to the direct-to-consumer advertising of prescription drugs." (U.S.)

> Direct-to-consumer ads "have the potential to be exploited by pharmaceutical marketers." (U.K.)

But Big Pharma spends $30 billion a year on medical marketing. That represents a lucrative revenue stream for mainstream media. According to a 2019 report from Dartmouth University, published in the *Journal of the American Medical Association:*

> "From 1997 through 2016, medical marketing expanded substantially, and spending increased from $17.7 to $29.9 billion, with direct-to-consumer advertising for prescription drugs and health services accounting for the most rapid growth, and pharmaceutical marketing to health professionals accounting for most promotional spending."

This included a total of 4.6 million ads, including an astonishing 663,000 TV commercials per year. This combination of direct-to-consumer advertising and the cultivation of doctors delivers an effective "one-two punch for knockout sales," according to an industry trade letter. Then there are the ads that do not tout a particular product, but are drug industry propaganda, pure and simple. The medical journalist Shannon Brownlee did a take-down of this practice in 2003. She used as an example a series of ads by Novartis, the giant Swiss manufacturer of cancer drugs. Each ad ran a photo of an actual cancer patient. One, which ran in *Scientific American*, read:

> "To life! Novartis and Rabbi Sklarz drove his cancer into remission in just 56 days."

It carried this quote:

> "'When I was struck with cancer, I needed lots of help: Thanks to Novartis, I got it.'"

The ad made no mention of the role of the Rabbi's doctors in achieving this remission. As Shannon Brownlee put it:

> "The ads aren't selling a product. They're selling hope."

And hope sells, even when the reality is far, far different.

Of course, when others, such as alternative practitioners, use individual testimonials to tout their treatments, this is considered the height of quackery. In "28 Ways to Spot Quacks and Vitamin Pushers," the quackbuster Stephen Barrett, MD, has this to say about testimonials:

> "If people tell you that product X has cured their cancer, arthritis, or whatever, be skeptical....Testimonial evidence is forbidden in scientific articles, is usually inadmissible in court, and is not used to evaluate whether or not drugs should be legally marketable."

But what is called arrant quackery in alternative medicine is perfectly acceptable when used to promote the products of Big Pharma.

In the 1930s, advertising to cancer patients was a sure sign of quackery. Now it is ubiquitous.
Source: Works Progress Administration, 1938

## Chapter 4. How to rig a trial

> **"The function of the formal controlled clinical trial is to separate a handful of true advances from a legion of false leads and unverifiable clinical impressions."**
>
> —*William Thomas Beaver, MD, Professor of Pharmacology, Georgetown University*

The $1.2 trillion in revenue of the pharmaceutical industry ultimately depends on the results of clinical trials. These are human experiments that are carried out with the permission, or informed consent, of test subjects. Clinical trials are considered the pinnacle of a rigorous system of new drug development. They form the basis of all U.S. Food and Drug Administration, European Medicines Agency, and other regulatory approvals of new drugs.

We focus here on the FDA because, according to a 2019 article in *JAMA Internal Medicine*:

> "Among regulators, the U.S. Food and Drug Administration is uniquely important. Its decisions not only affect the population of the United States, but often influence decisions in other countries."

Many people believe that the clinical trial system is a crown jewel of Western science, a reliable foundation stone for evidence-based medicine. But, in our view, the system is rigged to make dubious, toxic and expensive drugs appear both safe and effective. The dry rot of Big Pharma's influence has affected the FDA as well.

By selecting which patients are allowed into clinical trials, doctors can make drugs appear better than they are. They do this by including and/or excluding large segments of the population from the trials in question. In fact, according to Catherine Y. Spong, MD, of the National Institutes of Health:

> "Up to 59% of the U.S. population is made of groups who are usually not included in clinical trials."

According to Dr. Spong, the commonly excluded are:

> "...children, the elderly, pregnant women, lactating women, people with chronic diseases, people with intellectual or physical disabilities, people with mental health diagnoses, and those in organ failure."

That's quite a few people! Similarly, according to another NIH official:

> "Those who take part in research are younger and healthier than the population that will eventually have access to the drug being studied. They are also more heavily skewed toward Caucasians."

Each of these criteria guarantees that participants in clinical trials are unrepresentative of many of the real world patients who will ultimately receive the drug in question. This single fact makes most new cancer drug trials unreliable.

One can easily find many descriptions of this problem in the standard medical literature. It is talked about openly at large meetings of cancer doctors. For example, at the 2019 ASCO annual meeting, Dr. R. Donald Harvey, of Emory University, told a large group of oncologists:

> "...trial results end up not representing the patients we would treat in the real world."

Many other medical leaders have made the same point:

- 2013: "Stringent inclusion and exclusion criteria...makes application of a study's findings to real-world contemporary clinical practice highly questionable."
- 2015: "Clinical trials involve selected patients who are treated according to protocols that might not represent real-world practice."
- 2017: "Extrapolating results from adult clinical trials to the treatment of children may be inappropriate and possibly harmful."
- 2018: "Results from novel therapeutics trials are not always generalizable to real-world patients."
- 2018: "Results from clinical trials may not mirror 'real world' patient outcomes."

One very significant finding came from a 2018 German study of multiple myeloma, a cancer of blood plasma cells. Researchers looked at the outcomes in what they called clinical trial eligible versus clinical trial ineligible patients. To be clear, the first group were eligible for clinical trials because they had been chosen for their better all-around health status. The latter patients had been excluded because of various health and social problems. The differences in treatment outcomes were dramatic.

Progression-free survival in the trial ineligible patients was just 16.2 months compared to 27.3 months for the trial eligible patients. When it came to all-important overall survival, among the trial ineligible patients it was 34.2 months vs. 58.6 months among trial eligible patients. Simply put, patients who were younger, healthier, and wealthier lived almost twice as long as the ineligible patients.

The exclusion of less promising test patients can be subtle. It is mainly carried out through predetermined inclusion and exclusion criteria for participants. But there is usually no medical necessity that certain patients be excluded. This is done simply to improve the final figures in terms of both effectiveness and toxicity.

A 2018 workshop sponsored by the FDA and Duke University concluded:

> "Clinical trial patient inclusion and exclusion criteria are far too rigid, often based on outdated notions, and the whole subject needs to be reimagined to include a more representative sample of the population."

Carefully selected patients will have better responses, with fewer and less severe side effects, than a group of real world patients. But the inclusion of these real world patients would also greatly diminish the *alleged* benefit of new drugs, and therefore make FDA approval less likely.

## Race as a factor

According to the American Cancer Society's *Cancer Facts & Figures for African-Americans, 2019-2021:*

> "Collectively blacks have the highest death rate and shortest survival of any racial/ethnic group in the U.S. for most cancers. Black men also have the highest cancer incidence rate."

Yet, it has often been noted that racial and ethnic minorities are less likely to enroll in cancer clinical trials than are whites. Here are some representative quotations:

- 2014: "The proportion of minority patients enrolled in cancer clinical trials remains persistently low."
- 2014: "Less than two percent of the National Cancer Institute's clinical trials focus on any racial/minority population as their primary emphasis."

- 2017: "This underrepresentation of minorities in research trials persists."
- 2019: "Minority U.S. populations are underrepresented in cancer clinical trials.... Black patients constitute less than 4% of all patients enrolled across multiple trials."
- 2019: "Suboptimal race reporting and representation (especially in blacks and Hispanics) occurs regularly in landmark oncology trials...."

Clearly there is insufficient societal will to significantly increase the representation of people of color in clinical trials. Another possibility is that drug companies and their representatives prefer white patients, with higher socio-economic status, in order to inflate the perceived effectiveness of their drugs.

## Age as a factor

There is another important variable: age. Cancer is largely a disease of seniors:

> "Slightly more than half of all cancers in 2009 occurred in adults aged equal to or greater than 65 years" and "70% of cancer-related deaths occur in patients aged 65 years and over."

At the same time, seniors only represent one third of the adult participants in cancer clinical studies. As a result, older people are seriously underrepresented in cancer clinical trials. A report from the Yale University School of Medicine showed how clinical trial enrollment decreases with age. Thus, while 3% of those 64 or younger enrolled in trials, this fell to 1.3% in the 65-to-74-year-old age group, and plummeted to 0.5% in those older than 74. Put another way, the likelihood of a person over 74 being enrolled in a cancer trial is one-sixth that of someone under 65.

What impact does advanced age have on the outcome of trials? Elderly people in a clinical trial are at increased risk of more frequent and severe side effects, and are therefore more likely to need delays in their treatment, or might even drop out or die. According to scientists at the Cork University Hospital in Ireland:

> "The prevalence of adverse drug reactions increases with age, with twice as many patients aged 65 years and older being hospitalized because of adverse drug reaction-related problems than

their younger counterparts."

There is evidence that many cancer drugs do not work as advertised in older patients. For example, a 2018 study of the cancer drug Xeloda found that patients aged 70 years or older experienced more serious adverse effects than younger patients. The rate of hand-foot toxicity in those 70 or older was nearly double that of patients below that threshold. The drug dosage had to be reduced in one-third of the younger patients versus in 82.5% of the elderly ones.

In cases like this, the severe side effects of an experimental treatment almost certainly led to the death of some older participants. Beside the human tragedy, this would depress the survival rate and possibly cause a delay, suspension or cancellation of the trial. Thus, a drug's proponents have a practical reason to keep the elderly out of their trial. In sum, a report from the M.D. Anderson Cancer Center accurately summarized the overall situation:

> "Older adults are vastly underrepresented in clinical trials, in spite of shouldering a disproportionate burden of disease and consumption of prescription drugs and therapies, restricting treatments' generalizability, efficacy, and safety."

In 2012, Kevin S. Scher, MD, and Arti Hurria, MD, wrote:

> "Although new agents may be successful in the treatment of healthier, younger adults, information is limited on how to apply these new agents to older adults who represent the majority of patients receiving treatment."

A 2018 study at The Mount Sinai Hospital, New York, found that elderly patients with metastatic bladder cancer who were treated in the community setting did much worse than patients enrolled in a clinical trial. Elderly patients treated in the community setting who were receiving chemotherapy had a survival of 8.5 months. But in the clinical trial, the median overall survival was 18.5 months.

At the very least, one cannot assume that a treatment that was approved based on a younger population will perform as expected in older people.

## Performance status as a factor

Another important factor is the patients' overall performance status. According to a 2015 article in the journal *JAMA Oncology:*

> "Performance status is a score that estimates the patient's ability to perform certain activities of daily living without the help of others."

Nowadays, performance status is usually measured on a scale established by the Eastern Cooperative Oncology Group (ECOG). To enter most cancer trials, patients are required to have an ECOG performance status of 0, which means fully active, or of 1, which means they are able to carry out all their normal tasks. Patients with an ECOG status of 2 are excluded from most trials. Yet a ECOG 2 patient is still ambulatory and capable of all self-care and is up and about more than 50% of waking hours. They are mainly unable to carry out work activities. There is usually no good reason to exclude such patients from clinical trials. That is, unless the researchers wanted trial participants to be unrepresentative of the real world patient population.

According to a 2015 *JAMA Oncology* article:

> "Many clinical trials...are restricted to more fit patients, such as those with a performance status of 0 to 1.... Because nearly all anticancer treatments have potentially serious adverse effects, the risks of using certain treatments in low performance status patients may far exceed the benefits."

Ian F. Tannock, MD, of Princess Margaret Cancer Centre and the University of Toronto, has written as follows:

> "Eligibility criteria for clinical trials are important to determine whether their results are applicable to patients seen in daily practice."

In a bluntly honest 2019 interview with *ASH Clinical News,* Professor Tannock explained this point with particular reference to performance status:

> "Researchers can conduct a trial in 2,000 patients and identify a difference of a few days in survival. It might be statistically significant, but it's not clinically important. Moreover, those individuals selected for the trial were quite possibly heavily selected to have high performance status. When

> you try to see this same small difference in the general patient population, the effect is smaller and the toxicity is higher."

In fact, we know that in the real world, overall survival declines as one descends the performance scale. In a German study of chemotherapy for metastatic bladder cancer, the "median survival time for patients with ECOG status 0, 1, and 2 was 45, 12, and 10.5 months respectively." In other words, all other things being equal, patients who had an excellent ECOG score of 0 lived four times as long as patients with the same type and stage of cancer but with a worse performance status.

Italian oncologists similarly explained how performance status is crucial for the outcome of a lung cancer trial:

> "Performance status is… a strong predictor of survival and adverse events…. But the vast majority of prospective phase III trials had been conducted stratifying patients according to performance status."

By stratifying they mean limiting the trial to people with a superior performance status. That fact alone powerfully boosts the outcome of clinical trials. In a clinical trial of over 1,000 lung cancer patients who were being treated with standard chemotherapy, there was also a close correlation between performance status and median overall survival:

- A very good performance status of 0 was associated with 13.5 months overall survival.
- A good performance status of 1 was associated with 10.6 months overall survival.
- A worse performance status of 2 was associated with 5.9 months overall survival.

Further confirmation came from a 2019 study of kidney cancer patients treated at U.S. Veterans Administration (VA) hospitals. VA patients are more representative of the real world than those normally included in most clinical trials. Of 220 kidney cancer patients treated at the VA, almost two-thirds had their therapy held up or reduced because of side effects. Yet it is the results of clinical trials, rather than real world figures, that are usually quoted to patients trying to make treatment decisions.

Many have proposed eliminating the performance status requirement entirely and allowing anyone with a proper diagnosis to join a trial. A panel of experts from the American Society of Clinical Oncology, Emory University, and the FDA told their colleagues at the 2019 ASCO annual meeting:

> "Narrower criteria should only be used based on a compelling scientific rationale for exclusion."

They were pleading with their colleagues to let more patients into the trial system. This would help overcome the dearth of volunteers for clinical trials, upon which all evidence-based medicine ultimately rests. Most oncologists know very well about this flaw in the clinical trial system, but no one does anything about it. I believe this is because having narrow criteria ultimately serves the interests of Big Pharma. In this way, less promising patients are systematically excluded before they can depress results and force the FDA to reject a potentially profitable new drug.

## Income as a factor

Another way of skewing results is by systematically reducing the participation of poor and working class people. This is also widely discussed in the scientific literature, but nothing substantive is ever done to correct this. People abroad often have an exaggerated sense of the average American's wealth, based on Hollywood movies, webcasts and TV shows. But here are some sobering facts about wealth disparities in America:

- 72% of Americans live in a state of financial uncertainty.
- Almost half of all Americans exist at or near the poverty level.
- 15 million American workers earn less than $10 an hour.
- Four in ten American adults are unable to cover an unexpected expense of $400.
- 87 million Americans are medically uninsured or underinsured.

So there is both extensive poverty and a general lack of resources in much of the U.S. But clinical trials systematically discourage the participation of low income individuals. This creates unrepresentative results, which are not applicable to most of the population.

A 2016 study at the Fred Hutchinson Cancer Research Center, Seattle, confirmed that:

> "Patients with annual household incomes below

> $50,000 were 27% less likely than patients with higher incomes to participate in clinical trials.... Participation rates were lowest for patients with annual incomes of less than $20,000."

Participants in clinical trials are five times less likely to be on Medicaid (health insurance for poor people) than non-participants. And patients were also half as likely to join a trial if they lived in an area with high unemployment. According to a 2018 study from Yale University, people living in low and middle income U.S. counties are more likely to die of cancer than those living in higher income neighborhoods.

In America, the median income of counties ranges from $22,000 to $122,000 per year. The annual cancer death rate in high income counties was 186 per 100,000 versus 230 per 100,000 in low-income counties. Among the factors leading to these stark disparities are unaffordable care and low quality care.

Naturally, drug companies want to populate their clinical trials with the healthiest and wealthiest patients they can find, to inflate the response curves and decrease the severity of side effects. This sort of manipulation is especially deceptive when good results are used to gain accelerated approval from the FDA.

## The treatment center as a factor

In the U.S., clinical trials are usually centered in one or more of the nation's 49 comprehensive cancer centers. The much sought-after designation, which is assigned by the National Cancer Institute, places them among the top 3% or 4% of all 1,500 cancer treatment centers in the United States.

For various reasons, results at comprehensive cancer centers tend to be better than at the typical community hospital. For example, a 2015 study showed that:

> "Patients treated at one of a handful of specialized cancer centers collectively had a 9% higher survival rate over five years when compared to cancer patients treated at community hospitals...."

To quote the veteran science journalist Sharon Begley, clinical trial participants at specialized cancer centers are:

> "...better plugged in to the health care system (or they wouldn't have found a trial in the first place), better educated, and wealthier (it's often necessary

> to travel multiple times to where the trial is being conducted)."

In a 2015 California study of ovarian cancer, only 8.1% of ovarian cancer patients were treated at comprehensive cancer centers. Yet survival from ovarian cancer was:

- 43.4 months at community hospitals
- 52 months at high-volume hospitals
- 78 months at comprehensive cancer centers

Community hospitals and practices, which serve 85% of U.S. cancer patients, are ill equipped to deal with complex new treatments, with their rare and life-threatening side effects. But by restricting clinical trials to the comprehensive cancer centers, one also achieves an unrealistic result, which then is not applicable to the majority of patients.

## Reform of the process

Over the years there have been numerous attempts to increase the number of real world patients. None of these voluntary schemes worked. Finally, in 1993, the U.S. Congress responded to concerns about unequal access to clinical trials by enacting the National Institutes of Health Revitalization Act. This act mandated a greater representation of women and minority group patients in NIH sponsored research. The public was assured at the time that:

> "Ensuring broad access to research studies is an important aim of national research policy."

But 10 years later, scientists from Yale University conducted a comprehensive review in the *Journal of the American Medical Association* on how well the Revitalization Act was working. This revealed the following:

> "Enrollment in cancer trials is low for all patient groups. Racial and ethnic minorities, women, and the elderly were less likely to enroll in cooperative group cancer trials than were whites, men, and younger patients, respectively. The proportion of trial participants who are black has declined in recent years."

A 2019 study in *JAMA Oncology* from top medical institutions confirmed this defect:

> "Race and race subgroup analysis reporting occurs infrequently, and black and Hispanic races are consistently underrepresented compared with their burden of cancer incidence in landmark trials that led to FDA oncology drug approvals."

In 2019, this problem was the focus of a meeting at the American Society of Clinical Oncology (ASCO) convention. They too issued recommendations for expanding acceses to clinical trials. And once again, top researchers warned that in general clinical trial results are not representing patients treated in the real world.

We have had 25 years of Congressionally mandated reforms that ended up with few positive changes. Although everyone involved pays lip service to greater inclusiveness, the current system could actually benefit Big Pharma in a number of ways. If clinical trials were made truly representative of the general population, fewer drugs would pass muster with the FDA.

There is no proof that Big Pharma is pursuing such a policy. But two doctors, Kevin S. Scher, MD, and the late Arti Hurria, MD, alluded to this at least as a possibility. In a 2012 article in the *Journal of Clinical Oncology,* they hinted at how Big Pharma could profit from the fact that many real world patients do not join these trials:

> "Drug manufacturers and researchers are incentivized to perform positive studies that lead to drug approval. Populations, such as older adults, with increased toxicity risks, are assumed to fare less well and are under-represented in clinical trials."

## Downplaying side effects

Cancer drugs typically cause a wide array of side effects. But clinical trial reports usually downplay side effects to make drugs appear safer and more tolerable than they really are.

Cancer clinical trials, wrote Australian researchers in 2017, "may not reflect the reality of chemotherapy side effects in routine clinical practice." In particular, certain factors are manipulated to have side effects appear milder than they really are:

- Patients who are at greater risk of drug complications are often excluded from clinical trials.

- Safety monitoring is more intensive in clinical trials than in routine care thus leading to expedited palliation of symptoms.
- Simultaneously, the reporting of drug side effects may be selective, only giving common or serious side effects, while ignoring the full scope of what patients experience.
- Side effects in clinical trials are reported by the clinicians themselves, who may under report their number and severity.

## Ignoring research misconduct

In 2015, there was an article in *JAMA Internal Medicine* with the provocative title,

> "Research Misconduct Identified by The U.S. Food And Drug Administration: Out of Sight, Out of Mind, Out of The Peer-Reviewed Literature."

In it, the author, Professor Charles Seife, points out that every year, the FDA inspects numerous clinical trial sites and occasionally finds "evidence of substantial departures from good clinical practice," as well as outright research misconduct.

> "However, the FDA has no systematic method of communicating these findings to the scientific community, leaving open the possibility that research misconduct detected by a government agency goes unremarked in the peer-reviewed literature."

Most instances of research misconduct remains hidden from the medical profession and, by extension, the general public. Professor Seife found 57 published clinical trials for which FDA inspectors had found significant evidence of one or more of the following violations:

- Falsification or submission of false information
- Problems with side effects reporting
- Trial protocol violations
- Inadequate or inaccurate record keeping
- Failure to protect the safety of patients

These violations were frequent. Yet the facts were not revealed to the public:

> "Only 3 of the 78 publications (4%) that resulted from trials in which the FDA found significant violations mentioned the objectionable conditions or practices found during the inspection. No corrections, retractions, expressions of concern, or other comments acknowledging the key issues identified by the inspection were subsequently published."

In one egregious case, a researcher falsified documents in a number of trials of chemotherapy for stomach cancer:

> "The researcher hid the patient's impaired kidney and liver function, and the first dose of the treatment proved to be fatal. The researcher pleaded guilty to fraud and criminally negligent homicide and was sentenced to 71 months in prison.
>
> "Although this episode is described in detail in FDA documents, as well as court documents, none of the publications in the peer-reviewed literature associated with the chemotherapy study in which the patient died have any mention of the falsification, fraud, or homicide."

## Chapter 5. Case study: Avastin

On very rare occasions the FDA shows some backbone, although this is a rare exception to the rule. The following saga demonstrates what can be done, when there is the political will to act in the public's interest. This episode took place in 2011, when the FDA rescinded one of the approved indications for the blockbuster drug Avastin. But eight years later the astonished FDA staff was still referring to this episode as Armageddon.

Since 2004, Avastin has been a huge money-maker for the giant Swiss pharmaceutical company, Roche, and its American subsidary, Genentech. According to the insider website, *Fierce Pharma*:

> "Roche has been milking everything it can from Avastin since winning approval for the drug to treat colon cancer a decade ago, pushing for label indications to rake in stellar sales. In August 2014, the company nabbed an FDA OK to use its med to treat cervical cancer. A few months later, the agency signed off on Avastin in combination with chemotherapy as a treatment for platinum-resistant ovarian cancer, delivering another win to the Swiss drugmaker."

In 2007, Genentech proposed Avastin as a treatment for advanced breast cancer. But when it brought its evidence before the Oncology Drug Advisory Committee (ODAC), the committee, surprisingly, turned it down. Most ODAC members agreed that the data they presented was simply not compelling.

But, in an unusual move, FDA officials overruled their own advisors and gave the company accelerated approval for Avastin's use in breast cancer. This approval was based on a small trial called E2100, which showed a 5.5 month increase (from 5.8 months to 11.3 months) in progression-free survival for the two-drug combination of Avastin and Abraxane.

Avastin soon became one of the top selling cancer drugs of all time, in part because of the addition of the huge breast cancer market. Each year the drug had "nearly $7 billion in global annual sales, including $3 billion in America."

However, as the ODAC members had figured out, Avastin didn't actually work in breast cancer. According to the oncologist Frederick C. Tucker, MD, writing in the *New York Times (2011)*:

> "The criteria for full approval was that Avastin not worsen overall survival and that the drug provide clinically meaningful progression-free survival."

Not worsening overall survival was a pretty low bar for continued FDA approval. After all, water could meet that criterion. And no one could explain what was meant by clinically meaningful progression-free survival, since progression-free survival itself is *not* clinically meaningful (being a surrogate endpoint).

Then two subsequent trials of Avastin in breast cancer, called Avado and Ribbon-1, were a disaster. In the Avado trial, a small increase in progression-free survival was not statistically significant. In fact, at one dose, placebo performed better than Avastin. In the second trial, Ribbon-1, involving 1,300 patients, scientists looked at overall survival, not just progression-free survival. Breast cancer patients were randomly assigned to either a standard form of chemotherapy plus Avastin or the same chemo plus placebo. Here was the key finding:

> "No statistically significant differences in overall survival between the placebo- and Avastin-containing arms were observed."

As the ODAC members saw, on a statistical basis, the drug did not work in advanced breast cancer. Not deterred, Genentech/Roche changed tack and claimed that Avastin improved patients' quality of life. However, according to Dr. Tucker, the "quality-of-life data were incomplete, sketchy and, in some cases, non-existent."

The best that a Genentech/Roche spokesman could say was that "health-related quality of life was not worsened when Avastin was added." That was a weak rationale for a drug that at the time cost $88,000 per patient per year.

But in 2011, the agency had a new commissioner, Margaret Hamburg, MD, who thought it irrational to allow a drug to be sold when it clearly did not work. She agreed with her cancer advisory board and took the unusual step of revoking the FDA's prior approval of Avastin for breast cancer. As she stated at the time:

> "It is clear that women who take Avastin for metastatic breast cancer risk potentially life-threatening side effects without proof that the use of Avastin will provide a benefit, in terms of delay in tumor growth, that would justify those risks. Nor is there evidence that use of Avastin will either help them live longer or improve their quality of life."

The FDA's decision provoked "a firestorm of criticism," according to Dr. Tucker:

> "The decision was denounced by some politicians as health care rationing, and by breast cancer patients who feared that they would be deprived of a drug that they felt had helped them immensely."

Roche pulled out all the stops in their effort to block Dr. Hamburg. It launched an aggressive campaign to get the FDA to reconsider its decision. In fact, the company stood to lose $500 million to $1 billion a year in revenue because of the FDA's partial ban. Their chief ploy was to claim to speak for desperate cancer patients who wanted this (ineffective) drug. As part of this, Roche launched a massive public relations campaign to pressure Dr. Hamburg to change her mind:

> "Oncologists recounted their successes, and patients who were doing well on Avastin argued for its continued approval. But anecdote is not science."

The mainstream media was its compliant self. Typical was a November 2011 story from the Associated Press. It began this way (note the loaded terms):

> "The government delivered a blow to some desperate cancer patients Friday as it ruled that the blockbuster drug Avastin should no longer be used to treat advanced breast cancer."

The story quoted a grateful patient saying, "It saved my life!" This publicity blitz was followed by demonstrations organized by allegedly independent patient groups, and tear-filled public sessions in which people held up large pictures of their cancer-stricken relatives. Perhaps these were real patients with real grievances, but it all seemed beautifully choreographed. It is known that Big Pharma also forms, supports and deploys phony patient groups, in a practice called "Astroturfing" (or fake grassroots activism).

The pressure on FDA was immense, but, much to her credit, Dr. Hamburg stood her ground. She insisted that the FDA should only approve this drug if it actually increased overall survival, which it clearly did not. Dr. Hamburg was the last FDA director to actually enforce the law and go against the wishes of Big Pharma. She was also among the few who did not exit through the revolving door to drug company employment. She went on to become chairperson of the board of the American Association for the Advancement of Science (AAAS), publisher of *Science* magazine.

In 2015, Dr. Hamburg was replaced as FDA Commissioner by Robert Califf, MD, of Duke University, Durham, North Carolina. Dr. Califf, by contrast, was very cozy with the drug industry. According to *Forbes:*

> "Califf's industry ties run deep. He worked closely with drug companies in the best possible way: convincing them to do large, expensive, and, for Duke, profitable clinical trials that helped prove the effectiveness of major medicines."

According to government documents, between 2013 and 2018 Dr. Califf personally received $114,000 in general payments from various drug companies. In 2013 his biggest contributor was Genentech, the American division of Roche, manufacturer of Avastin.

Margaret Hamburg, MD, former commissioner of the FDA.

Photo: Abe1inc01n10g

## Chapter 6. Tumor responses

A long time ago, shrinking tumors was considered the most important thing that a cancer drug could do. Now, even the FDA downgrades the importance of tumor shrinkages. According to its very influential *Guidance for Industry* (2018):

> "In the 1970s, FDA usually approved cancer drugs based on objective response rate, determined by tumor assessments from radiological tests or physical examinations. In the early 1980s…FDA determined that cancer drug approval should be based on more direct evidence of clinical benefit, such as improvement in survival, improvement in a patient's quality of life, improved physical functioning, or improved tumor-related symptoms. These benefits may not always be predicted by, or correlate with, the objective response rate, i.e., tumor shrinkages."

This is an amazing statement. At least, on paper, the FDA acknowledges patient benefit as the only true measure of a drug's merit. Yet, in practice, the FDA continues to be swayed by changes in the size of the tumor. Here are some examples:

- In 2015, FDA approved the drug Lynparza for the treatment of ovarian cancer, based on an overall response rate of 34%, of which just 2% were complete responses.
- In 2017, FDA approved the drug Rubraca for advanced ovarian cancer based on an "investigator-assessed objective response rate of 54%."
- In 2019, FDA approved Yescarta for large B-cell lymphoma based on an objective response rate of 72%.

We are not discussing here whether or not these particular drugs are safe and effective. We are just showing that FDA has not abandoned tumor shrinkages as a basis for drug approval. Far from it. This uncertain measurement of value is very much alive, and figures in the approval of many drugs.

The problem is that in recent years FDA has more and more been granting accelerated approval to new cancer drugs, without requiring proof of improved overall survival.

As evidence of how unreliable tumor shrinkages are, here are half a dozen instances in which an improved tumor shrinkage rate did not correlate with improved overall survival:

- Breast Cancer (2008): "No endpoint could be demonstrated as a good surrogate for overall survival in these trials."
- Breast Cancer (2016): "No endpoint was judged to be valid surrogate for overall survival at the metastatic setting."
- Gastro-Esophageal Cancer (2017): "Disease-free survival and…complete response did not correlate with overall survival, and should not be used as surrogate end-points in patients with gastro-esophageal cancer…. overall survival should still represent the primary end-point."
- Immune Checkpoint Drugs (2017): The results indicated a weak correlation between tumor shrinkages and overall survival.
- Lung Cancer (2017): With certain exceptions, "no endpoint was judged to be valid surrogate for overall survival."
- Lung Cancer (2018): In many studies there was no correlation between tumor shrinkages or progression-free survival and actual overall survival.

In other words, one still has to do the difficult, expensive and time-consuming work of calculating overall survival to know if a cancer drug works, in any meaningful sense. Or, to quote this famous paraphrase of Euclid:

> "There is no royal road to science, and only those who do not dread the fatiguing climb of its steep paths have a chance of gaining its luminous summits."

## Bending the rules

The oncologist Vinay Prasad, MD, and others have shown how often the FDA bends its own rules and approves drugs without proof of increased overall survival.

For example, between 2006 and 2018, the FDA approved drugs for 85 separate cancer indications. Of these 85 indications, only 32 (38%) were based on regular approval, while the majority received accelerated approval. Only about one-fifth of these accelerated approvals were later converted to regular approvals through a belated proof of overall survival benefit. The rest showed only an advantage in a surrogate endpoint, such as the response rate.

Which makes us wonder, wasn't the point of granting accelerated approval to get promising drugs to market faster, while the sponsor continued with studies to show real life prolongation?

Big Pharma and its mouthpieces try to convince us that FDA needs to water down its once rigorous requirements in order to speed up the approval process. Speed is everything! But the FDA should only approve drugs that have actually been proven to work. And despite what some vocal advocates may say, in the end, it is the cancer patient who suffers when the FDA cuts corners on behalf of Big Pharma. The individual patient, as well as society as a whole, deserves to know the truth about all cancer drugs. And this can only come about through painstaking and honest work.

# Section IV: Corruption of Oncology

## Chapter 1. The Cancer Industry revisited

In December 2016, the U.S. Congress passed the 21st Century Cures Act. This authorized $6.3 billion in funding, mostly for the National Institutes of Health. One purpose of this law, from the point of view of Big Pharma, was to have the U.S. taxpayer foot the bill for new drug development, while leaving their rapacious profit system in place.

$1.8 billion was dedicated to cancer research, in what was called the Beau Biden Cancer Moonshot initiative. The underlying premise was that cancer can be controlled or cured through the precise targeting of mutations within any individual's tumor. I do not think that this is feasible, and I shall explain why.

There are innumerable mutations within most cancers, and so one would need a drug for each of these. First of all, there is the cost of researching, developing and marketing scores of new drugs. Let us assume that the system of reviewing and approving new drugs remained the same as it has been for the past 50 years.

In 2020, the Tufts Center for Drug Development estimated the cost of developing a new drug at $2.6 billion per drug. More moderate estimates range from $648 million to $1.4 billion per drug. But even at the low end we are talking about the expenditure of many more billions of dollars just for R&D.

### $1 Million per patient

As for the individual patient, the average price of a new cancer drug in recent years has been $150,000 per year. However, the retail price of Xalkori is $211,308 per year. Other targeted drugs include Yescarta for $373,000, Vitrakvi for $393,600 and Kymriah for $475,000 per patient. According to Carl B. June, MD, who developed Kymriah, Novartis's actual production cost is just $20,000, while the other 95% or so is profit. According to an NPR report, this $475,000 is:

> "...the cost of the drug itself; in addition, many patients experience serious side effects that can land them in a hospital intensive care unit for weeks, pushing treatment costs to more than $1 million."

An article in *Health Affairs* by Harvard researchers put the problem this way: Drugs Don't Work If People Can't Afford Them.

Kite Pharma, a division of Gilead Sciences, has priced Yescarta at $373,000 per infusion. As a result, the U.K.'s National Institute for Health and Care Excellence said No to Yescarta because of its outrageous price. A few months later the company buckled under and negotiated a lower price.

Even if we assume a price of $150,000 per patient per year, if one administered six such drugs, this would bring the cost per patient to almost $1 million. In the U.S. there are about 1.8 million new cases of cancer each year. Therefore, to provide every new cancer patient in the U.S. with such drugs would cost the country about $1.8 trillion dollars. That is more than half of the $3.4 trillion that the Internal Revenue Service collects in tax revenue annually. Half of all tax dollars would have to go for the treatment of cancer.

This is a system out of control, in which a few super wealthy drug companies dictate prices to the government, with no oversight. Congress as a whole is bought and paid for by giant corporations. According to opensecrets.org, pharmaceutical and health product companies spent over $228 million on lobbying efforts in 2019. This money went to 415 out of 435 voting members of the House of Representatives and 98 out of 100 Senators. This is what we mean by bought and paid for.

Pharmaceutical companies employed a total of 1,419 lobbyists, of whom 65% were former government employees. Their trade organization, the Pharmaceutical Research & Manufacturers of America, or PhARMA, spent $22.8 million. Pfizer alone spent $8.7 million, employing 11 lobbying firms in the process, Roche spent $8.4 million while Bristol-Myers Squibb spent $6.1 million. All of this ultimately helps them control the Congress and hamstring any movements for reform.

In 1980, I wrote a book, *The Cancer Industry,* about the structure and activity of the cancer establishment. Since then, the field has grown to gargantuan proportions that were unimaginable 40 years ago. Until 2019 there were ten companies that dominated the worldwide cancer drug marketplace. With the merger of Bristol-Myers Squibb and Celgene that number was reduced to nine. These companies are, in order of their projected sales, Bristol-Myers Squibb (with Celgene added), Roche, Merck, Pfizer, AstraZeneca, Johnson & Johnson, Novartis, AbbVie, and Astellas.

## Size of the market

Overall, cancer drug sales in 2019 were projected to be $120 billion. This is about 10% of overall drug sales worldwide. The cancer drug industry is multinational, with a strong U.S. dominance. The United States represents 45% of the global pharmaceutical market. In 2019, five out of the top nine drug companies were based in the U.S. Even the Swiss firm, Roche, an industry leader, is highly dependent for its profits on its American branch, Genentech.

For some companies, cancer drugs provide a large share of their overall revenue. More than 60% of Roche's pharmaceutical revenue comes from cancer drugs. Bristol-Myers Squibb also derives over 65% of its total revenue from cancer drugs, even before the Celgene merger. The latter's flagship cancer drug, Revlimid, similarly provided 65% of Celgene's total revenue. As the *Wall Street Journal* commented in 2019:

> "Many pharmaceutical companies expect cancer treatments to drive growth in the coming years."

According to the head of Roche's pharmaceuticals division:

> "Cancer is getting crowded; there are too many people chasing too few targets."

Companies who were previously more interested in general medicine, like Pfizer, GlaxoSmithKline, and AstraZeneca, are now moving into the cancer arena. This is mainly because of the potential for high returns, and of course a corrupted regulatory system. Plus, of course, cancer remains a huge market worldwide. These nine corporations dominate the cancer drug field.

In fact, six of the 15 top-selling drugs in the world, including three of the top five, are treatments for cancer. These six top-selling cancer drugs are:

- Revlimid $9.7 billion — Bristol-Myers Squibb
- Keytruda $7.2 billion — Merck
- Herceptin $7.1 billion — Roche
- Avastin $7.0 billion — Roche
- Rituxan $6.9 billion — Roche
- Opdivo $6.7 billion — Bristol-Myers Squibb

Because of the worldwide patent system, *each drug* constitutes a legal monopoly for 20 years after its invention. According to one consumer advocate:

> "This monopoly power results from the patents we grant to pharmaceutical companies for novel medicines. Once they are granted patents on their prescription drugs, drugmakers tend to have monopoly pricing power for these drugs…they can charge whatever they would like…."

Technically, there is a state of limited competition, in which a market is shared by a small number of producers or sellers. More than a century ago the author Frank Norris called this sort of market domination The Octopus, because of its stranglehold on all aspects of economic life. Big Pharma is the Octopus of the 21st Century.

## Consolidation of pharma

Twenty-five years ago, a drug industry newsletter noted:

> "The major players in the pharmaceutical industry have…joined in the consolidation of the industry. Smaller companies are finding it increasingly difficult to compete in terms of product lines and market share, and the larger companies are moving in and forming even larger organizations" through acquisitions and mergers.

Today this process of consolidation continues, although there are many small biotech firms with patents on one or two molecules which they hope to sell to the industry leaders.

George Lundberg, MD, editor of the *Journal of the American Medical Association,* once described drug companies as "marketing cartels that run things in the United States." The way they earn their profits, he added, is "simply quintessential capitalism."

## Biotherapeutics, Inc.

The exploitation of cancer patients began in earnest in the 1980s. In 1984, ahead of Dr. Steven Rosenberg's big announcement of interleukin-2, his NCI colleagues Robert Oldham, MD, and William H. West, MD, left government service and started a company to offer immunotherapy on a fee-for-service basis. Their for-profit company was called Biotherapeutics, Inc. of Franklin, Tennessee.

Clearly this was in advance of any proof that such treatments were safe or effective. It was also an end run around the FDA's stringent regulations. In the wake of Rosenberg's dramatic pronouncements, Drs. Oldham and West began to offer a version of the IL-2 treatment. Their target audience was the many patients whose hopes had been raised by Rosenberg's media appearances, only to discover they could not get into the government's program.

Drs. Oldham and West did some over-the-top promotions. West called IL-2 "the most important thing that has happened in cancer in history." They and their financial backers calculated that there was a large segment of the cancer population that was ready and willing to pay to get IL-2.

Some in the nonprofit sector condemned Biotherapeutics as an "expensive scam" or "capitalism in its most predatory form." The *Washington Post* called it "a therapeutic back door that medicine's opinion leaders are anxious to see slammed shut." Some National Cancer Institute scientists complained that "the company exploits its clients, mires its doctors in impossible conflicts of interest, and excludes the poor." All of which was true. Here is a revealing paragraph from a 1988 report in *The Scientist:*

> "In their desperate search for a cure, Oldham predicted, cancer patients would flock to his door, wallets in hand. Plenty of other people agreed, and they put up $40 million to launch the company and stake their claim to a share of the profits."

Biotherapeutics was publicly traded and thus had to answer to venture capitalists and stockholders. But the underlying issue was that IL-2 just didn't work well in most common kinds of cancer, and word of its toxicity was spreading. Eventually the company went bankrupt. However, not to be deterred, its backers soon became the center of an even greater controversy. This was the promotion of the ineffective, highly toxic and super-expensive treatment for stage IV breast cancer with high-dose chemotherapy.

## High-dose chemo profits

The main motivation was the same: simple greed. One also saw medical school professors competing for professional acclaim; some oncologists looking to profit from an expensive and complicated procedure; hospitals struggling to shore up their bottom line; and a corporation, Response Oncology, that packaged this dangerous and ineffective treatment for mass consumption. And as always in the background was Big Pharma, which quietly made a fortune providing the drugs for the procedure.

The particular regimen varied somewhat from clinic to clinic. But typically patients were given a high-dose combination of toxic drugs such as cyclophosphamide, cisplatin, and carmustine, with or without the addition of melphalan. Most of these drugs were manufactured by Bristol-Myers Squibb.

How much money did drug companies actually make from the high-dose chemo scandal? I cannot find any scholar who has addressed, much less answered that question. So let us make a rough guess. By most accounts, 41,000 American women took the high-dose chemotherapy treatment for breast cancer. Since each procedure cost about $100,000, overall, the gross income was around U.S. $4.1 billion. Figures vary, but about 20% of that total cost was spent for the purchase of drugs. Therefore, Big Pharma's share was approximately U.S. $800,000,000 in sales over the 15-year course of the scandal. But this aspect never came to the public's attention. Big Pharma was never held to account.

## What the market will bear

The drug industry's response to anger over price gouging has been to step up its lobbying efforts. Having no rational justification other than their own supersized profits, they are bribing Congress into silence. According to Fierce Pharma, in 2019 the single largest source of Big Pharma lobbying was Pfizer, Inc.:

> "Pfizer dropped a whopping $5.13 million in the first quarter, well on its way to matching or surpassing its 2018 total spending of $11.41 million."

In part because of this systematic undermining of American democracy, anger over the cost of prescription drugs has reached the boiling point. A 2019 poll by the Kaiser Family Fund found that 79% of the American public thinks that the cost of prescription drugs is unreasonable, and 80% think that drug company profits are a major factor in those costs. When Americans were asked how much they trust pharmaceutical companies to price their drugs fairly, only 3% said they trusted them a lot, while a whopping 74% indicated distrust.

But these high prices are a direct outcome of U.S. Congressional decisions. Congress approved the Medicare Modernization Act (MMA) of 2003 by a single vote at three in the morning. This led to the current pricing outrage. The MMA, a lengthy bill written in dense legalese, forbids Medicare from negotiating the price of medications, as most other countries do.

This has resulted in an unusual situation where even some conservative Republicans (who voted to pass the bill in 2003) are now clamoring for what the *Wall Street Journal* calls "standbys of the left: foreign importation and pricing penalties." A headline at *Open Secrets* summed up the current impasse at curbing drug prices:

> "Efforts to Reduce Drug Prices Stall Amid Pharmaceutical Lobbying"

According to that article:

> "Ambitious legislation designed to curtail these rising costs is stalled as pharmaceutical companies spend tens of millions of dollars lobbying against the measures."

The outrageous pricing of new drugs—especially cancer drugs—has become one of the most volatile political issues of our time. In their campaign against high drug prices, the American Association of Retired Persons explained the rules of the game this way:

> "In a world of strong patent laws and limited regulation of pricing, for-profit pharmaceutical companies have extraordinary power to charge what they want for the medicines they offer."

What most people do not realize, however, is that the safety and effectiveness of these drugs are equally suspect and worthy of intense scrutiny.

## Cost of treatment

Treating the side effects of drugs multiplies the costs to the patients. For the last decade, some top oncologists have been warning about these escalating cancer drug prices.

For example, Leonard B. Saltz, MD, chief of colon cancer therapy at Memorial Sloan Kettering Cancer Center, has said the sticker price is just the starting point. For drugs like Kymriah, he advised consumers to think of the $475,000, the drug's list price, as parts, not labor. That figure includes:

> "No money for doctors; no money for nurses; no money for pharmacists; no money for real estate, heat, and lights; no money for the needles, the IV tubing, the IV fluids, the anti-nausea medicines, the other chemotherapies that are given…."

Saltz took this issue head on in his plenary speech to the 2015 American Society of Clinical Oncology meeting. He told 25,000 oncology colleagues, including many with financial ties to Big Pharma:

> "These drugs cost too much. Cancer-drug prices are not related to the value of the drug. Prices are based on what has come before and what the seller believes the market will bear."

Another oncologist who has called out Big Pharma on its pricing is Hagop Kantarjian, MD, a leading leukemia specialist at the M.D. Anderson Cancer Center, Houston. Dr. Kantarjian has written forcefully on the topic:

> "High cancer drug prices are a worsening trend in cancer care and are affecting patient care and our health care system. In the United States, the average price of cancer drugs for about a year of therapy increased from $5,000 to $10,000 before 2000 to more than $100,000 by 2012, while the average household income has decreased by about 8% in the past decade…. Bound by the Hippocratic Oath, oncologists have a moral obligation to advocate for affordable cancer drugs."

In 2013, in an unprecedented move, Dr. Kantarjian and 120 of his professional colleagues co-signed an editorial expressing their concerns about the high prices of new cancer drugs and the continuously rising prices of older ones. Nothing ever came of this protest.

## The great Taxol giveaway

Little noticed in the debate over prices is the fact that Americans foot the bill twice for cancer drugs: first, as taxpayers who support research, and then as consumers.

Government tax money pays for most basic research and development of new drugs. It then, by law, allows Big Pharma to charge whatever it likes for these drugs. Little or nothing comes back to consumers for their role in enabling these discoveries. Dr. Kantarjian made this same point:

> "Although 85% of cancer basic research is funded through taxpayers' money, Americans with cancer pay 50% to 100% more for the same patented drug than patients in other countries."

For 2019, U.S. taxpayers provided the National Cancer Institute with \$5.74 billion in funding, not counting an extra \$400 million per year for the Beau Biden Cancer Moonshot. That brings the National Cancer Institute total appropriation to over \$6 billion for that year.

In recent years, the government has contributed to the development of virtually all new drugs. According to a 2018 report in the *Proceedings of the National Academy of Sciences:*

> "National Institutes of Health funding contributed to published research associated with every one of the 210 new drugs approved by the Food and Drug Administration from 2010 to 2016. Collectively, this research involved more than 200,000 fiscal years of National Institutes of Health project support (1985–2016) of grant funding totaling more than \$100 billion."

And, in the end, Big Pharma has been the ultimate beneficiary of this \$100 billion. For after the National Institutes of Health has done the difficult work, the drug companies reap the rewards of this public research, which is their ticket to superprofits. This is another example of what Joseph Stiglitz, PhD, has referred to as "a system where you socialize the losses and privatize the gains."

The clearest example of how this works was Bristol-Myers Squibb's acquisition in the 1990s of the right to exclusively market the blockbuster cancer drug Taxol. Taxol was developed entirely at U.S. taxpayer's expense. The National Cancer Institute maintained a natural product screening program, under the direction of a research chemist, Jonathan L. Hartwell, PhD. Dr. Hartwell's lifelong goal was to discover natural botanical products that might prove effective against cancer. As part of that program, scientists at the U.S. Department of Agriculture sent the National Cancer Institute some samples of the bark of the Pacific yew tree (*Taxus brevifolia*). Susan B. Horwitz, PhD, of Albert Einstein Medical Center, Bronx, NY, showed that Taxol could kill cancer cells in a very unusual and efficient way.

The NCI spent a total of $32 million on the preclinical and clinical studies of the drug. But, to commercialize it, the NIH, parent agency of the NCI, signed a cooperative agreement with Bristol-Myers Squibb. From the public's point of view, this was one of the worst deals in history. It gave the New Jersey company a longterm monopoly on marketing this drug. According to an older article, "Success Story: Taxol," at the NCI website:

> "To date, Taxol is the best-selling cancer drug ever manufactured. Annual sales of the drug peaked in 2000, reaching $1.6 billion."

NCI cultivated what it called a special relationship with Bristol-Myers Squibb, and touted the company's portfolio of oncology agents. But in the *Story of Taxol,* two professors from the University of Manchester, U.K., described the revolving door between Bristol-Myers Squibb and the National Cancer Institute:

> "It was not unusual for senior NCI people to end up working for Bristol-Myers Squibb. Robert Wittes was just the latest in a line of transfers. John Douros, who was chief of the Natural Products Branch was another, as was Stephen Carter, who had been Deputy Director of the Division of Cancer Treatment between 1967 and 1975, and was subsequently employed by Bristol-Myers Squibb from 1981 until 1995."

In the 1980s, Bristol-Myers Squibb owned patents on 10 of the 50 cancer drugs on the market. In 1984, according to *Forbes*, the company sold $153 million in chemotherapy drugs, making it the preeminent American manufacturer. It controlled close to 50% of the domestic anticancer market.

The links between Bristol-Myers Squibb and Memorial Sloan-Kettering Cancer Center were particularly strong:

- Lewis Thomas, MD, the president of Memorial Sloan-Kettering, was also a paid director of the company.
- Richard M. Furlaud, the CEO of the company, was on the MSKCC Board of Overseers, as well as on its Institutional Policy Committee.

- Richard L. Gelb, chairman of the board of Bristol-Myers Squibb, was chairman of the board of managers of Sloan-Kettering Institute.
- James D. Robinson, chairman of American Express, was vice chairman of the MSKCC board and also a director of Bristol-Myers Squibb.
- Robert Wittes, MD rotated among top jobs at MSKCC, NCI and Bristol-Myers Squibb, winding up as MSKCC's physician-in-chief.

According to the Government Accounting Office, the NIH spent a total of $484 million developing Taxol. It then agreed to a small payment from Bristol-Myers Squibb of $16 million for an eight year monopoly. Bristol-Myers Squibb's total expenditure on the drug was $143 million. But over the next decade it raked in over $9 billion from the government's work.

"The whole thing was a sweetheart deal," was how James Love, director of the Taxpayer Assets Project in Washington, D.C., summarized the Taxol scandal. Once Bristol-Myers Squibb had secured its patents, it used methods, both fair and foul, to extend its legal monopoly. Ultimately, in 2002, it faced legal sanctions:

> "Attorneys general from 29 states accused Bristol-Myers Squibb of illegally profiting through several fraudulent schemes to keep lower-priced generic versions of Taxol, a life-extending cancer drug, off the market."

In 2003, Bristol-Myers Squibb paid $100 million in fines for overcharging for Taxol. It also reached a $670 million agreement to end claims that it used its patents to thwart generic competition for the drug. It could afford to pay these fines, because it had received $9 billion in sales. This was just one of the ways that Big Pharma found to profit from cancer patients and the general public.

## The phony coupon scheme

The result of Big Pharma's machinations can be devastating to the individual patient. Paying for cancer treatment contributes to the financial ruin of many. According to a 2019 *CNBC* report:

> "...66.5% of all U.S. bankruptcies were tied to medical issues—either because of high costs for care or time out of work. An estimated 530,000

> families turn to bankruptcy each year because of medical issues and bills."

But the sight of cancer patients going bankrupt and being kicked out of their homes is not good public relations for drug companies. They fear that this might lead to Congressional action on their outrageous prices. So, in response, most Big Pharma firms now offer discounts or coupons to lower, or even eliminate, the cost of their drugs to some individual consumers.

This turns out to be a clever ruse. *Kaiser Health News* has called drug discount coupons a case of deceptive generosity, part of the "jockeying for profits in the lucrative pharmaceutical industry."

This 2019 American Association of Retired Persons (AARP) headline says it all:

> "The Hidden Costs Behind Prescription Drug Company Discounts: Coupons and charity keep list prices high, costing insurers and governments more."

That is because these discount coupons explicitly do not apply to Medicare or insurance companies. Medicare is actually required by law to pay the full price, which is exclusively set by the drug company. AARP relates the story of one myeloma patient, Pamela Holt, who got the drug Revlimid with no out-of-pocket costs. But there was a catch to the company's largesse:

> "Sounds wonderful, yes? But it's not so simple. Medicare—that is, taxpayers—still must pay the remainder of the drug's more than $250,000 annual tab. Experts say the seemingly generous charitable aid that Holt receives is actually intended to reduce public pressure for drugmakers to lower their prices. It helps Holt and others like her, but at the cost of the nation's rising health care budget."

"It's really just a racket," Holt said. A Congress bribed through copious campaign donations has decreed that in the U.S. no Medicare bargaining over drug prices is allowed. This is why many Americans go to Canada to purchase their drugs; the Canadian government negotiates lower prices for its citizens. But in the U.S. this legal prohibition on price negotiations has cost the people billions of dollars through higher taxes, insurance premiums, deductibles, and other charges to the public.

## Political capital

American politicians of all stripes have made political capital out of fighting cancer. In December 1971, President Richard M. Nixon launched the government's war on cancer with a promise to cure the disease in time for the American Bicentennial in 1976. Obviously, that never happened. Lately, American politicians have been making even more grandiose statements and impossible promises.

For example, in 2019, the Democrat Joe Biden and the Republican Donald Trump waged a war of words over who would own the cancer franchise. First, Biden said:

> "I promise you, if I'm elected President, you're going to see the single most important thing that changes America. We're gonna cure cancer."

Then, a few days later, in launching his 2020 campaign, President Trump countered:

> "We will come up with the cures to many, many problems, to many, many diseases—including cancer and others and we're getting closer all the time."

Despite these claims, half a century after Nixon declared war on cancer, many patients still experience the poor to mediocre performance of most cancer drugs. There is a huge gap between the expectations raised by politicians exploiting the hopes of cancer patients and the harsh reality of ineffective, toxic and outrageously expensive drugs.

The NCI once asked the Institute of Medicine (now the Health and Medicine division of the National Academy of Sciences) "to develop a set of recommendations to improve the federally funded cancer clinical trials system." In 2010, this resulted in a book called *A National Cancer Clinical Trials System for the 21st Century*. This book frankly exposed many of the flaws in cancer drug testing. The authors concluded that the system was not conducting clinical trials in a way that was likely to improve the care of real world patients.

In one telling paragraph, they exposed many of the same points we are making in this book:

> "Most cancer treatments available today are effective in only a minority of patients.... As a result, many patients undergo costly treatments and endure the side effects of those treatments without

> deriving any benefit.... An alternative treatment that might be more effective for a patient's particular disease is delayed or forgone."

So who were these radical critics, with their talk of beneficial alternative treatments and the like? Well, they were actually pillars of the establishment:

1. John Mendelsohn, MD, President of the M.D. Anderson Cancer Center, an internationally acclaimed leader in the field of medicine.
2. Harold L. Moses, MD, Director Emeritus at the Vanderbilt-Ingram Cancer Center and a past president of the American Association for Cancer Research.
3. Sharyl J. Nass, PhD, Director of the National Cancer Policy Forum at the National Academies of Sciences, Engineering, and Medicine.

This Institute of Medicine critique of the clinical trial system never reached the general public. In the intervening years, there was zero publicity given to this book. But in 2014, top leaders of the American Society of Clinical Oncology (ASCO) affirmed the conclusions of this report. They warned that the whole cancer clinical trial system was:

> "...sluggish and costly, resulting in small, incremental improvements in overall survival."

The head of ASCO's Cancer Research Committee, Lee M. Ellis, MD, of the M.D. Anderson Cancer Center, questioned the validity of most cancer drug trials. He told the *ASCO Post:*

> "Far too often, clinical trials result in a statistical endpoint...that doesn't translate into a meaningful benefit for patients."

The ASCO Research Committee included 50 of the most prominent names in oncology, including professors from Harvard, Johns Hopkins, Yale, and Duke universities. But again, no one paid the slightest attention to these sweeping criticisms directed at the status quo from inside the cancer establishment itself.

## Chapter 2. The chemotherapy concession

A doctor once called the relationship between Big Pharma and oncology almost incestuous. But one cannot understand this twisted relationship without understanding the chemotherapy concession. This was a scheme by which some oncologists profited by administering high-priced drugs in their offices and hospitals. In doing so, they acted as both physicians and drug salesmen, although patients were usually unaware of the latter role.

Quite amazingly, the online archive of the American Society of Clinical Oncology (ASCO), which has articles on every aspect of cancer, has only a single mention of the chemotherapy concession. According to John Vernon Cox, DO, writing in the 2013 *ASCO Connection*:

> "The traditional structure of oncology practice revolves around the buy and bill chemotherapy concession."

Dr. Cox alluded to the shrinkage of dollars from buy and bill, a phrase that would be unfamiliar to any but oncology insiders. A 2015 ASCO publication also proposed the reform of the buy and bill system for outpatient chemotherapy. Buy and bill was defined as follows:

> "Currently, [oncology] practices purchase drugs and then bill insurers, colloquially called buy and bill. Reimbursement for these drugs is the largest source of gross revenue for oncology practices, and as the prices of cancer drugs have grown over time, these purchases have had significant impact on the financial health of practices...."

The chemotherapy concession has been called oncology's "dirty little secret." I gained insight from an oncologist who took part in a group practice in the late 1990s. He wrote that although government regulators saw it as a clear conflict of interest, the practice continued for many years because it was so profitable. He stated the following:

> "The most cynical of oncologists simply selected drugs for incurable stage IV patients and described it as 'palliative chemotherapy.' Their choice of drugs was guided by which provided the biggest profit margin between what they could buy it for

> and what the Centers for Medicare & Medicaid Services or private insurance would reimburse us for. In the late 1990s, a lymphoma patient would be treated with six cycles of the drug combination R-CHOP, which was worth about $40,000 in chemotherapy profits."

This was $40,000 over and above what doctors normally earned for administering the treatment. Put another way, providing drugs to a single lymphoma patient was worth more at that time than the average American family earned in a year.

According to one of the few people to study the question, Jennifer L. Malin, MD, of the University of California at Los Angeles, in 2012 the chemotherapy concession accounted for 65% of revenue in a typical oncology practice, "dwarfing the income from evaluation and management."

In the U.S., at that time, the average salary of an oncologist was around $250,000. (It is currently about $360,000.) But if two-thirds of their income came from the behind-the-scenes sale of chemotherapy drugs, then some oncologists were making three quarters of a million dollars per year. This put them into the top one percent of all earners, bringing in thirty times the salary of the average American worker.

Until 1999, the public had no inkling that the chemotherapy concession even existed. But in that year, at a Medicare meeting in Baltimore, a gastroenterologist complained that the government had reduced his reimbursement rate for colonoscopies from $400 to $108. All of the doctors in his internal medicine group were hurting, he said, except for the medical oncologists, whom he said were making a fortune running their in-office retail pharmacies. This offhand remark alerted attendees to the fact that oncologists were selling drugs at a profit in their offices.

The "chemotherapy concession" was named and discussed in a *Journal of the National Cancer Institute* article in 2001. But it only became common knowledge in 2003, through an article by the *New York Times* reporter Reed Abelson. She revealed:

> "At a time when overall spending on prescription drugs is soaring, cancer specialists are pocketing hundreds of millions of dollars each year by selling drugs to patients—a practice that almost no other doctors follow."

Essentially, some oncologists who gave injections and infusions in their offices were stockpiling these drugs at a deep discount and then billing Medicare or other insurance plans the full retail price. In a follow-up article in 2006, Abelson wrote:

> "One government study said that cancer doctors, or oncologists, were receiving discounts as high as 86 percent on some chemotherapy drugs. The doctors then pocketed the difference."

Professor Joseph P. Newhouse of Harvard University told the *New York Times* that oncologists treated a greater number of patients because they had been making so much money under the old system, "these markups were a substantial portion of their income."

All this took place against a backdrop of the increasing standardization and monopolization of cancer care in America. This meant that, increasingly, small and independent practices were forced to either join bigger organizations or go out of business entirely.

The beginning of the end for the independent oncologist was Congressional passage of the 340B Drug Pricing Program in November 1992. This scheme, whose legal basis was the Veteran Health Care Act of 1992, protected specified government-supported clinics and hospitals from drug price increases, while giving them access to price reductions.

> "340B required drug companies to provide discounts of 20 to 50 percent to hospitals and clinics that treat low-income and uninsured patients."

But it was quickly side-tracked from its original beneficial goal. According to reporter Andrew Pollack of the *New York Times:*

> "The program allows hospitals to use the discounted drugs to treat not only poor patients but also those covered by Medicare or private insurance. In those cases, the hospital pockets the difference between the reduced price it pays for the drug and the amount it is reimbursed."

Thus, the financial benefit of the chemotherapy concession increasingly went to big hospitals and larger practices instead of, as formerly, to the small independent practices. As a result at least 400 independent practices became part of hospitals in recent years.

The chemotherapy concession further declined with the passage of the Medicare Modernization Act (MMA) of 2003. This dramatically cut reimbursements for cancer drugs given in most private practices. However, the MMA did not cut reimbursement rates to hospitals or large oncology organizations, such as the giant US Oncology. This was founded in 2004 and soon became a branch of the drug distribution giant McKesson. This organization now handles the finances of over 1,200 seemingly independent oncologists across the United States. (This is the same McKesson that is heavily implicated in the opioid crisis.)

According to my informants, it is these giant groups that now reap the rewards of the chemotherapy concession, with far fewer opportunities for independent oncologists to do the same. US Oncology in particular enjoys economies of scale. It is able to obtain discounts due to its large-volume purchases and a large number of participating clinics.

The Medicare Modernization Act of 2003 had some other unexpected effects on the practice of oncology. For instance, it increased the likelihood that some cancer patients would receive chemotherapy. It also changed the types of drugs that patients received, since some practices began to make treatment decisions based on its impact on their income, rather than purely on the patient's welfare. According to the *New York Times:*

> "Many doctors ended up prescribing chemotherapy for more of their patients, to make up for lower prices [due to Medicare cuts]."

Dr. Malin analyzed the records of 200,000 lung cancer patients treated between 2003 and 2005 and found that oncologists, under the 2003 Medicare Modernization Act, were giving more extensive and expensive treatments. Previously, 16.5% of such patients received chemotherapy. After the law went into effect this rose to 18.9% of patients. This 2.4% difference may not seem like much, but it was enormous when applied to the general cancer population, which is over 1,700,000 new U.S. cases each year.

According to University of Southern California Professor Mireille Jacobson, PhD, writing in a RAND Corporation report in 2010, the MMA:

> "...actually increased the likelihood that lung cancer patients received chemotherapy,... Physicians switched from dispensing the drugs that experienced the largest cuts in profitability, carboplatin and Taxol, to other high-margin drugs, like Taxotere."

Oncologists of course tried to fight back against the charge of profiteering. In fact, according to Memorial Sloan-Kettering's Larry Norton, MD, then the president of ASCO:

> "We're just trying to break even."

"Breaking even" for some people meant bringing in three quarters of a million dollars per year. But the net result of the Medicare Modernization Act has been the precipitous decline in independent cancer clinics. According to one oncologist I spoke to:

> "There has been a concerted effort to rid the map of independent smaller centers. I have heard over and over again at many mainstream conferences, that each and every patient should first be considered for a clinical trial. While I wish this was because large numbers of patients are getting breakthrough drugs, this is not the case, since the vast majority of phase I trials provide negligible value.
>
> "Then why? Because it works for Big Pharma, insurance and the big institutions. Pharma gets its drugs tested. Insurance is off the hook for drug costs during the study period, and institutions make far more money running trials than caring for patients. Is there any wonder why smaller independent cancer clinics have become nearly extinct?"

## Millions from anemia drugs

In 2010, the *New York Times* published an article, "Doctors Reap Millions for Anemia Drugs." It revealed that drug companies were paying some oncologists to prescribe anti-anemia medications, since anemia is a common side effect of chemotherapy:

> "Two of the world's largest drug companies are paying hundreds of millions of dollars to doctors every year in return for giving their patients anemia medicines, which regulators now say may be unsafe at commonly used doses.... The payments give physicians an incentive to prescribe the medicines at levels that might increase patients' risks of heart attacks or strokes."

The two companies in question were Johnson & Johnson and Amgen. The payments were "an important source of profit for doctors and [kidney dialysis] centers." The *Times* also reported that a single oncology practice in the Pacific Northwest, consisting of six cancer doctors, "received $2.7 million from Amgen for prescribing $9 million worth of its drugs last year." $2.7 million in incentives divided six ways is $450,000 apiece. And that's just from a single company to a single clinic for a single class of drugs. But the drugs in question can have considerable toxicity. One oncologist commented on the companies' rewards program:

> "The deal was so good. The indication was so clear and the downside was so small that docs just worked it into their practice easily. Now it's much scarier than that. We could really be doing harm."

Although the authors called for "further research...to understand the impact of these financial incentives," no such studies have been published. In fact, PubMed lists a grand total of three studies on the topic, the latest of which appeared in 2013. Its conclusion:

> "A substantial proportion of oncologists, who are not paid a fixed salary, report that their incomes increase when they administer chemotherapy and growth factors [such as for anemia]."

## Dubious role of medical journals

One might think that medical journals, with their peer-review system of quality control, would hold the line against biased, erroneous and fraudulent research. But because of the pervasive influence of Big Pharma, many have become active participants in deception.

Here are the conclusions of four top medical journal editors after a lifetime of involvement in the field. Marcia Angell, MD, was an editor of the *New England Journal of Medicine* for 25 years. She later wrote *The Truth About Drug Companies: How They Deceive Us and What To Do About It.*
According to Dr. Angell:

> "It used to be that drug companies would hand their new drug over to an academic center to have it tested, and then they sat back and waited, Now they're intimately involved in every step along the way, and they treat academic researchers more like hired hands."

She also had choice words to say about the entanglements of

doctors who take drug company money.

These researchers think:

> "...what these companies are after are their brains, but they're really after the brand. To buy a distinguished senior academic researcher, the kind of person who speaks at meetings, who writes textbooks, who writes journal articles—that's worth 100,000 salespeople."

George D. Lundberg, MD, was for 17 years the top editor of the *Journal of the American Medical Association.* In his book, *Severed Trust,* he wrote:

> "U.S. pharmaceutical companies remain a world model for creating devious methods to get physicians and patients to do what the companies want, whether or not it is in the best interest of the patient."

Jerome P. Kassirer, MD, was for eight years the editor-in-chief of the *New England Journal of Medicine.* In 2004, he wrote *On the Take: How Medicine's Complicity with Big Business Can Endanger Your Health.* The people "on the take" were his fellow doctors, who had been corrupted by Big Pharma. As he wrote:

> "Away from the eyes of the public, the pharmaceutical industry captures the loyalty of physicians with gifts and lavish meals, pays them as consultants (even though they do little or no consulting), funds their research, and pays for the expenses of their continuing education. Equally obscured is the willingness of many doctors to accept this largesse."

Finally, Richard Smith, MD, was an editor of the *British Medical Journal* for 25 years. He concluded that much of the research in medical journals is "fraudulent, prone to bias and deeply flawed." In his 2006 book, *The Trouble with Medical Journals,* he stated that:

> "...many of the ethical difficulties of medical journals arise in their relationship with pharmaceutical companies."

Medical journals have become, by and large, "creatures of the drug industry." They are packed with studies that are conceived and carried out by industry. Although they bear the names of celebrated doctors, they are often ghost written by hired hands of the pharmaceutical companies themselves.

Professor Charles Seife expanded on this point in a 2014 *Scientific American* article, "How Drug Company Money is Undermining Science":

> "The entanglements between researchers and pharmaceutical companies take many forms. There are speakers' bureaus: a drugmaker gives a researcher money to travel—often first class—to gigs around the country, where the researcher sometimes gives a company-written speech and presents company-drafted slides.
>
> "There is ghostwriting: a pharmaceutical manufacturer has an article drafted and pays a scientist (the 'guest author') an honorarium to put his or her name on it and submit it to a peer-reviewed journal. And then there is consulting: a company hires a researcher to render advice."

## Payments to clinical trial doctors

Society has entrusted doctors who perform clinical trials with a solemn duty. This is to find out which medicines actually benefit the highly vulnerable population of cancer patients. Many cancer doctors and nurses carry out this duty with care and compassion. They are a huge asset to the community.

At the same time, a distressing number of people involved in clinical trials are not the impartial judges the public believes them to be. They are receiving payments from the very companies whose products they are evaluating.

Taking money from a Big Pharma firm, while evaluating its products, is a huge conflict of interest. How can doctors be objective about the hand that feeds them? Once patients realize how things stand, how can they trust recommendations that come from such doctors? There is a pervasive conflict of interest in the medical field when it comes to the evaluation of clinical trials. According to NutritionFacts.org:

> "Every single one of eight reviews covering over a thousand studies found that research funded by industry is more likely to make conclusions that are favorable to industry. "

In the words of Professor Charles Seife in *Scientific American* (2012):

> "In the past few years the pharmaceutical industry has come up with many ways to funnel large sums of money—enough sometimes to put a child through college—into the pockets of independent medical researchers who are doing work that bears, directly or indirectly, on the drugs these firms are making and marketing."

According to the sociologist Eric Campbell, PhD, a professor of medicine at Harvard Medical School.:

> "There isn't a single sector of academic medicine, academic research or medical education in which industry relationships are not a ubiquitous factor."

In 2018, the Canadian sociologist, Professor Sergio Sismondo, wrote an entire book, *Ghost-Managed Medicine,* showing in great detail how "Big Pharma's invisible hands" manipulate, from start to finish, the entire process of approving new drugs.

Similarly, Justin E. Bekelman, MD, of the Yale University School of Medicine, showed that one-fourth of all clinical trial investigators have ties to the drug industry. And these are generally the key opinion leaders, the senior authors of papers on a new drug. In addition, Dr. Bekelman showed that:

> "Roughly two thirds of academic institutions hold equity in start-ups that sponsor research performed at the same institution."

A start-up company's new drug may be worth millions, or even billions, of dollars to the patent holder. So when a university or a hospital owns part of a start-up company, and then conducts research on its own product, how objective is that likely to be? This is more than a hypothetical question. It has been shown that there is a 3.6 times greater chance of a study arriving at a positive conclusion when funding comes from a private company than when it comes from nonprofits or government. Dr. Bekelman concluded:

> "Financial relationships among industry, scientific investigators, and academic institutions are widespread. Conflicts of interest arising from these ties can influence biomedical research in important ways."

Bekelman is being diplomatic in his criticism. In fact, Big Pharma now controls every phase of the clinical trial system. This is an international scandal, in just the way that lack of any testing for safety and efficacy was, in the days of the thalidomide disaster. And the cause of both is clear. In the words of Senator Estes Kefauver, co-author of the FDA reform law of 1962, it is the "corrosive influence of unrestrained greed."

Photo credit: Kmimtz66

## Chapter 3. Open Payments

For details on payments by Big Pharma to American doctors you need to consult a U.S. government website named Open Payments. This website was a result of the Physician Payments Sunshine Act of 2010, a bold attempt to:

> "...increase the transparency around the financial relationships between health care providers and medical product manufacturers."

Open Payments keeps track, to the penny, of the money that flows from Big Pharma to doctors and hospitals across the U.S. It makes that information freely available to the general public in an admirably transparent way. So people who are interested in understanding oncology's relationship to Big Pharma should familiarize themselves with this invaluable site.

Dr. Vinay Prasad has called Big Pharma money paid to doctors "the cancer growing in cancer medicine." He does not exaggerate. At this writing, Open Payments provides information for the years 2013 through 2018. This shows that during this five-year period Big Pharma paid out $43.22 billion dollars in numerous transactions with American doctors and hospitals. To be clear, this is not a payment for goods or services in the normal sense. It is mainly for the purchase of goodwill.

These payments come in various forms. Here I am mainly discussing what Open Payments calls general payments, and not research funds, which are listed in a separate category.

- General payments are not associated with a research study. They come in the form of cash, directly into the personal bank accounts of individual doctors for their private use.

- Big Pharma made these general payments to over one million individual doctors for their personal use between 2013 and 2018.

- Out of the $43.22 billion, $15.23 billion was in the form of personal payments to individual doctors.

- Another $26.57 billion went for research funding. Since government funding is often inadequate to carry out full-scale clinical trials, Big Pharma money has become essential to medical scientists and to their hospitals. It is another way that Big Pharma powerfully influences trials of new drugs.

- In addition, doctors in this period received $1.42 billion in

> stock in these same companies. Sometimes this involves gifts of stock options, which enable the recipient to buy a company's stock at a deep discount.

General or personal payments are almost always sanitized as reimbursement for some alleged service or other. These can be disguised as (to quote an FDA disclaimer statement):

> "Investments, consulting, expert witness testimony, contracts, grants, teaching, speaking, writing, patents and royalties, and primary employment."

Whether or not this practice conforms to the legal definition of bribery, or corruption, these doctors have put themselves at risk of violating the Hippocratic Oath. They have aligned their own financial interests with those of Big Pharma. At the very least, these drug companies quite reasonably can expect that the doctors will maintain a positive attitude towards them and their products.

In a broader sense, doctors taking drug company money are unlikely to take the consumer's side in any dispute with industry. Thus, those seeking to reform the current situation have lost their most powerful potential allies in the fight, who are America's doctors. It explains why very few oncologists, as a rule, are fighting back against the outrageous cost of modern medications.

A related term for this is influence peddling. This is defined as the use of power or influence on someone else's behalf in return for money or favors. In particular, the $15.23 billion given in personal payments has had a pervasive and corrupting influence on the process of new drug testing, and thereby on the whole oncology profession.

## Spinning the results

Well-placed doctors can influence the medical profession and the public's perception of a clinical trial's outcome. These individuals, called key opinion leaders, or KOLs, are of crucial importance to Big Pharma.

We all know how, in a previous era, doctors were used by the tobacco industry to tout the safety of their cancer-causing products. Big Tobacco even claimed to have proof of benefit from "distinguished doctors in clinical tests" reported in "authoritative medical journals."

Today, we may be less naive, but doctors are still used to tout the benefits of unproven and dangerous drugs.

Generally, in a clinical trial, KOLs occupy the top positions. According to Jeffrey J. Meffert, MD, of the University of Texas Health Science Center, San Antonio:

One of many advertisements showing doctors supporting the tobacco industry

> "Key opinion leaders…are the experts in their field upon whom we depend for original research leading to disease understanding and new therapies…. KOLs are used not only to lend credibility to claims of efficacy and safety but also to promote anecdotal and off-label use of these medications to increase industry profits."

There are even KOL management companies, which are employed by industry "to turn those involved in medical education and research into efficient and productive members of the sales force." That's what these doctors have become: members of Big Pharma's sales force.

There is nothing haphazard about Big Pharma's recruitment of the leaders of oncology. Top authors in the pay of Big Pharma control the phrasing of the paper, especially its summary, or Abstract. This is often the only part that many people, including doctors, read. Abstracts also influence the way that medical journalists interpret the study for the general public.

So by controlling the precise wording, one can control the impact of even a negative study on the market. There is a name for this practice: spin.

Spin, in a medical context, has been defined in the *Journal of the American Medical Association*:

> "The use of specific reporting strategies…to highlight that the experimental treatment is beneficial,

> despite a statistically *nonsignificant* difference for the primary outcome, or to distract the reader from statistically *nonsignificant* results."

## How common is spin?

In articles on cancer treatment, spin is pervasive. A 2013 study from Princess Margaret Hospital, Toronto, analyzed the situation in regard to breast cancer clinical trials:

> "Of 164 included trials, 33% showed bias in the reporting of the primary endpoint and 67% in the reporting of toxicity.... Only 32% of articles indicated the frequency of grade 3 and 4 toxicities in the abstract."

A follow-up study of cancer trials found biased reporting in 47% of the abstracts of papers that had failed to find a statistically significant difference between the two arms of the study. The Princess Margaret researchers concluded:

> "Bias in reporting of efficacy outcomes is common for studies with a negative primary end-point and can lead to off-label misuse of experimental therapies, if they are approved for other indications. Toxicity is under-reported...leading to a biased view of the safety of new treatments."

The widescale practice of spin in oncology is part of the promotion of Big Pharma's interests by physicians who are aligned with its goals. It is little different than the blatant payments to doctors of a previous era who endorsed the products of Big Tobacco.

Sometimes the influence seems to go beyond spin. Consider a 2009 study of medical conflict of interest in the American Cancer Society journal, *Cancer*. The authors, from the University of Michigan, looked at a total of 1,434 oncology studies. They found conflicts of interest in 45% of the papers whose authors were medical oncologists. Analyzing the same data for the influential *New England Journal of Medicine,* the figure was 61%. Medical oncologists had the highest degree of conflict of interest of all physicians surveyed.

But the most disturbing part of that paper is in a table titled Outcomes of Randomized Trials. This table showed that clinical trials in which oncologists had a conflict of interest more frequently reported positive results. Doctors who were taking money from Big

Pharma arrived at positive overall survival results for the experimental drug twice as often as those who were not on the take (29% versus 14%). At the same time, doctors on the take came up with a negative result in just a single instance, or one percent of the time. It looks as if some doctors manipulate trial data—or at least its interpretation—to make the results come out in favor of Big Pharma's latest drug. Some of these themes can be illustrated through the career of one man, José Baselga, MD.

## Chapter 4. The case of Dr. Baselga

In 2018, José M. Baselga, MD, PhD, was at the top of his profession. Born in Spain, he had worked his way up the professional ladder to become Physician-in-Chief of Memorial Sloan-Kettering Cancer Center in New York City, America's largest private cancer center.

In 2007, he had co-authored an article in the journal *Nature*, "Keeping Faith With [Clinical] Trial Volunteers," in which he called for complete transparency about potential conflicts of interest. He and his colleagues wrote:

> "We support calls by the World Medical Association and others to expand disclosure of funding sources and financial conflicts of interest to potential [clinical] trial participants."

In a 2017 paper, of which he was first author, he claimed that he had no conflicts of interest. However, in August 2018, the *New York Times* revealed that Baselga was actually receiving huge secret payments from the drug industry. He thereupon revised his no conflict statements in various journals and admitted to receiving payments from a variety of companies in the cancer field. These companies included Roche and its American division Genentech, Novartis, AstraZeneca, Eli Lilly, as well as a dozen lesser-known entities.

Dr. Baselga then was forced out under pressure from his Memorial Sloan-Kettering Cancer Center boss, Craig B. Thompson, MD. A few months later, Baselga was hired as vice president and director of R&D of the giant European drug firm, AstraZeneca. In an interview, Baselga insisted that "the move to the corporate world with AstraZeneca clearly puts the matter behind him."

What led to his abrupt departure from Memorial Sloan-Kettering Cancer Center were his enthusiastic statements about Roche's new drugs, especially taselisib.

Breast cancer patients who received this experimental drug, plus an FDA-approved drug, Faslodex, were said to have a lower risk of their cancer worsening compared to those who received Faslodex plus a placebo (sugar pill).

In a 2018 clinical trial, taselisib extended progression-free survival by two months versus a placebo. That was 7.4 months for taselisib versus 5.4 months for the placebo. But the more meaningful overall survival data was not released.

Meanwhile, there were grade 3 or 4 (severe or life-threatening) instances of diarrhea in 12% of the taselisib patients, severe lowering of blood sugar in 10%, inflammation of the colon in 3%, and mouth sores in 2% of patients. Fully 17% of patients discontinued treatment due to its toxicity. While the positive effects were not good at all, the side effects were just awful. Yet on June 2, 2018, speaking at the American Society of Clinical Oncology meeting in Chicago, Baselga enthused about the results of this clinical trial. Among other things, he said:

> "Our findings are proof that targeting this pathway in breast cancer is effective."

At the same time, his own institution, Memorial Sloan-Kettering Cancer Center, put out a press release on the topic. Under a full-scale portrait of Dr. Baselga was the following caption:

> "Memorial Sloan-Kettering Cancer Center Physician-in-Chief José Baselga says the new results are 'incredibly exciting' for improving the treatment of advanced breast cancer."

Incredibly exciting? All that taselisib had done was to extend progression-free survival by two months. And that is a largely meaningless measure of benefit to cancer patients. In fact, on the very next day, Roche executives pulled the plug on this "incredibly exciting" drug and all similar agents. The headline at one trade website said it all:

> "Roche dumps its…effort on taselisib after researchers track poor survival edge, harsh side effects for breast cancer."

But Baselga's performance around taselisib, and other drugs, had raised eyebrows. He insisted that he had nothing to declare, all the while sounding like a drug salesperson. Soon, investigative journalists from the *New York Times* and *ProPublica* were on his case, to see if he was receiving payments from taselisib's manufacturer, Roche. Using public databases, including the U.S. government's Open Payments website, they unearthed a network of financial ties, not just to Roche, but to many other drug companies as well:

> "At a conference this year… [Baselga] put a positive spin on the results of two Roche-sponsored clinical trials that many others considered disappointments, without disclosing his relationship to the company. Since 2014, he has received more than $3 million from Roche in consulting fees…."

These three million dollars were the payment from one

company to one doctor, who vigorously promoted their products. Four decades ago, in my book, *The Cancer Industry,* I revealed the same type of conflict of interest at that institution. But the revelation of the more than three million dollar payment on the front page of the *New York Times* led to a public rebuke of Dr. Baselga from Memorial Sloan-Kettering Cancer Center, his abrupt resignation in September 2018, and a scandal that reverberated for months through the giant cancer center.

Dr. Baselga was publicly criticized by Craig B. Thompson, MD, president and CEO of Memorial Sloan-Kettering Cancer Center. In a letter to the staff, Dr. Thompson wrote about the invisible line between personal advancement and corruption, a line that Dr. Baselga had crossed. And he blamed himself for not keeping better track of his subordinates:

> "José reported to me, and I wish I had done more to keep him away from the line. While Dr. Baselga has acknowledged his mistakes and resigned, this has not brought closure.... It has led to discussions of whether we still know where the right side of the line is."

Then it turned out that, in the previous year, Thompson himself had received $300,000 per year as a board member of one of the biggest cancer drug manufacturers, Merck. He also received $70,000 in cash from another drug maker and $215,050 in its stock. Open Payments revealed that between 2013 and 2018 Dr. Thompson received $86,298.24 in personal funds, mainly from Merck and Pfizer. This was on top of his annual compensation package from Memorial Sloan-Kettering Cancer Center, which alone was $6.7 million per year. Under pressure from the MSKCC board, Thompson resigned his position at Merck and Charles River Laboratories, but managed to maintain his job at the cancer center.

As part of the Baselga scandal, other top MSKCC researchers also revealed some of their own connections to Big Pharma. For example, Jedd D. Wolchok, MD, a pioneer of cancer immunotherapy, listed his affiliations with 31 companies. According to *ProPublica*:

> "The list of companies that pay [Dr. Wolchok] range from major manufacturers like Bristol-Myers Squibb and Merck, for whom he works as a paid consultant, to startups like BeiGene, Apricity and Adaptive Biotech, in which he reports owning stock options."

Open Payments revealed that between 2013 and 2018 Dr. Wolchok received $145,320.44 in personal payments and another $10,842,557.76 in associated research payments. The companies giving him personal payments were Bristol-Myers Squibb, Imclone, Amgen, Eli Lilly, Janssen Research, Genentech/Roche, Chugai, Medimmune, and Astellas. Most of this money came in the form of undefined consulting fees.

Globally speaking, these are just a few of the drug industry connections that investigative reporters and Open Payments have revealed. In truth, it is nearly impossible to find a major cancer clinical trial in which the key opinion leaders are not taking personal payments from Big Pharma, including the companies whose products they are investigating. By doing so, these doctors compromise the integrity of trials and raise the fundamental question of whether these clinical trials really do show effectiveness for the drugs under study.

## Chapter 5. Regulating the regulators

**"But who will guard the guardians?"**

*—Juvenal, 2nd Century C.E. (Quis custodiet ipsos custodes?)*

The Food and Drug Administration (FDA) is the main federal agency charged with protecting the U.S. public's health. According to the agency's website:

> "FDA is responsible for the oversight of more than $2.5 trillion in consumption of food, medical products, and tobacco. FDA-regulated products account for about 20 cents of every dollar spent by U.S. consumers."

In particular, the FDA's decisions control the success or failure of all drugs marketed in the U.S. This is important because although the U.S. contains just 4.3% of the world's population, it constitutes 45% of the market for prescription drugs.

For it to fulfill its function, it is essential that the FDA remain independent of Big Pharma's corrosive influence, and especially that it be impartial in judging the merits and demerits of particular drugs. But, according to Michael Carome, MD, a former Health and Human Services official, speaking to *PBS NewsHour:*

> "Instead of a regulator and a regulated industry, we now have a partnership. That relationship has tilted the agency away from a public health perspective to an industry friendly perspective."

Partnership and friendliness sound like intrinsically good things. But what we are actually looking at is something quite sinister. It is in fact the regulatory capture of the FDA by the drug industry, which began in earnest with the Reagan presidency. In fact, Reagan's very first executive order, #12291, required the FDA along with other agencies to carry out a "cost-benefit analysis" of their regulations. This looked at regulation from the industry's point of view, with an emphasis on reducing "the burdens of existing and future regulations." According to one student of that era, Reagan's deregulation policies:

> "...left the FDA so financially vulnerable that it depended on the economic involvement of the industry.... The era of New Right conservatism

> during the Reagan era built the foundation that led to the regulatory capture of the Food and Drug Administration."

In fact, according to Professor John Abraham of King's College London:

> "The regulatory state and the pharmaceutical industry work largely in partnership and behind a cloak of secrecy."

A 2018 study in *Science* showed that many FDA officials put in time at the agency as a stepping stone to more lucrative employment. They leave FDA to work as employees, directors, consultants, or lobbyists for the very companies they previously regulated. This is called the revolving door, a well worn path to self-enrichment.

The revolving door between the FDA and industry rotates regardless of whether one political party or another is in power. Big Pharma works both sides of the political street. In fact, it may surprise readers to learn that in 2018 Big Pharma gave slightly more money to Democrats than to Republicans. Pharma always covers its bets, regardless of which party is currently in power.

The very useful Open Secrets website reveals that in 2018 the pharmaceutical industry spent a total of $283,440,000 on lobbying efforts. They employed a total of 1,451 lobbyists. Of these, 973, or 67.1%, were revolvers.

The latest ploy in 2019 is for big drug company executives to make large personal contributions to key Senators in order to block legislation that might reduce drug prices. According to the informative website, STAT news:

> "Top pharmaceutical CEOs have targeted a small group of Republican senators with roughly $200,000 in campaign donations in the past year.... Broadly, the contributions appear to target...those best positioned to influence legislation on Capitol Hill in a manner beneficial to drug companies."

President Trump's nomination of Scott Gottlieb, MD, as FDA Commissioner represented a new level of collaboration between the agency and the drug industry. Although Gottlieb is a medical doctor, his job for 10 years prior to joining FDA was as a partner at New Enterprise Associates, the world's largest venture capital firm, managing assets of $20 billion.

In fact, Gottlieb was an investing partner in their healthcare division. After he was nominated to head the FDA, he expressed his intention to recuse himself "for one year from any agency decisions involving about 20 healthcare companies he worked with," including Bristol-Myers Squibb, GlaxoSmithKline, and Vertex Pharmaceuticals.

Then, less than two years into the job, Gottlieb suddenly quit as FDA Commissioner. A few months later, he was hired as a director of Pfizer. Pfizer directors receive an average of $187,091 per year for attending eight meetings. One Senator called on Gottlieb to resign his board seat at Pfizer, arguing that:

> "This kind of revolving door influence-peddling smacks of corruption, and makes the American people rightfully cynical and distrustful about whether high-level Trump officials are working for them, or for their future corporate employers."

Gottlieb's replacement as FDA Commissioner was Norman Sharpless, MD, Director of the UNC Lineberger Comprehensive Cancer Center, Chapel Hill, North Carolina. Sharpless once described himself as an academic entrepreneur. He is a co-founder of G1 Therapeutics, a pharmaceutical company "focused on advancing innovative therapies in multiple oncology indications," and of Sapere Bio. Sharpless reputedly has $6 million of his own money tied up in G1.

Here are some other revolvers who have served as FDA Commissioners:

- 1999-2001: Jane E. Henney, MD. After leaving the FDA, Henney joined the board of directors of AstraZeneca, as well as Cigna Corporation, AmerisourceBergen and the China Medical Board.

- 2002-2004: Mark McClellan, MD, PhD, now a professor of Business, Medicine and Health Policy at Duke University, is a director of Johnson & Johnson, Cigna, Alignment Healthcare, and Seer.

- 2006: Lester M. Crawford, MD, who pleaded guilty to "lying and conflict-of- interest charges in connection with stock he and his wife owned in companies regulated by the FDA."

- 2006-2009: Andrew von Eschenbach, MD, who serves as a director of BioTime, a biotechnology company, and on the advisory boards of Johnson & Johnson, Chugai Pharmaceuticals, Arrowhead Research Corporation, and other drug companies.

A *Kaiser Health News* article showed that:

> "Hundreds of people have glided through the 'revolving door' that connects the drug industry to Capitol Hill and to the Department of Health and Human Services [parent department of the FDA]."

*Science's* investigative reporter, Charles Piller, explained the influence of these FDA revolvers:

> "FDA staffers play a pivotal role in drug approvals, presenting evidence to the agency's advisory panels and influencing or making approval decisions. They are free to move to jobs in Pharma, and many do...."

One prominent critic of the practice, Vinay Prasad, MD, and his Oregon colleagues investigated the FDA's revolving door in the *British Medical Journal* in 2016. To quote a summary of his report:

> "[Dr. Prasad] tracked 55 FDA reviewers in the hematology-oncology field from 2001 through 2010....Of the 26 reviewers who left FDA during this period, 15 of them, or 57.7%, later worked or consulted for the biopharmaceutical industry."

Dr. Prasad asked the following rhetorical questions:

> "If you know in the back of your mind that your career goal may be to someday work on the other side of the table, I wonder whether that changes the way you regulate? Are you more likely to give [Big Pharma] the benefit of the doubt? Are you less likely to beat them up hard over [using bad data in drug studies]?"

David S. Egilman, MD, a professor of family medicine at Brown University in Rhode Island, and an expert on the corporate corruption of science, has said that the FDA is "outmanned and out-financed by industry." He continued:

> "A single FDA officer generally has major responsibility for the approval of a drug in a process that involves negotiation with a host of industry physicians, scientists, lawyers, and marketing experts over a number of years. This psychologically, scientifically, and financially imbalanced relationship...puts the agency at risk

> of being captured by the economic interests it regulates."

According to salary.com, in 2019 the average salary of an FDA clinical trials data analyst was about $66,000. Compare that to the average base pay of a Washington, D.C. lobbyist, which was almost twice that ($124,000). In other words, by keeping their mouths shut, FDA employees can double their income if they go over to the "dark side."

### Crucial role of user fees

One of the ways that the drug industry has weakened the FDA has been through the political process. By funding pro-industry politicians they have been able to lessen FDA's ability to act independently and vigorously in the public interest.

Professor John Abraham of King's College, London, has thoroughly documented this process:

> "The FDA was subject to severe budgetary cuts during the Reagan Administrations, which reduced the number of employees from 8,200 in 1979 to 7,000 in 1987. Over the same period Congress had passed 20 new laws giving the FDA new responsibilities in both the food and drug area.... To avert budgetary disaster the pharmaceutical industry agreed to partly fund the agency via users' fees... but only in exchange for explicit acceleration of regulatory review defined by industry demands."

A key turning point in the history of the FDA was passage of the Prescription Drug User Fee Act of 1992. In fact, Professor Stephen J. Ceccoli, a historian of the agency, has written that passage of this Act represented the fourth "distinctive regime" in the regulation of new medicines. It is a regime marked by "deregulation" and "efficiency."

According to Professor Donald W. Light in his essay "Institutional Corruption of Pharmaceuticals and the Myth of Safe and Effective Drugs":

> "The authorization of user fees in 1992 has turned drug companies into the FDA's prime clients, deepening the regulatory and cultural capture of the agency. Industry has demanded shorter average review times and, with less time to thoroughly

> review evidence, increased hospitalizations and deaths have resulted. Meeting the needs of the drug companies has taken priority over meeting the needs of patients."

So what are these user fees, and how do they compromise the FDA? The agency itself describes user fees this way:

> "The Prescription Drug User Fee Act authorizes FDA to collect fees from companies that produce certain human drug and biological products. Since the passage of [this Act], user fees have played an important role in expediting the drug approval process."

As of 2019, the fee for reviewing a drug with clinical data is over $2.5 million. Because of the Reagan and G.H.W. Bush cuts, the FDA is kept seriously underfinanced. FDA should have received appropriations to thoroughly evaluate all the products of industry. Instead, it had to turn to industry itself to pay for these evaluations. This put the FDA in a dependent position vis-à-vis Big Pharma. From that point forward, the FDA was working for the very industry it was supposed to be regulating. The law passed the Senate by a unanimous voice vote in 1992. According to the *New York Times:*

> "The legislation...signifies a major change in the relationship between the Food and Drug Administration and the industry it monitors."

David Kessler, MD, then the FDA Commissioner, agreed to hire 600 new examiners not to better scrutinize new drugs but to speed drug approval. The law, which was seen as a great advance in the era of HIV/AIDS, actually undercut the close examination of all new drugs. Instead, it was mainly about rushing poorly tested drugs to market. It was also a huge money maker for industry. According to the *New York Times:*

> "The companies may make millions of dollars at the same time they pay new fees to the Government. The FDA estimates that companies may earn an average of $10 million for each additional month they have a drug on the market."

The initial user fee was $100,000 per drug, rising to $233,000 in five years. But since, according to the FDA, drug companies would earn $10 million for each additional month they had a drug on the market, they essentially turned a $100,000 fee into $120,000,000 per year in the blink of an eye. And that was per drug!

At the same time, President George H.W. Bush and the Congress cut the budget request for the National Institutes of Health by $200 million, "the first time in memory that Congress has not given the institutes a more generous budget than the Administration asked for," according to the *New York Times.*

This further weakened the position of the public sector compared to private interests. The net result was that the FDA effectively became an arm of the industry it was meant to regulate. At the present time, user fees pay for at least 65 percent of the drug approval process. This is what economists mean by regulatory capture. According to a 2018 investigation by journalists at *ProPublica,* "FDA Repays Industry by Rushing Risky Drugs to Market":

> "As pharma companies underwrite three-fourths of the FDA's budget for scientific reviews, the agency is increasingly fast-tracking expensive drugs with significant side effects and unproven health benefits."

The *ProPublica* article is very revealing:

> "The FDA is increasingly green-lighting expensive drugs despite dangerous or little-known side effects and inconclusive evidence that they curb or cure disease. Once widely assailed for moving slowly, today the FDA reviews and approves drugs faster than any other regulatory agency in the world."

## Advisory panel conflicts

Big Pharma has also meddled with the FDA advisory process. According to a 2018 report in *Science,* some FDA advisory panel members are also in the pay of the drug industry.

Advisors are routinely questioned about potential sources of bias before beginning their deliberations on a new drug. But nothing is asked about payments occurring after the completion of the evaluation. In an exposé, *Science* focused on the giant multinational drug maker, AstraZeneca, and its blockbuster drug, Brilinta. The advisory panelists seemed free of conflict before the start of the approval process. But after AstraZeneca received approval for Brilinta, it made large payments to four members of the review panel. According to *Science*:

> "As Brilinta's sales took off later…AstraZeneca… showered the four with money for travel and advice. For example, those companies paid or reimbursed …Jonathan Halperin of the Icahn School of Medicine at Mount Sinai in New York City more than $200,000 for accommodations, honoraria, and consulting from 2013 to 2016."

Mainly because of this approval, Brilinta earned AstraZeneca $1.3 billion in 2018, with earnings rising at a rate of 21% per year. So a few million dollars in general payments to key advisory board members is a tiny price to pay, if it smooths the way to FDA approval.

As part of its cancer drug review process, FDA relies heavily on the Oncology Drug Advisory Committee (ODAC). The stated purpose of ODAC is as follows:

> "The Committee reviews and evaluates data concerning the safety and effectiveness of marketed and investigational human drug products for use in the treatment of cancer and makes appropriate recommendations to the Commissioner of Food and Drugs."

The FDA rarely overrides its chief cancer advisors. But how much influence does Big Pharma have over ODAC? The drug industry has its own permanent representative on the committee. This enshrines the idea that FDA and the industry are partners in a collaborative effort, rather than in a potentially adversarial relationship. For the period 2016 to 2019 this representative has been P. K. Morrow, MD, a Vice President of Amgen.

By using Open Payments, one gets an insight into the allegiance of the medical oncologists on the panel. Between 2013 and 2018, some ODAC members received significant amounts of money from leading cancer drug manufacturers. These are some of the same companies whose products come before ODAC for its recommendations. Why doesn't the FDA make these members recuse themselves? At the start of each meeting, the FDA does conduct a *pro forma* examination of ODAC members for conflicts of interest. But after this formal review, typically, another FDA employee declares ODAC members to be free of significant conflicts:

> "FDA has determined that members and 11 temporary voting members of this committee are in compliance with federal ethics and conflict of interest laws."

But does this really mean that ODAC members and other advisors are free of conflicts of interest? Not necessarily. FDA simply declares their known conflicts of interest to be less significant than the agency's need for their opinions. As an FDA staffer put it:

> "Congress has authorized FDA to grant waivers to special government employees and regular federal employees who have potential financial conflicts when it is determined that the agency's need for a special government employee's services outweighs his or her potential financial conflict of interest."

This is almost comical, as if an advisor could not be swayed by thousands (or millions) of dollars in consulting fees and research funding. And, as if the knowledge of these particular oncologists is so precious that FDA could not find equivalent expertise among the thousands of other U.S. oncologists who have no such conflicts of interest.

In 2018, there were 11 non-staff members at the ODAC meeting. Six received general payments, in the form of cash and other gifts for their own use, usually in addition to research funds for their hospitals. Between 2015 and 2018 these were:

1. Brian Rini, MD, Cleveland Clinic, who received almost $300,000 in personal payments from Pfizer, Roche, Merck, GlaxoSmithKline, Novartis and over $20 million in associated research funding (mostly from Pfizer).

2. Alice T. Shaw, MD, PhD, Massachusetts General Hospital, who received over $207,000 in personal funds from Pfizer, Roche, Novartis, and others. She also brought in over $9.5 million in associated research funding.

3. Grzegorz S. Nowakowski, MD, Mayo Clinic, who received over $147,000 in personal payments from Celgene, Bayer, AbbVie, etc. He also received over $3.1 million in associated research funding, mostly from Celgene.

4. Vassiliki A. Papadimitrakopoulou, MD, M.D. Anderson Cancer Center, who received personal payments of over $142,000 from AstraZeneca, Celgene, Merck, Janssen, AbbVie, Novartis, AstraZeneca, Bristol-Myers Squibb, and Lilly.

5. Gregory J. Riely, MD, Memorial Sloan-Kettering Cancer Center, who received over $69,000 in personal funds from Pfizer, Novartis, Merck, Roche, Squibb and Celgene.

6. Alberto S. Pappo, MD, St. Jude Children's Research Hospital, who received over $33,000 from Bayer, Eli Lilly, AstraZeneca and Merck and over $515,000 in associated research funding from Merck, Novartis, Bristol-Myers Squibb, AstraZeneca and Roche.

## Role of Congress

The FDA is under the executive control of the U.S. Department of Health and Human Services (HHS). Why then don't higher ups clean up the drug regulatory mess at the FDA? Don't look for much action there. The present head of HHS is a Trump appointee named Alex Azar. He was for five years president of the giant drug firm Eli Lilly. He was also a top Big Pharma lobbyist. He is also a top-level revolver, having previously served as HHS's general counsel from 2001 to 2007.

While at Eli Lilly, Azar personally:

> "...built a substantial financial portfolio now worth $9.5 million to $20.6 million, and he was paid nearly $2 million in his final year at the company."

Other drug company executives and lobbyists who followed the revolving door into the Trump administration:

- Keagan R. Lenihan, chief of staff of the FDA, joined the administration after being top lobbyist for the $208 billion drug and distribution giant McKesson.
- Lance Leggitt, was the chief of staff at HHS from 2017 to 2018. In that year he became Deputy Assistant to President Trump on domestic policy. He previously worked for the law firm Baker, Donelson, which represents many major drug clients.
- Robert Lighthizer, the U.S. Trade Representative in charge of negotiating drug policies, "most recently worked at the law firm representing Pfizer, Merck, and Abbott, among others."
- Scott Gottlieb, MD, who served as head of the FDA, has ties to GlaxoSmithKline and Bristol-Myers Squibb, and has been on the board of directors of eight pharmaceutical companies. He is a member of the product investment board at GlaxoSmithKline, the world's sixth-largest pharmaceutical company. He resigned from the FDA and soon afterwards became a director of Pfizer.

- Joseph Grogan, who worked for the FDA, became director of Global Regulatory Affairs for Amgen and a lobbyist for Gilead Sciences, but now reviews health care regulations for the U.S. Office of Management & Budget.

But this problem of revolvers is not unique to one particular party or administration. The sociologist Timothy M. Gill, PhD, has shown that both major parties are riddled with conflicts at the highest level. A majority of presidential cabinets include corporate elites, defined as individuals who previously held high-ranking managerial positions in corporations. As to the percentage of revolvers in recent administrations, it was 64% under George W. Bush, 52% for Obama, and 72% for Trump, the latter being the highest level of the past half-century. But, overall, says Gill:

> "There is little difference between Democrat and Republican administrations on their corporate appointments, with Republicans appointing only a bit more (54%) than Democrats (48%)."

Open Secrets shows that drug and health care product companies spent $283,440,000 on lobbying in 2018. They employ an army of over 1400 lobbyists (13% of the total in Washington). Most of these lobbyists are former high-level government employees, including many revolvers from the FDA. The Pharmaceutical Research and Manufacturers of America alone spent almost $28 million on lobbying Congress. The biggest individual spender was Pfizer, Inc., which alone spent $11,450,000 on lobbying in 2018.

Drug companies gave $27.5 million to Congressional reelection campaigns in 2018. In fact, out of 435 voting members of the House of Representatives, 415 took Big Pharma's money, as did 98 out of 100 U.S. Senators. The average payment to a member of the Senate is around $90,000 and around $40,000 in the House. At least 20 Senators received more than $220,000 and one, Bob Casey, received over half a million dollars. A big reason for all this lavish spending is to keep FDA regulations concerning drug approvals weak. Drug lobbyists pushed for the 21st Century Cure Act to get the FDA:

> "...to rely less on randomized controlled trials when deciding whether or not to put a new drug on the market."

## Chapter 6. Revelations from Goldman Sachs

There are indications that Wall Street consciously prefers stabilization of a disease rather than its cure. When companies turn an acute disease into a chronic one, it becomes more profitable for them. In April 2018, a top analyst for Goldman Sachs, the Wall Street investment firm with almost one trillion dollars in assets, let the cat out of the bag. Ms. Salveen Richter issued a report advising pharmaceutical companies not to offer actual cures for cancer. Ms. Richter is a vice president of the company. Her report, *The Genome Revolution*, expressed concerns that the genetic revolution might be *too* effective at eliminating diseases. She therefore asks a rhetorical question:

> "Is curing patients a sustainable business model?"

Her answer was no. She suggested that companies think twice before offering treatments that actually cured people. The full report was available only to Goldman Sachs clients. But *CNBC* got a copy and quoted from it:

> "The potential to deliver 'one shot cures' is one of the most attractive aspects of gene therapy. However, such treatments offer a very different outlook with regard to recurring revenue versus chronic therapies. While this proposition [of one-shot cures, ed.] carries tremendous value for patients and society, it could represent a challenge for genome medicine developers looking for sustained cash flow."

Sustained cash flow. That of course is Wall Street's bottom line. The Richter report was so blatant. They used to hide their greed.

# Section V: Fixing the Cancer Drug Scandal

## Chapter 1. Recommendations

*With Wayne Jonas, MD — see Acknowledgments*

1. Institute a single-payer *Medicare for All* system, which will guarantee excellent care to all, not as a privilege, but as a human right, as per Senator Bernard Sanders' Medicare for All Act of 2019.
2. Open up the clinical trial system. At the present time, as few as 41% of adult cancer patients even qualify for clinical trials and fewer than 5% participate. This means that patients in the general population cannot be sure that the results of clinical trials apply to them. By eliminating restrictive admission criteria, the number of potential participants could be greatly increased.
3. Trial participants should look like the affected patient population. Patients in clinical trials should be a microcosm of the population affected by the disease, in terms of age, sex, race, income, performance status and education. In that way, patients will have greater assurance that approved treatments will actually benefit and not harm them.
4. Patients should be paid to participate. And they should be offered generous compensation for all direct and indirect expenses incurred as a result of participating in clinical trials. That includes paid leave from their jobs, help with quality child care, reimbursement for travel to and from the trial, and good accommodations and meals for themselves and their designated caregivers.
5. Use overall survival as the main endpoint. Progression-free survival and objective response rates may be useful surrogate endpoints in early stage or exploratory trials. But surrogate endpoints are an insufficient basis for the approval of new cancer drugs. Trials should be patient centered and should therefore focus on real benefits.

6. Eliminate accelerated approval. The FDA should phase out accelerated approval and half a dozen other programs that lead to the rapid approval of new cancer drugs. Accelerated approval is often presented as a boon to patients. But this is pro-industry propaganda. It is mainly of benefit to the big drug companies.
7. Withdraw approval of unproven drugs. The FDA should withdraw approval from any drug that has not been proven to actually help people live longer or better. This can be done, as former Commissioner Margaret Hamburg, MD, showed in the case of Avastin for breast cancer. There should be a housecleaning of unproven drugs by the FDA.
8. End drug industry corruption of the clinical trial system. Make it illegal for the pharmaceutical industry to offer money to any doctor involved in a clinical trial. Anyone found hiding such payments should be barred from participating in future clinical trials, and face criminal charges.
9. Reform the Oncology Drug Advisory Committee. It should primarily be made up of cancer patients, health activists and truly independent oncologists. Its focus should be on patient centered outcomes, which means increased overall survival and improved quality of life. The drug industry should no longer have a seat at the table where drug approvals are being discussed.
10. Fund non-conventional treatment research. At least 5% of all drug profits should by law go to governmental or non-profit agencies to conduct research on non-patented and other minimally profitable approaches. Such approaches would include lifestyle changes: (e.g. diet, exercise, mental health); out-of-patent, repurposed or off-label drugs; and natural products that are directed towards the prevention and treatment of cancer.
11. Ethical investing. Require that all money being held by governmental programs, such as Social Security and Medicare, only be invested in ethically responsible companies, that do not undermine or harm social good. This would include the avoidance of investing in rapacious drug companies.

12. Better Cures Act. Replace the 2016 21st Century Cures Act with a 21st Century Better Cures Act. This will require that all new cancer drugs actually benefit patients through increased overall survival and improved quality of life.
13. Patent laws. Change patent laws to tie financial rewards to patient benefit. Eliminate the "valley of death," in which treatments that have demonstrated effectiveness disappear because they fail to meet the industry's bloated financial goals.
14. Revolving door. Close the notorious revolving door by banning Federal employees from working for Big Pharma or their lobbyists for at least five years. Do not allow Big Pharma representatives to later serve in government.
15. Lobbying. Eliminate Big Pharma lobbying of Congress, as part of a comprehensive reform of the widespread bribery of Congress through campaign contributions.
16. Advertising. Outlaw all direct-to-consumer pharmaceutical advertising, following the lead of the European Union and more than 100 other countries.
17. Negotiations. Allow Medicare, National Institutes of Health, and all other government agencies, such as the Department of Defense and the Veterans Administration, to negotiate to bring down the price of drugs, as is normally done in most other countries. Refuse to approve any outrageously priced cancer drugs.

## Chapter 2. Why nationalize?

**"I would be willing to accept almost any degree of socialization if we could only get some results in the field of cancer."**

*—James Ewing, MD, Chief Pathologist, Memorial Hospital, and author of* Neoplastic Diseases, *1928*

On July 18, 2019, *JAMA Oncology* published a viewpoint article, "Beyond Parity and Toward Socially Owned Anticancer Drug Research." This called for the elimination of private ownership of cancer drugs. It proposed instead the creation of a publicly funded cancer drug enterprise. This socially owned agency would develop and market all new cancer drugs. As a public resource, it would drastically lower prices, end the exploitation of cancer patients, and create an equitable distribution network, providing reasonably priced licenses to other countries.

The author of this article was Ian Neff, MS, a PhD candidate at the Oregon Health & Science University, Portland. This was the first time, to my knowledge, that a major medical journal has published a carefully reasoned proposal to nationalize any portion of the drug industry.

The American Medical Association, under Dr. Morris Fishbein, fought for years against any form of socialized medicine, or, as Fishbein called it medical Soviets. For decades he cast the national debate over universal health insurance as one of Americanism versus Sovietism. By doing so, said a historian, he aroused fears of a Communist takeover of the American medical system.

The National Cancer Institute, National Library of Medicine, and other branches of the National Institutes of Health, at their inception were attacked as socialistic by *JAMA* editor Morris Fishbein and others.

Such hard-line attitudes are far less common today, especially among young people. Some readers may still object that a nationalization of the cancer drug business would be un-American. However, nationalization is hardly unprecedented. The *New York Times* wrote:

> "The United States has a culture that celebrates laissez-faire capitalism as the economic ideal, but the practice is sometimes different. Over the past century, the U.S. government has nationalized railways, coal mines and steel mills, and it has even

> taken a controlling interest in banks when that was deemed to be in the national interest."

According to a *CBS News* report, "A History of Corporate Nationalization":

> "During World War I, the government nationalized railroads, telegraph lines and the Smith & Wesson Company. During World War II, it seized railroads, coal mines, midwest trucking operators, and many other companies including, briefly, retailer Montgomery Ward."

In 2008 the U.S. government took a controlling interest in General Motors, as part of its $80.7 billion bailout of the American auto industry. In September 2008 (under George W. Bush's Republican administration) it took direct control of the two mortgage giants, Freddie Mac and Fannie Mae, putting them into conservatorship under the Federal Housing Finance Agency. The U.S. Treasury then invested billions of dollars "to prop them up and minimize damage to the housing market."

The government also forced a restructuring and leadership change of the insurance giant American International Group (AIG). It took ownership of 79.9% of AIG's equity, replaced its top executives, and exercised veto power over all important decisions.

It may be objected that, had it not done so, the global economy might have collapsed. But for cancer patients and their relatives, the current crisis is a matter of life and death, and relief is more urgent than rescuing an insurance company.

Despite "Reaganomics," not everything can, or should, be run for a profit. In our opinion, cancer drugs should fall into the nonprofit category. For the majority of poor people, life without public education, welfare, food stamps, Social Security, Medicare, and Medicaid would be a nightmare. These public programs are enormously popular, and 74 percent of Americans say that Social Security benefits should not be reduced in any way.

However, at the time these programs were instituted, they were bitterly opposed by the American Medical Association and other conservative organizations. When President Truman proposed a national health insurance plan in 1945, Dr. Fishbein hit back:

> "The movement for placing American medicine under the control of the Federal Government through a system of federal compulsory sickness insurance is the first step towards a regimentation

> of utilities, of industries, of finance, and eventually of labor itself. This is the kind of regimentation that led to totalitarianism in Germany and the downfall of that nation."

Truman's bill did not pass, and 75 years later we are still debating the same issue, as the only industrialized country in the world without a national health insurance program. In 1962 President John F. Kennedy vehemently called for a national medical program to cover everyone, but this campaign was cut short by his assassination.

The cancer drug industry is admittedly booming. But it is this very success, fueled by the most outrageous drug prices the world has ever seen, that has created the current crisis. It is now dire enough (from the consumer's point of view) to require a sweeping solution.

Because of the staggering cost of new cancer drugs, said Ian Neff, the question is not whether to control prices but how. Neff demolished the argument that drug manufacturers and consumers are engaged in a free exchange between autonomous agents who meet on a level playing field in the marketplace:

> "Of course, people prefer to survive rather than die of cancer. Therefore, market pricing cannot be a free exchange between autonomous agents when patients' survival depends on a narrow range of options. Many will pursue survival and tolerate any cost, including insurmountable debt.... This relegates the patient to a lower station, reinforcing an unjust asymmetry of power. The patient has his or her life at stake, while the manufacturer only risks money."

Neff argues that there is a solution, which is:

> "...replacing for-profit drug development with a socially owned model in which the public funds development and owns the resulting product."

There are some models for this. In Canada, there is a new government agency whose purpose is to bring gene and cell therapies to Canadians at an affordable price. The National Research Council of Canada is funding the Human Health Therapeutics Research Centre, whose first project is to revive a $1 million-per-person drug, Glybera, that disappeared from the market because a drug company did not think it was profitable enough.

According to the Canadian government:

> "The National Research Centre of Canada will coordinate a national effort to increase the affordability and accessibility of these ground-breaking technologies—in collaboration with academic facilities, research centres and networks, clinicians, hospital centres and others—to enable a national ecosystem for health innovation in the area of cell and gene therapies."

For the U.S., we are proposing a similar government-owned enterprise, centered at the National Institutes of Health, to research, produce and market cancer drugs. In cooperation with universities, it would innovate new drugs. But, to be clear, it would also *manufacture* both existing and new cancer drugs to guarantee their availability to patients in need. This is necessary since the U.S. has been hit in recent years by crippling shortages of essential drugs such as vincristine for childhood leukemia, BCG (Bacillus Calmette-Guérin) for bladder cancer, and many other medications that are just not profitable enough for rapacious drug companies. In fact, a University of Pennsylvania survey of oncologists:

> "...found 83 percent had dealt with shortages by delaying cancer treatments, omitting doses, using second-choice drugs, or sending patients elsewhere."

*STAT News* accurately identified the root cause of the problem. These generic drugs are now in the public domain, and so do not generate the profits of patented agents that Big Pharma demands:

> "Companies have very little incentive to manufacture a drug like BCG. Although it's been used to fight cancer since the 1970s, it isn't easy to produce. And priced at a relatively modest $100-$200 a dose, it's not a drug that companies are rushing to make, even if it's no longer patented; right now, Merck is the only manufacturer for the U.S. and European markets. BCG, in other words, is an example of a medically important drug that gets neglected because it fails to generate a lot of money for its maker."

We predict that in the U.S. and elsewhere there will be broad support for the nationalization of the cancer drug industry. Although the question has never been posed as such, a 2017 Harris poll did show that:

> "...over 70% of Americans support increasing federal spending on cancer research, even if it adds to the deficit or raises taxes."

This same opinion poll, commissioned by the American Society of Clinical Oncology, found that 91% of the public thought the cost of cancer drugs was too high, and 86% believed that the federal government should regulate the price of cancer drugs to lower their cost.

In fact, cancer drug development is, to a great degree, already nationalized. Research conducted by the Center for Integration of Science and Industry showed that every one of the 210 new drugs approved by the FDA between 2010 and 2016 was based on federally funded studies. As we have shown, a 2018 article in the *Proceedings of the National Academy of Sciences* reported:

> "Collectively, this [federally funded] research involved more than 200,000 years of grant funding, totaling more than $100 billion. The analysis shows that more than 90% of this funding represents basic research."

Then, at the end of this lengthy and costly research and development process, mainly done at NIH-funded institutions, Big Pharma companies swoop in and put the finishing touches on all that publicly funded research. They and they alone then patent the new cancer drugs, which become the exclusive property of a few profit-driven corporations. They receive a legal monopoly to sell the drug at whatever price they choose for a period of 20 years.

The American consumer, whose taxes paid for the original research, is charged again for accessing these same drugs. Desperate patients have nowhere else to go to get their drugs. Nowadays, cancer drugs typically cost from $150,000 for immune checkpoint inhibitors to $475,000 for a single infusion of Kymriah.

According to Dean Baker, a senior economist at the Center for Economic and Policy Research:

> "The drug industry wants us to believe the government can fund good basic research, but is incapable of developing and testing new drugs. That is, of course, not true. A Center for Integration of Science and Industry analysis shows the enormously important government role in developing

> new drugs. We should start asking questions about how the government can see the process through so [new drugs] could be sold at generic prices the day they are approved by the FDA."

The U.S. government already has the talent and the superstructure to take over every aspect of the drug development process. It would only require a new law to complete the changeover and have these agencies and institutions finish the job and develop and market new drugs.

On two occasions, the NCI came very close to not just developing, but producing essential cancer drugs. This was the case with Adriamycin, in which the NCI not only helped test the drug, but helped fill out the New Drug Application to the FDA. In the case of Taxol, the NCI paid for the development of the drug from start to finish, but then handed a monopoly on the source material, Pacific yew derivatives, to Bristol-Myers Squibb, in what Congressman Ron Wyden and others called a shameless sweetheart deal.

Currently, most of the expenses associated with new cancer drugs goes to advertising and promotion, which are essentially unnecessary, and to the salaries and bonuses of top executives, as high as $25 million per individual, or for buybacks to inflate stock market prices, and other useless expenses that the patient must ultimately bear.

Enormous sums are spent in effect bribing members of the U.S. Congress, corrupting key opinion leaders, assailing the public with direct-to-consumer advertising, and the like. If you want to know how much could be saved by nationalizing the cancer drug industry, consider information from the Pew Charitable Trusts. It shows that clinical trials constitute a mere sliver of the total expenditure of drug companies.

Overwhelmingly, drug companies' expenses are for sales promotion, including $15 billion for face-to-face sales and promotional activities; $5.7 billion for free samples of medication provided to physiciansand $2.1 billion for promotional meetings and mailings, print advertisements, and direct-to-consumer pharmaceutical advertising. This is wasteful activity whose only purpose is to jack up the sales of generally unproven drugs. All that waste would stop under a nationalized cancer drug industry. Actual clinical trial expenses come to $130 million, which is a tiny fraction of the overall spending.

Following our suggestions, doctors would go back to receiving information on new drugs via non-commercial sources, such as professional meetings and medical journals. There is certainly no need for them to waste their time with drug company representatives. This practice harks back to the disreputable past of the drug industry when so-called snake oil salesmen roamed the land. And, in fact, according to *Modern Healthcare,* fewer drug rep visits lead to lower drug costs.

Ian Neff agrees that phasing out the role of Big Pharma would be a boon to cancer patients:

> "Eliminating expenses from advertisement, executives, and shareholder profit could make socially owned drugs affordable to any patient."

But genuine research and development would in fact be expanded, so that all new drugs would ultimately be tested in randomized controlled trials that were truly representative of the real world patients who will ultimately receive these treatments.

Neff realized that there will be critics who say that:

> "...eliminating the profit motive will disincentivize the best and the brightest from researching cancer treatments."

However, he convincingly argued that it is researchers in white coats, not executives in white collars, who deserve to be rewarded for innovations:

> "The chief executive officers and shareholders who benefit most from windfall profits are not the scientists making life-saving breakthroughs. We should recognize researchers who benefit humanity, but we should reward scientists rather than executives."

Neff concludes his *JAMA Oncology* opinion piece this way:

> "On behalf of the patients and the United States, we need to advocate for solutions that address the price and supply of anticancer drugs.... Social investment in cancer would be politically popular, remove the profit-driven misalignment of research priorities, and promote both equity and innovation in cancer care."

Unless we strike at the root of the problem—which includes the bribery of politicians through bottomless campaign contributions—we will never fix the cancer drug scandal, much less find solutions to the other problems identified in this book.

## Section VI: Further Reading

Angell, Marica, MD. *The Truth About the Drug Companies: How They Deceive Us and What to Do About It.* New York: Random House, 2005. An outstanding critique of drug industry from one of the most famous medical journal editors.

Bach PB, Saltz LB and Wittes RE. In Cancer Care, Cost Matters. *The New York Times* [op-ed], October 14, 2012. A breakthrough op-ed in which three prominent Memorial Sloan-Kettering Cancer Center (MSKCC) oncologists announced the hospital's refusal to give a new cancer drug (Zaltrap) to their patients because of its outrageous price.

Bach, PB, Saltz LB. "Raising the Dose and Raising the Cost: The Case of Pembrolizumab in Lung Cancer," *J Natl Cancer Inst. 2017 Nov 1;109(11).* doi: 10.1093/jnci/djx125.Everything Bach and Saltz write on the topic of drug pricing is worthwhile.

Bekelman JE, Li Y, Gross CP. Scope and impact of financial conflicts of interest in biomedical research: a systematic review. *JAMA* 2003:289:454-465. A major study of conflicts of interest in medical research, focused on cancer. Formerly of Yale, Bekelman is now Associate Professor of Radiation Oncology at the University of Pennsylvania.

Begley, Sharon. Do cancer clinical trials exaggerate the real-world benefits of drugs? *StatNews.com,* November 21, 2016. A very fine medical writer reflects on how clinical trials overstate the effectiveness of treatments in the real world.

Brownlee, Shannon. Health, Hope and Hype. Why the media oversells medical 'breakthroughs'. *Washington Post* commentary, August 3, 2003; Page B1. A veteran science journalist's account of how health writers promote dubious treatments.

Chen, Caroline. FDA repays industry by rushing risky drugs to market. *ProPublica,* June 26, 2018. Exposé of how "pharma companies underwrite three-fourths of the FDA's budget for scientific reviews."

Fauber, John and Chu, Elbert. The Slippery Slope: Is a Surrogate Endpoint Evidence of Efficacy? *MedPage Today,* October 26, 2014. A critique of the concept of progression-free survival. Fauber has won more than two dozen national journalism awards.

Fauber, John and Chu, Elbert. The Slippery Slope: Risks and Confusion: When approval is based on a surrogate, durable benefits are difficult to find. Part Two of the "Slippery Slope" special report from *MedPage Today* (see above).

Deyo, Richard A. and Patrick, Donald L. *Hope or Hype: The Obsession with Medical Advances and the High Cost of False Promises.* New York: Amacom, 2005. A sweeping critique of the false claims of medical breakthroughs.

Gøtzsche, Peter C. *Deadly Medicines and Organised Crime: How Big Pharma has Corrupted Healthcare.* London, U.K.: Radcliffe Publishing, 2013.

Hall, Shannon and Winters, Dan. Bad science and breast cancer. "How could so many oncologists ignore basic principles of science?" *Discover,* August 2002.

Herder, Matthew. The FDA and Sarepta: a window into the real world of drug regulation. *STAT News,* Sept. 3, 2019. A penetrating analysis of the relationship between the FDA and drug companies, with a special focus on post-market studies.

Jaklevic, Mary Chris. How one bit of medical jargon fuels public confusion about cancer treatments. *HealthNewsReview.org.* October 22, 2019. Good description of how the use of progression-free survival confuses patients and benefits drug companies.

Leaf, Clifton. *The Truth in Small Doses: Why We're Losing the War on Cancer-and How to Win It.* New York, NY: Simon & Schuster, 2013. An insightful critique of the war on cancer by the editor-in-chief of *Fortune,* who is also a cancer survivor.

Light, DW, Lexchin J, Darrow JJ. Institutional corruption of pharmaceuticals and the myth of safe and effective drugs. *Journal of Law Medicine and Ethics,* 2013. Written while at Safra Center for Bioethics by an outstanding critic of American medicine.

Löwy, Ilana. *Between Bench and Bedside: Science, Healing and IL-2 in a Cancer Ward.* Cambridge, Mass.: Harvard University Press, 1996. A perceptive study of the IL-2 story by a skilled observer.

Lundberg, George. *Severed Trust. Why American Medicine Hasn't Been Fixed.* New York: Basic Books, 2001. A classic from the long-time editor of the *Journal of the American Medical Association.*

Mailankody, Sham, Prasad, Vinay. Five years of cancer drug approvals: innovation, efficacy, and costs. *JAMA Oncology* 2015;1:539-540. Anything these two iconoclastic critics of Big Pharma write is worthwhile.

Martinez, Vanesa. Cancer could be thousands of different diseases. *Irish Times,* March 29, 2018. Perceptive reporting from a young Irish researcher and science journalist.

Meffert, Jeffrey J. Key opinion leaders: where they come from and how that affects the drugs you prescribe. *Dermatologic Therapy,* May 6, 2009.

Miessler, James. Cancer Trials: Is Progression-Free Survival Enough? *Center Watch,* October 8, 2018. A fine critique of the concept of progression-free survival.

Neff, Ian. Beyond parity and toward socially owned anticancer drug research. *JAMA Oncol.* Published online July 18, 2019. doi:10.1001/jamaoncol.2019.2291. A cogently argued case for the "social ownership" of the cancer drug industry.

Oxfam. *Prescription for Poverty: Drug Companies as Tax Dodgers, Price Gougers, and Influence Peddlers.* 2018. How drug companies exploit the less developed parts of the world.

Piller, Charles. FDA's revolving door: Companies often hire agency staffers who managed their successful drug reviews. *Science.* July 5, 2018. One of a series of excellent investigative reports that journalist Charles Piller has written for *Science.* Piller is a founding board member of the Center for Public Integrity.

Postrel, Virginia. Will cancer breakthroughs pass economic test? *Austin American-Statesman (Bloomberg News)*, November 11, 2012. Insightful analysis of the fallacy behind so-called precision medicine.

Prasad, Vinay. Revolving door between government and industry: Future jobs of FDA's haematology-oncology reviewers. *BMJ* 2016;354:i5055. Vinay Prasad is an outstanding critic of fraud and deception in the medical field. Everything he writes about Big Pharma is worth reading.

Rettig, Richard A, et al. *False Hope: Bone Marrow Transplantation for Breast Cancer.* New York: Oxford University Press, 2007. Originally written for the RAND Corporation, this is the classic account of the "high-dose chemotherapy" fiasco.

Scher, Kevin S. and Hurria, Arti. Under-representation of older adults in cancer registration trials: known problem, little progress. *Journal of Clinical Oncology,* 2012;30:2036-2038. A perspective analysis of why and how older cancer patients are under-represented in clinical trials. Sadly, Arti Hurria, MD, died in a Los Angeles traffic accident in 2018.

Seife, Charles. How drug company money Is undermining science: The pharmaceutical industry funnels money to prominent scientists who are doing research that affects its products—and nobody can stop it." *Scientific American,* November 21, 2012. Everything Charles Seife writes on the subject of Big Pharma is worthwhile.

Sismondo, Sergio. Ghost-Managed Medicine: Big Pharma's Invisible Hands. Manchester, U.K.: Mattering Press, 2018. Trenchant analysis of the manner in which Big Pharma manipulates clinical trials, from a leading Canadian sociologist.

Smith, Richard. *The Trouble with Medical Journals,* London: Royal Society of Medicine Press, 2006. Yet another testimony, this one from the former executive editor of the *British Medical Journal* on the corrupting influence of Big Pharma on publishing.

## Acknowledgments

One colleague who offered very detailed and helpful comments on this book is my long-time scientific collaborator, Tibor Bakacs, MD, PhD, DSc, of the Alfréd Rényi Institute of Mathematics of the Hungarian Academy of Sciences. Since the early 1990s, Dr. Bakacs and I have worked closely on different aspects of the cancer problem. We initially helped in the evaluation of a form of Newcastle Disease virus vaccine for cancer. More recently, we co-authored articles in the peer-reviewed literature on the potential, and the peril, of immune checkpoint inhibitor drugs. Our most recent collaboration is a paper on cancer immunotherapy for the *Scandinavian Journal of Immunology*.

Wayne Jonas, MD, of Alexandria, VA, gave me crucial help with the policy recommendations, for which I am grateful. In the 1990s, he was the director of the NIH Office of Alternative Medicine. Dr. Jonas has also served as Director of the World Health Organization Center for Traditional Medicine; Director of the Medical Research Fellowship at Walter Reed Army Institute of Research. He is a Lieutenant Colonel in the U.S. Army Medical Corps, and currently serves as a Clinical Professor of Family Medicine at Georgetown University, and Executive Director of the Samueli Integrative Health Programs.

I want to thank Professor Thomas Seyfried, PhD, author of *Cancer as a Metabolic Disease,* for providing detailed guidance for the chapter on metabolic therapy. I also want to thank David J. Hess, PhD, author of *Evaluating Alternative Cancer Therapies,* for providing detailed suggestions on the organization of the book, most of which proved very valuable in making the text more readable. So too did an eagle-eyed reader, Elaine Lissner.

As always, my family's help has been indispensable. Thanks also to the following for reading and/or commenting on various issues: Ferre Akbarpour, MD, Huntington Beach, California; Drs. Keith and Penny Block, Skokie, Illinois; Stephen Hoption Cann, PhD, British Columbia; Damian Dupuy, MD, Providence, Rhode Island; Nancye Files, Ellsworth, Maine; James Gordon, MD, Washington, DC; Charlotte Gyllenhaal, PhD, Skokie, Illinois; Johan Haux, MD, PhD, Skövde, Sweden; Monica Hughes, PhD, Auckland, New Zealand; Ralf Kleef, MD, Vienna, Austria; Michael Lerner, PhD, Bolinas, California; Dwight McKee, MD, California; Elizabeth Curtis Moss, Blue Hill, Maine; Michael Retsky, PhD, Boston, Massachusetts; Mark Rosenberg, MD, Boca Raton, Florida; and Shimon Slavin, MD, Tel Aviv, Israel.

Any errors are the author's sole responsibility.



*Quotations:* Generally speaking, the quotations are as they appear in the sources. However, occasionally we have abridged, rearranged or altered them slightly to conform with the general style of the book. This includes the use of trade names instead of generic names for drugs, and an avoidance of acronyms and abbreviations, which may be unfamiliar to readers.

# Endnotes

*The page numbers and the bold words refer to the beginning of a paragraph in the text. Medical journal articles can be accessed through the National Library of Medicine's pubmed.gov Most newspaper articles have been accessed through newspapers.com and other proprietary websites.*


## Preface to book

vii **We landed in our present mess** Cited from the foreword to Gøtzsche, Peter C. *Deadly Medicines and Organised Crime: How Big Pharma Has Corrupted Healthcare.* London, U.K.: Radcliffe Publishing, 2013, p. xi.

vii **To the average person** American Cancer Society, *Cancer Facts & Figures 2020,* ACS: Atlanta, GA. 2020.

vii **In response to this catastrophe** NCI Budget and Appropriations, Accessed: January 2020. https://www.cancer.gov/about-nci/budget

## Section I, Chapter 1

1 **People go where the money is** Berenson, Alex. Incentives limit any savings in treating cancer. *New York Times,* June 12, 2007.

1 **This is not to deny** PDQ Pediatric Treatment Editorial Board. PDQ Cancer Information Summaries: Childhood Acute Lymphoblastic Leukemia Treatment (PDQ®) Health Professional Version. Published online: October 22, 2019.

2 **Cancer journalism usually hails** Kolata, Gina. Advances elusive in the drive to cure cancer. *New York Times,* April 23, 2009.

2 **The much touted recent drops** Kolata, Gina. Hopeful glimmers in long war on cancer. *New York Times,* November 4, 2013.

3 **Allison stated** James Allison, Nobel Prize in Physiology or Medicine 2018. Dec 7, 2018. https://www.youtube.com/watch?v=0kuh7G9CP9Y&t=5s Accessed: January 2020.

3 **This was in line with a 2017** Salas-Vega S, Iliopoulos O, Mossialos E. Assessment of overall survival, quality of life, and safety benefits associated with new cancer medicines. *JAMA Oncol* 2017;3(3):382-390. doi:10.1001/jamaoncol.2016.4166

4 **These drugs are limited** Haslam A, Prasad V. Estimation of the percentage of US patients with cancer who are eligible for and respond to checkpoint inhibitor immunotherapy Drugs. *JAMA Netw Open* 2019;2(5):e192535. doi:10.1001/jamanetworkopen.2019.2535.

4 **In the first randomized trial of Yervoy** Hodi FS, O'Day SJ, McDermott, DF, et al. Improved survival with ipilimumab in patients with metastatic melanoma. *N Engl J Med* 2010; 363:711-723. DOI: 10.1056/NEJMoa1003466

4 **These drugs are also** Andrews, Audrey. Treating with checkpoint inhibitors—figure $1 million per patient. *Am Health Drug Benefits.* 2015 Aug; 8(Spec Issue): 9. PMID: 26380599; PMCID: PMC4570079.

4 **We observed a 91% incidence** Shoushtari AN, Friedman CF, Navid-Azarbaijani P, et al. Measuring toxic effects and time to treatment failure for nivolumab plus ipilimumab in melanoma. *JAMA Oncol* 2018;4(1):98-101. doi: 10.1001/jamaoncol.2017.2391.

4 **In patients receiving immune** Thallinger C, Füreder T, Preusser M, et al. Review of cancer treatment with immune checkpoint inhibitors. *Wien Klin Wochenschr* 2018; 130(3): 85–91. doi: 10.1007/s00508-017-1285-9

4 **But how many hospitals** Clifford, Kirstiann. Nurses on the front lines of immunotherapy. March 05, 2019. www.mdanderson.org/publications/cancerwise/nurses-on-the-front-lines-of-immunotherapy-CAR-T-cell-therapy-managing-side-effects.h00-159301467.html Accesssed: January 2020.

## Section I, Chapter 3

8 **Throughout the twenties** Strickland, Stephen. Politics, *Science and Dread Disease. A Short History of the United States Medical Research Policy.* Cambridge, Mass.: Harvard University Press, 1972.

9 **Gilman and Goodman had found** Hazell, Sarah. Mustard gas – from the Great War to frontline chemotherapy. *Cancer Research U.K.* website. 2014. Accessed: January 2020.

## Section I, Chapter 4

12 **The cigarette has justly been called** Proctor RN. The history of the discovery of the cigarette–lung cancer link: evidentiary traditions, corporate denial, global toll. *Tob Control.* 2012 Mar;21(2):87-91. doi: 10.1136/tobaccocontrol-2011-050338

12 **In World War II the U.S.** Cavallo, Jo. A leading light in cancer advances, Mary Lasker used wealth and connections to increase funding for medical research. *ASCO Post* September 15,

2012. Accessed: December 2019.

12 **It is often stated that doctors** Abbe, Robert,MD [1851-1928]. Cancer of the mouth: the case against tobacco. *N York Med J.* July 3, 1915;102:1-4. Reprinted as a booklet in Philadelphia by A.R. Elliott, July 3, 1915.

12 **Tobacco has a predominant influence** Ewing, James. *Neoplastic Diseases. A Treatise on Tumors.* Philadelphia: W.B. Saunders, 3rd edition. 1922, p. 841 *inter alia.*

13 **Ernst Wynder led the anti-cigarette** Fields N, Chapman S. Chasing Ernst L Wynder: 40 years of Philip Morris' efforts to influence a leading scientist. *Journal of Epidemiology & Community Health* 2003;57:571-578 doi: 10.1136/jech.57.8.571

13 **Between 1962 and 1979 RJR** Cheadle EA. MRC grant request Memorial Sloan-Kettering... June 14,1985. *RJ Reynolds Records; Congressman Bliley Philip Morris Collection.* https://www.industrydocuments.ucsf.edu/docs/kyfd0097 Accessed: January 2020.

13 **Cigarettes were recognized as the cause** Proctor RN. The history of the discovery of the cigarette–lung cancer link: evidentiary traditions, corporate denial, global toll. *Tob Control* 2012;21:87-91. doi: 10.1136/tobaccocontrol-2011-050338

14 **Basic biomedical research is necessary** Mintz. Morton. Directors Face Smoke Screen. *Washington Post,* April 28, 1982.

14 **Reed says he does not believe** Ibid. (Mintz)

14 **What Philip Morris does not state** Ibid. (Mintz)

14 **Between 1962 and 1979 R.J. Reynolds** Gardner MN, Brandt AM. "The doctors' choice is America's choice": The physician in US cigarette advertisements, 1930-1953. Am J Public Health 2006 Feb;96(2):222-32. doi: 10.2105/AJPH.2005.066654

15 **In 1946, R.J. Reynolds launched** Little, Becky. When cigarette companies used doctors to push smoking. Before studies showed that cigarettes caused cancer, tobacco companies recruited the medical community for their ads. *History.com* website. September 11, 2019. Accessed: January 2020.

16 **Fishbein helped stave off efforts** Proctor RN. "Everyone knew but no one had proof": Tobacco industry use of medical history expertise in US courts, 1990-2002. *Tob Control* 2006 Dec;15 Suppl 4(Suppl 4):iv117-25. doi: 10.1136/tc.2004.009928

16 **Cigarette smoking is responsible for more** Tobacco-related mortality. Smoking and Tobacco Use. Centers for Disease Control and Prevention (CDC). January, 2018. https://www.cdc.gov/tobacco/data_statistics/fact_sheets/health_effects/tobacco_related_mortality/index.htm Accessed: January 2020.

16 **According to Professor Proctor** Proctor RN. The history of the discovery of the cigarette–lung cancer link: evidentiary traditions, corporate denial, global toll *Tob Control* 2012;21:87-91. doi: 10.1136/tobaccocontrol-2011-050338

## Section I, Chapter 5

17 **In the 1950s and 1960s, a group** Saxon, Wolfgang. Emerson Foote, 85, who headed large advertising agencies, dies. *New York Times,* July 8, 1992, p. 73.

16 **The antismoking effort** Kolata, Gina. Hopeful glimmers in long war on cancer. *New York Times,* November 4, 2013.

17 **Overwhelmingly, the emphasis of** In 1927, J.H. "Jock" Whitney "inherited the bulk of his father's vast fortune of over $200 million," of which $23 million was in British-American Tobacco and $15 million in Liggett and Myers stock. John N. Ingham, *Biographical Dictionary of American Business Leaders,* Westport, Connecticut: Greenwood Press, 1983, p. 1617.

18 **Promising a quick cure was a vote-getter** DeVita Jr. VT, Chu E. A history of cancer chemotherapy. *Cancer Res* November 1 2008'68(21)8:643-8653; doi: 10.1158/0008-5472.CAN-07-6611

19 **One can trace the evolution** American Society of Clinical Oncology (ASCO). Society History. https://www.asco.org/about-asco/overview/society-history Accessed: January 2020.

19 **In 1975, a sliver of clinical trials** Cohn. Meredith. Industry funds six times more clinical trials than feds, research shows. *The Baltimore Sun,* Dec. 15, 2015. https://www.baltimoresun.com/health/bs-hs-trial-funding-20151214-story.html Accessed: January 2020.

20 **Finally, a new Italian-American** Gutman, James. Hercules unit eyes big future. *Morning News.* Wilmington, Del. March 11, 1975, p. 29.

20 **No pharmaceutical firm is going to take on** Greenberg, Daniel. For sale of cancer drug. *Science & Government Report,* Volume 2, 1972, p.67.

20 **For better or for worse, that's the business** Hendershot, Steve. When life happens. *Illinois Tech.* Fall 2019. https://magazine.iit.edu/fall-2019/when-life-happens Accessed: January 2020.

21 **Big Business became unapologetically** Blatt. David. Prosperity policy: rethinking the corporation. *The Journal Record.* September 11, 2019. https://journalrecord.com/2019/09/11/prosperity-policy-rethinking-the-corporation/Accessed: January 2020.

21 **Companies must obey the law** Murray, Alan. America's CEOs seek a new purpose for the corporation. *Fortune.* August 19, 2019. https://fortune.com/longform/business-roundta-

ble-ceos-corporations-purpose/ Accessed: January 2020; and Frakt, Austin. Reagan, Deregulation and America's exceptional rise in health care costs. *New York Times.* June 4, 2018.

21 **One result was that many** Welsh, Matt. The secret lives of professors. May 24, 2010. http://matt-welsh.blogspot.com/2010/05/secret-lives-of-professors.htm Accessed: January 2020.

22 **'Greed is good' was more than a** Frakt, Austin. Reagan, Deregulation and America's exceptional rise in health care costs. *New York Times,* June 4, 2018.

22 **All of a sudden the world** Abate, Tom. Boom in biotech stocks brings back memories of bubbles past / Industry observers say it won't burst like it did in '92. February 28, 2000. https://www.sfgate.com/business/article/Boom-in-Biotech-Stocks-Brings-Back-Memories-of-2799972.php Accessed: January 2020.

23 **Interferon shot cures high blood pressure** Newhouse News Service. Interferon shot cures high blood pressure in rats, study finds. *Arizona Republic,* Phoenix Arizona, April 5, 1990.

23 **Are interferons the cure for the common cold** Van Dellen, TR, MD. Are interferons the cure for the common cold? *Chicago Tribune,* Chicago, Illinois. August 19, 1974. p. 20.

23 **Interferon cures hepatitis** Anon. Reno Gazette-Journal, Reno, Nevada, 05 Aug 1990.

23 **Can virus-fighting interferons cure** Anon. The cancer battle. Can virus-fighting interferons cure humans? It works in animals. *Fort Lauderdale News,* Fort Lauderdale, Fla,17 Feb 1979.

23 **A stock market bubble formed around** Company Profiles: Interferon Sciences, Inc. Biocentury. https://bciq.biocentury.com/companies/interferon_sciences_inc Accessed: January 2020.

24 **Immunologists have remained** Hamblin, TJ. (Ed.). *Immunotherapy of Disease.* Springer, 1990. doi 10.1007/978-94-009-1844-3

24 **The NCI Director, Vincent** Lindenmann L, Schleuning W-D, editors. *Interferon: The Dawn of Recombinant Protein Drugs.* Berlin: Springer, 1990.

25 **In fact, the entire stock market** Case, John. Biotech Blues. *Inc.*, July 1, 1986.

25 **No one here had quite predicted** Ibid. (Case).

25 **Cancer killing wonder drug** Bylinsky, Gene. The anticancer company expands. *Fortune,* November 23, 1987.

25 **Ordinary white blood cells** Associated Press (Daniel Q. Haney). Ordinary white blood cells turned into cancer killers. *The Herald-Palladium,* Saint Joseph, Michigan, December 5, 1985.

25 **New therapy helps victims** Associated Press. New therapy helps victims fight cancer. *The Times-Tribune*, Scranton, Pennsylvania, December 5, 1985, p.1.

25 **The NCI was deluged with calls** Associated Press (Daniel Q. Haney). Hormone creates 'cancer hunters.' *The South Bend Tribune,* South Bend, Indiana. December 5, 1985, p. 3.

26 **One 29-year-old woman whose** Associated Press (Malcolm Ritter). Cancer therapy continues to show progress. *The Central New Jersey Home News.* New Brunswick, New Jersey, March 25, 1986, p. 29.

26 **Here is how their scientific** Rosenberg SA, et al. Observations on the systemic administration of autologous lymphokine-activated killer cells and recombinant interleukin-2 to patients with metastatic cancer. N Engl J Med. 1985 Dec 5;313(23):1485-92. doi: 10.1056/NEJM198512053132327

26 **So, all the favorable publicity** Löwy, Ilana. *Between Bench and Bedside: Science, Healing and IL-2 in a Cancer Ward.* Cambridge, Mass.: Harvard University Press, 1996.

26 **The cost of the new treatment** Altman, Lawrence K. Study of natural substance begins in effort to fight immune disease. *New York Times,* July 13, 1983, p. b5

27 **This was the world's first exposure** Piana, Ronald. Noted gastrointestinal oncologist Leonard Saltz, MD, tempers optimism with reality and factors cost into the equation of value in cancer care. *ASCO Post,* June 3, 2016. https://www.ascopost.com/issues/june-3-2016-narratives-special-issue/noted-gastrointestinal-oncologist-leonard-saltz-md-tempers-optimism-with-reality-and-factors-cost-into-the-equation-of-value-in-cancer-care/ Accessed: January 2020.

27 **But, as time went by, the IL-2** Moertel CG. On lymphokines, cytokines, and breakthroughs. *JAMA.* 1986;256(22):3141. doi:https://doi.org/10.1001/jama.1986.03380220107034

27 **In 1999 there was a follow-up** Michael B. Atkins, et al. High-dose recombinant interleukin 2 therapy for patients With Metastatic Melanoma: Analysis of 270 Patients Treated Between 1985 and 1993. Journal of Clinical Oncology 1999 17(7):2105-2105. doi 10.1200/JCO.1999.17.7.2105

28 **In a retrospective review** Moore MJ. Interleukin-2 in the treatment of unresectable or metastatic renal cell cancer: Time to write the obituary? Can Urol Assoc J. 2007 Mar;1(1):39. doi: 10.5489/cuaj.36.

29 **In the future, high-dose IL-2** DeVita VT, et al. Interleukin-2 (chapter). In: *Cancer: Principles and Practice of Oncology,* 11th edition, Philadelphia: Wolters Kluwer, 2019; and Yang JC, et al. Randomized study of high-dose and low-dose interleukin-2 in patients with metastatic renal cancer. *J Clin Oncol.* 2003 Aug 15;21(16):3127-32. doi: 10.1200/JCO.2003.02.122.

29 **But in 1998 Folkman's work** Gina Kolata. Hope in the Llb: A special report.; A cautious awe greets drugs that eradicate tumors in mice. *New York Times,* May 3, 1998, p.1.

30 **The clinical benefit is typically modest** Rebecca G. Bagley. Commentary on Folkman: Tumor angiogenesis factor. *Cancer Res* April 1 2016 (76) (7) 1673-1674; doi: 10.1158/0008-5472. CAN-16-0675.

## Section I, Chapter 6

31 **Between April 1945 and July 1947** Robert S. Stone, et al. Human Radiation Experiments. Atomic Heritage Foundation. www.atomicheritage.org › history › human-radiation-experiments July 11, 2017. Accessed: January 2020.

33 **In 2003, David F. Horrobin, MD, PhD** Horrobin DF. Are large clinical trials in rapidly lethal diseases usually unethical? Lancet. 2003 Feb 22;361(9358):695-7.

## Section I, Chapter 7

35 **Fifty years from now** Gina Kolata and Kurt Eichenwald. Health business thrives on unproven treatment, leaving science behind. *New York Times.* Oct. 3, 1999.

38 **But most reporters at the time** Elizabeth Whitney. New lung cancer treatment effective. *Tampa Bay Times,* St. Petersburg, Florida, 27 Mar 1976, Page 1

38 **Women with advanced breast** Kara Smigel, Women Flock to ABMT for breast cancer without final Proof, *JNCI: Journal of the National Cancer Institute,* 1995;87(13):952–955, https://doi.org/10.1093/jnci/87.13.952

39 **Oncology is big business** Rettig, Richard A, et al. *False Hope: Bone Marrow Transplantation for Breast Cancer.* Oxford, U.K.: Oxford University Press, 2007.

39 **Even small hospitals took out big ads** Anon. House calls, *The Times Leader,* Wilkes-Barre, Pennsylvania, 21 Sep 1999, p. 2.

40 **In 2003, the medical journalist Shannon** Brownlee, Shannon. Hope and hype. *The Journal Times,* Racine, Wisconsin,August 10, 2003, p. 31.

42 **In the late 1990s** Mello, Michelle and Brennan, Troyen A. The controversy over high-dose chemotherapy with autologous bone marrow transplant for breast cancer. *Health Affairs.* September/October 2001. https://doi.org/10.1377/hlthaff.20.5.101 Accessed: January 2020.

42 **In retrospect, we can see the reasons** Hall, Shannon and Winters, Dan. Bad science and breast cancer. *Discover.* August 21, 2002. http://173.226.48.202/2002/aug/featbad Accessed: January 2020.

43 **The day of reckoning came** Gaddy, Kristina. The fraudulent study that killed thousands of breast cancer patients. *OZY. The Daily Dose.* December 5, 2016.

44 **Bezwoda certainly deserved severe** Maugh, Thomas H and Mestel, Rosie. Key breast cancer study was a fraud. *Los Angeles Times,* April 27, 2001.

45 **He misled us, he misled the public** Denise Grady. Breast cancer researcher admits falsifying data. *New York Times.* February 5, 2000.

## Section I, Chapter 8

49 **According to a 2019 journal article** Aparisi F, Amado-Labrador H, Calabuig-Fariñas S, et al. Passenger mutations in cancer evolution. Cancer Rep Rev 2019;3: doi: 10.15761/ CRR.1000188

49 **Clinical trials are traditionally** Martinez V. Assessment of the efficacy and safety of olaparib monotherapy... Site: https://clinicaltrials.gov/ct2/show/NCT02000622?term=PARP+inhibitor&cond=breast+cancer&cntry=US&phase=2&rank=4 Accessed: January 2020.

50 **Cancer could be thousands of different diseases** Martinez, Vanesa. Early diagnosis critical: Catching this disease early means it has less time to develop. *Irish Times.* Dublin, Ireland, March 29, 2018

50 **According to Sir Michael Stratton** Stratton MR, Campbell PJ, Futreal PA. The cancer genome. *Nature.* 2009;458(7239):719-24. doi: 10.1038/nature07943.

50 **A review of COSMIC** Martincorena I, Campbell PJ. Somatic mutation in cancer and normal cells. Science. 2015;349(6255):1483-9. doi: 10.1126/science.aab4082. Epub 2015 Sep 24.

51 **To quote the NCI article** National Cancer Institute. The genetics of cancer, 2017. https://www.cancer.gov/about-cancer/causes-prevention/genetics Accessed: January 2020.

51 **The implications of this for drug companies** DiMasi JA, Grabowski HG, Hansen RW. Innovation in the pharmaceutical industry: New estimates of R&D costs, *Journal of Health Economics* 2016;47:20-33. doi: 10.1016/j.jhealeco.2016.01.012. Epub 2016 Feb 12; and Postrel, Virginia. Will cancer breakthroughs pass economic test? *Austin American-Statesman (Bloomberg News)*, November 11, 2012.

51 **But, as drugs become** Anon. (Press release).Pfizer reports second-quarter 2018 results. https://s21.q4cdn.com/317678438/files/doc_financials/Quarterly/2018/q2/Q2-2018-PFE-Earnings-Release.pdf Accessed: January 2020.

51 **In 2019 it was shown** Lin A, Giuliano CJ, Palladino A, et al. Off-target toxicity is a common mechanism of action of cancer drugs undergoing clinical trials. *Science Translational Medicine.* 2019;11(509). doi: 10.1126/scitranslmed.aaw8412.

52 **More than 180 previous studies** Begley, Sharon. Why so many cancer drugs fail: Genes

thought 'essential' for tumor survival are not, study finds. *StatNews.com,* September 11, 2019. https://www.statnews.com/2019/09/11/why-cancer-drugs-fail-genes-thought-essential-for-tumor-survival-are-not/ Accessed: January 2020.

52 **The researchers showed** Wong CH, Siah KW, Lo AW. Estimation of clinical trial success rates and related parameters. *Biostatistics.* 2019 Apr 1;20(2):273-286. doi: 10.1093/biostatistics/kxx069.

52 **Sheltzer's CRISPR findings** Vaux, DL. In defense of the somatic mutation theory of cancer. *Bioessays* 2011;33: 341-343. doi:10.1002/bies.201100022

53 **In fact, the FDA advisory board** Pfizer, Inc. Press Release. U.S. Food And Drug Administration approves pfizer's XALKORI® (crizotinib)... August 26, 2011. https://www.pfizer.com/news/press-release/press-release-detail/u_s_food_and_drug_administration_approves_pfizer_s_xalkori_crizotinib_as_first_and_only_therapy_specifically_for_patients_with_locally_advanced_or_metastatic_alk_positive_non_small_cell_lung_cancer Accessed: January 2020.

54 **For the Xalkori trial** Kwak EL, Bang YJ, Camidge DR, et al. Anaplastic lymphoma kinase inhibition in non–small-cell lung cancer. *N Engl J Med.* 2010 Oct 28;363(18):1693-703. doi: 10.1056/NEJMoa1006448

54 **But what really stood out** Ibid. (Kwak)

55 **Along came Alex** Peters S, Camidge DR, Shaw AT, et al. Alectinib versus Crizotinib in untreated ALK-positive non–small-cell lung cancer. August 31, 2017. *N Engl J Med* 2017; 377:829-838. doi: 10.1056/NEJMoa1704795; and American Hospital Association. Massachusetts General Hospital to receive AHA's inaugural Equity of Care Award. Jul 22, 2014. https://www.prnewswire.com/news-releases/massachusetts-general-hospital-to-receive-ahas-inaugural-equity-of-care-award-268160432.html Accessed: January 2020; and Kwak, *op.cit.*

56 **Xalkori was swiftly recommended** http://www.researchtopractice.com/component/node/32420?width=540&height=360; and https://www.fda.gov/media/114596/download; andhttps://openpaymentsdata.cms.gov/physician/717508/summary Accessed: January 2020.

56 **At the present time** https://openpaymentsdata.cms.gov/physician/200249/summary. Accessed: January 2020.

57 **How much would it cost** "The global oncology cancer drugs market was valued at $97,401 million in 2017, and is estimated to reach at $176,509 million by 2025, registering a CAGR of 7.6% from 2018 to 2025." Reportlinker, April 2, 2019. https://www.prnewswire.com/news-releases/the-global-oncologycancer-drugs-market-was-valued-at-97-401-million-in-2017–and-is-estimated-to-reach-at-176-509-million-by-2025–registering-a-cagr-of-7-6-from-2018-to-2025–300823104.html Accessed: January 2020.

58 **As sometimes happens with** Leaf, Clifton. Do clinical trials work? *New York Times,* op-ed. July 13, 2013.

59 **One of the drugs being tested** Barbor, Meg. No improvement in overall survival with addition of ganetespib to docetaxel in patients with non–small cell lung cancer. *ASCO Post* March 10, 2017. https://www.ascopost.com/issues/march-10-2017/no-improvement-in-overall-survival-with-addition-of-ganetespib-to-docetaxel-in-patients-with-non-small-cell-lung-cancer/ Accessed: January 2020.

61 **According to NCI officials** Shaffer, Anita T. Largest-ever precision medicine oncology trial ready for launch. Jun 01, 2015. *OncLive.com* https://www.onclive.com/conference-coverage/asco-2015/largest-ever-precision-medicine-oncology-trial-ready-for-launch Accessed: January 2020.

61 **At the 2018 ASCO meeting,** Eckhardt SG, Lieu C. Is precision medicine an Oxymoron? *JAMA Oncol* 2019;5(2):142–143. doi:https://doi.org/10.1001/jamaoncol.2018.5099

62 **The second NCI-MATCH** Chae YK, Vaklavas C, Cheng HH, et al. Molecular analysis for therapy choice (MATCH) arm W: Phase II study of AZD4547 in patients with tumors with aberrations in the FGFR pathway. Journal of Clinical Oncology 2018 36(15_suppl):2503-2503 doi: 10.1200/JCO.2018.36.15_suppl.2503

62 **Of 41 evaluable patients** Ibid. (Chae)

63 **So the results of the first** Press Release, National Cancer Institute. NCI-MATCH precision medicine clinical trial releases new findings, strengthens path forward for targeted cancer therapies. June 4, 2018. https://www.nih.gov/news-events/news-releases/nci-match-precision-medicine-clinical-trial-releases-new-findings-strengthens-path-forward-targeted-cancer-therapies Accessed: January 2020.

63 **Further results from the NCI-MATCH** ECOG-ACRIN Cancer Research Group. NCI-MATCH trial finds the combination of dabrafenib and trametinib effective.June 3, 2019. https://medicalxpress.com/news/2019-06-nci-match-trial-combination-dabrafenib-trametinib.html Accessed: January 2020.

64 **COSMIC contains a list** https://cancer.sanger.ac.uk/cosmic/census/tables?name=somatic Accessed: January 2020.

64 **At a time of general enthusiasm** Stratton MR. Campbell PJ, Futreal PA. The cancer genome. *Nature.* 2009 Apr 9;458(7239):719-24. doi: 10.1038/nature07943.

66 **Boston scientists once flippantly** Costa DB, Kobayashi SS. Whacking a mole-cule: clinical

activity and mechanisms of resistance to third generation EGFR inhibitors in EGFR mutated lung cancers with EGFR-T790M. *Transl Lung Cancer Res* 2015;4(6):809-15. doi: 10.3978/j.issn.2218-6751.2015.05.05.

## Section I, Chapter 9

67 **Immunosuppressed patients** Ribatti D. The concept of immune surveillance against tumors. The first theories. *Oncotarget* 2017;8(4):7175-7180. doi: 10.18632/oncotarget.12739.

68 **Despite nearly 50 years** Prehn RT. On the nature of cancer and why anticancer vaccines don't work. *Cancer Cell Int* 2005 Aug 1;5(1):25. doi: 10.1186/1475-2867-5-25.

69 **In 2016, the New York Times** Richtel, Matt. Immune system, unleashed by cancer therapies, can attack organs. *New York Times.* December 3, 2016.

69 **According to a 2016** Michot JM, Bigenwald C, Champiat S, et al. Immune-related adverse events with immune checkpoint blockade: a comprehensive review. *Eur J Cancer* 2016;54:139-148. doi: 10.1016/j.ejca.2015.11.016;

69 **Side effects are traditionally** Mirsoian A, Murphy WJ. Obesity and cancer immunotherapy toxicity. *Immunotherapy.* 2015;7(4):319-22. doi: 10.2217/imt.15.12.

70 **In 2017, Yale immunologist** Couzin-Frankel, Jennifer. Powerful new cancer drugs are saving lives, but can also ignite diabetes or other autoimmune conditions. *Science.* Nov. 15, 2017.

70 **Our extensive experience** Shoushtari AN, Friedman CF, Navid-Azarbaijani P, et al. Measuring toxic effects and ime to treatment failure for nivolumab plus ipilimumab in melanoma. *JAMA Oncol.* 2018;4(1):98-101. doi: 10.1001/jamaoncol. 2017.2391.

71 **In our view, it is counter** Michot JM, Bigenwald C, Champiat S, et al., *op. cit.*

73 **Take one such drug** Trefis Team. How important is Keytruda for Merck? *Forbes.com.* Aug 29, 2019. https://www.forbes.com/sites/greatspeculations/2019/08/29/how-important-is-keytruda-for-merck/#652562741b4d Accessed: January 2020.

73 **The majority of these agents** Yandell, Kate. The crowded field of checkpoint inhibitors. *Cancer Today,* April 3, 2019. https://www.cancertodaymag.org/Pages/cancer-talk/The-Crowded-Field-of-Checkpoint-Inhibitors.aspx Accessed: January 2020.

73 **What else is there** Anna Azvolinsky. First immunotherapy approved for breast cancer. March 13, 2019. https://www.cancertodaymag.org/Pages/cancer-talk/First-Immunotherapy-Approved-for-Breast-Cancer.aspx

74 **Do we just have too many** Kate Yandell. *op.cit.*

74 **Another strategy for a start-up** AGatlin, Allison. Will Big Pharma's giant maw scoop up these small-cap players? *Investors Business Daily,* December 26, 2018. https://www.investors.com/news/technology/big-pharma-pharmaceutical-companies-mergers/ Accessed: January 2020.

76 **One of the most significant** Sen S, Hess KR, Hong DS, et al. Impact of immune checkpoint inhibitor dose on toxicity, response rate, and survival: A pooled analysis of dose escalation phase 1 trials. *Journal of Clinical Oncology* 2018;36:15_suppl, 3077-3077 7; doi: 10.1200/JCO.2018.36.15_suppl.3077

77 **There were five times as many case** Renner A, Burotto M, Rojas C. Immune checkpoint inhibitor dosing: Can we go lower without compromising clinical efficacy? *J Glob Oncol* 2019 Jul;5:1-5. doi: 10.1200/JGO.19.00142.

77 **Here is how seven** Sen S, *op. cit.*

79 **A dose-response curve is generally evident** Frei E 3rd, Canellos GP. Dose: A critical factor in cancer chemotherapy. *The American Journal of Medicine,* October 1980, Volume 69, Issue 4, 585 - 594. doi: https://doi.org/10.1016/0002-9343(80)90472-6

79 **The FDA, says a leading cancer textbook** Bast, Robert C. Jr., et al. *Holland-Frei Cancer Medicine.* John Wiley & Sons, Mar 20, 2017, p. 601. Accessed: January 2020.

79 **However, in the past 20 years** Ibid. (Frei).

80 **A 2019 Journal of Global** Alex Renner, *op.cit.*

81 **Less than 5% of the population has coverage** Renner A, Burotto M, Rojas C.Immune checkpoint inhibitor dosing: Can we go lower without compromising clinical efficacy? *J Glob Oncol* 2019;5:1-5. doi: 10.1200/JGO.19.00142.

81 **Another study, from the Korean** Yoo SH, Keam B, Kim M, et al. Low-dose nivolumab can be effective in non-small cell lung cancer: alternative option for financial toxicity. ESMO Open. 2018;3(5):e000332. doi: 10.1136/esmoopen-2018-000332.

82 **Finally, we will mention** Postel-Vinay S, Aspeslagh S, Lanoy E, et al. Challenges of phase 1 clinical trials evaluating immune checkpoint-targeted antibodies, *Annals of Oncology* 2016;27:214–224, https://doi.org/10.1093/annonc/mdv550

82 **Changing the dosage** Goldstein DA, Gordon N, Davidescu M, et al. A phamacoeconomic analysis of personalized dosing vs fixed dosing of pembrolizumab in firstline PD-L1-positive non–small cell lung cancer, *JNCI: Journal of the National Cancer Institute,* 2017;109(11), doi: https://doi.org/10.1093/jnci/djx063

83 **Like most big corporations** https://www.merck.com/about/our-values/ Accessed: January 2020.

84 **Peter Bach, MD and** Bach PB, Conti Rena M, Muller RJ, et al. Overspending driven by oversized single dose vials of cancer drugs *BMJ* 2016; 352 :i788; and Daniel A Goldstein, et al., *op.cit.*

84 **This seemingly trivial factor** Bach, Peter, *op.cit.*

85 **The immune checkpoint inhibitors** Michot JM, Bigenwald C, Champiat S, et al. Immune-related adverse events with immune checkpoint blockade: a comprehensive review. *Eur J Cancer* 2016;54:139-148. doi: 10.1016/j.ejca.2015.11.016.

85 **Before the introduction** Albarel F. Long-term follow-up of ipilimumab-induced hypophysitis, a common adverse event of the anti-CTLA-4 antibody in melanoma. *Eur J Endocrinol.* 2015;172(2):195-204. doi: 10.1530/EJE-14-0845; and Faje, A. Immunotherapy and hypophysitis: clinical presentation, treatment, and biologic insights. *Pituitary* 2016;19:82–92 doi:10.1007/s11102-015-0671-4

86 **And, with that, we are only** Brahmer JR, et al. Management of Immune-related adverse events in patients treated with immune checkpoint inhibitor therapy: ASCO Clinical Practice Guideline. *J Clin Oncol.* 2018;36(17):1714-1768. doi: 10.1200/JCO.2017.77.6385

87 **After the very first infusion** Attarwala H. TGN1412: From discovery to disaster. *J Young Pharm.* 2010 Jul;2(3):332-6. doi: 10.4103/0975-1483.66810.

87 **There is no explanation** Steroids diminish survival benefits from ICIs in lung cancer. https://www.cancernetwork.com/asco-street-team/steroids-diminish-survival-benefits-icis-lung-cancer. Accessed: March 2020.

88 **Lower doses may reduce** Shiraj Sen, op,cit.

89 **There has been considerable** Cancer drugs don't always work as intended, researchers warn. *Science Daily,* September 11, 2019. https://www.sciencedaily.com/releases/2019/09/190911142837.htm Accessed: January 2020.

### Section I, Chapter 10

90 **The truth is that** CenterWatch Staff. Tufts CSDD report defends $2.9B total for drug development. March 21, 2016 *CenterWatch.* https://www.centerwatch.com/articles/15357 Accessed: January 2020.

90 **What is the actual benefit** Lin A, Giuliano CJ, Palladino A, et al. Off-target toxicity is a common mechanism of action of cancer drugs undergoing clinical trials. *Sci Transl Med* 2019 Sep 11;11(509). pii: eaaw8412. doi: 10.1126/scitranslmed.aaw8412..

90 **What did the critical observers** Schwaederle M, Zhao M, Lee JJ, et al. Impact of precision medicine in diverse cancers: A meta-analysis of phase II clinical trials. *J Clin Oncol.* 2015 Nov 10;33(32):3817-25. doi: 10.1200/JCO.2015.61.5997. Authors included Mendelsohn, et al.

91 **By testing enough subgroups** Schulz KF, Grimes DA. By testing enough subgroups: subgroup and interim analyses. *Lancet.* 2005;365(9471):1657-61. doi :https://doi.org/10.1016/S0140-6736(05)66516-6

### Section II, Introduction

93 **The current scientific understandin** Calabrese EJ. A Failed cancer paradigm: implications for cancer risk assessment and patients. J Cell Commun Signal. 2019 Sep;13(3):271-272. doi: 10.1007/s12079-019-00526-6. Epub 2019 Aug 5. We have slightly abridged the quotation.

93 **Complementary oncology** https://www.thieme.com/books-main/complementary-medicine/product/3006-complementary-oncology

93 **I can see why people** U.S. DHHS. What is the U.S. opioid epidemic? https://www.hhs.gov/opioids/about-the-epidemic/index.html Accessed: January 2020.

### Section II, Chapter 1

96 **In many ways, mitochondria** Martin WF, Mentel M. The origin of mitochondria. *Scitable by Nature Education,* 2010. https://www.nature.com/scitable/topicpage/the-origin-of-mitochondria-14232356/

96 **These organelles were first observed** Anon. College Biology Volume 2 of 3, An Open Education resource by Textbook Equity. ISBN-13: 9781312395336

97 **Cancer cells tend to have** Anon. News release, University of Colorado. Cancer cells greedy for glucose. Oct 01, 2018. https://www.technologynetworks.com/cancer-research/news/cancer-cells-greedy-for-glucose-310141 Accessed: January 2020.

98 **But after World War II** Medes G, et al. Metabolism of neoplastic tissue. IV. A study of lipid synthesis in neoplastic tissue slices in vitro. *Cancer Res* January 1 1953 (13) (1) 27-29; and Hans Krebs. *Otto Warburg Cell Physiologist Biochemist and Eccentric.* Phila.: Ishi Press, 2019.

98 **There is renewed attention** Vander Heiden MG, Cantley LC, Thompson CB. Understanding the Warburg effect: the metabolic requirements of cell proliferation. Science. 2009 May 22;324(5930):1029-33. doi: 10.1126/science.1160809.

99 **Selling PET devices** News AIM via COMTEX Press Release. PET-CT scanner device market

determine a spectacular expansion and productive *Impact* 2018-2026. June 21, 2019.

**99 One of the most robust** Vaux, D.L. In defense of the somatic mutation theory of cancer. Bioessays, 2011;33:341-343. doi: 10.1002/bies.201100022

**100 Exhibit A was the first** Ardito F, Giuliani M, Perrone D, et al. The crucial role of protein phosphorylation in cell signaling and its use as targeted therapy (Review). *Int J Mol Med.* 2017 Aug;40(2):271-280. doi: 10.3892/ijmm.2017.3036.

**100 It is now a proven fact** Gottschalk S. Imatinib (STI571)-mediated changes in glucose metabolism in human leukemia BCR-ABL-positive cells. *Clin Cancer Res* 2004;10(19):6661-8. doi: 10.1158/1078-0432.CCR-04-0039

**100 A significant reduction** De Rosa V, Monti M, Terlizzi C, et al. *Int J Mol Sci.* 2019 Jun 27;20(13):3134. doi: 10.3390/ijms20133134; and Vitiello GA, Medina BD, Zeng S, et al. Mitochondrial inhibition augments the efficacy of imatinib by resetting the metabolic phenotype of gastrointestinal stromal tumor. *Clin Cancer Res* 2018;24(4):972-984. doi: 10.1158/1078-0432. CCR-17-2697.

**101 There are clear indications** Gorini S, De Angelis A, Berrino L, et al. Chemotherapeutic drugs and mitochondrial dysfunction: focus on doxorubicin, trastuzumab, and sunitinib. *Oxid Med Cell Longev* 2018 Mar 18;2018:7582730. doi: 10.1155/2018/7582730; and Varga ZV, Ferdinandy P, Liaudet L, et al. Drug-induced mitochondrial dysfunction and cardiotoxicity. *Am J Physiol Heart Circ Physiol.* 2015 Nov;309(9):H1453-67. doi: 10.1152/ajpheart.00554.2015.

**101 There is also evidence** Sarosiek KA, Ni Chonghaile T, Letai A. Mitochondria: gatekeepers of response to chemotherapy. *Trends Cell Biol* 2013 Dec;23(12):612-9. doi: 10.1016/j.tcb.2013.08.003.

**101 Other scientists pointed out** Burke PJ. Mitochondria, bioenergetics and apoptosis in cancer. *Trends Cancer* 2017;3(12):857-870. doi: 10.1016/j.trecan.2017.10.006.

**102 In Cancer as a Metabolic Disease** Seyfried, Thomas. *Cancer as a Metabolic Disease: On the Origin, Management, and Prevention of Cancer.* Hoboken, New Jersey: John Wiley & Sons, 2012.

**102 Professor Seyfried has raised the following** In an email correspondence with the author, October 2019.

**102 Normal tissues were found** Yizhak K, Aguet F, Kim J, et al. RNA sequence analysis reveals macroscopic somatic clonal expansion across normal tissues. *Science* 2019 Jun 7;364 (6444). pii: eaaw0726. doi: 10.1126/science.aaw0726.

**103 Metformin may stop the growth:** https://www.cancer.gov/about-cancer/treatment/clinical-trials/intervention/metformin-hydrochloride Accessed: January 2020.

## Section II, Chapter 2

**104 Then, in 2014** Slavin S, Moss RW, Bakacs T. Control of minimal residual cancer by low dose ipilimumab activating autologous anti-tumor immunity. *Pharmacy Res.* 2014 Jan;79:9-12. doi: 10.1016/j.phrs.2013.10.004. Epub 2013 Nov 4.

**104 Kleef's use of lower doses** https://www.ncbi.nlm.nih.gov/pubmed/?term=Bull+JM%5B-Author%5D+hyperthermia; and Kleef R, Moss R, et al. Complete clinical remission of stage IV triple-negative breast cancer lung metastasis administering low-dose immune checkpoint blockade in combination with hyperthermia and interleukin-2. *Integr Cancer Ther.* 2018 Dec;17(4):1297-1303. doi: 10.1177/1534735418794867.

**106 With better patient selection** June C, Warshauer J, Bluestone J. Is autoimmunity the Achilles' heel of cancer immunotherapy?. *Nat Med* 23, 540–547 (2017) doi:10.1038/nm.4321

**106 As I go around the country** Richard D. Klausner, MD. Cancer, minorities & the medically underserved. The role of the National Cancer Institute. First published: 09 November 2000 https://doi.org/10.1002/(SICI)1097-0142(19981015)83:8+<1703::AID-CNCR7>3.0.CO;2-Y

## Section II, Chapter 3

**107 In 18 detailed monographs** Nauts, Helen Coley. *Beneficial Effects of Immunotherapy (Bacterial Toxins) on Sarcoma of the Soft Tissues, Other than Lymphosarcoma.* End results in 186 determinate cases with microscopic confirmation of diagnosis, 49 operable, 137 inoperable. Monograph no. 16, New York: Cancer Research Institute, 1975.

**109 There is an extraordinary chart** Göhring, Einar. *Active Fever Therapy with MBV - Coley's Toxins: The Perfect Storm of Cytokines.* Neopubli GmbH, April 9, 2019.

**110 Some people might think** MacAdams, Donald H. *The Reinvention of Coley's Toxins,* self-published, 2018. Available via Amazon.com.

**110 In the 1970s, Mrs. Nauts** Data on funding from Form 990 (2017): https://pdf.guidestar.org/PDF_Images/2018/131/837/2018-131837442-1040b078-9.pdf Accessed: January 2020.

**110 A final hurdle** Matthew Tontonoz. Whatever happened to Coley's toxins? *Cancer Research Institute website.* April 02, 2015. https://www.cancerresearch.org/blog/april-2015/what-ever-happened-to-coleys-toxins Accessed: January 2020.

**110 How can one say this** Julie Karbach, Neumann A, Brand K, et al. Phase I clinical trial of mixed bacterial vaccine (Coley's toxins) in patients with NY-ESO-1 expressing cancers: Immunological effects and clinical activity. *Clin Cancer Res* 2012:(18-19)5449-5459; doi: 10.1158/1078-0432.CCR-12-1116

## Section III, Chapter 1

**113 The use of surrogate endpoints** Prasad V, Kim C, et al. The strength of association between surrogate end points and survival in oncology: A systematic review of trial-level meta-analyses. *JAMA Intern Med* 2015;175(8):1389–1398. doi:https://doi.org/10.1001/jamainternmed.2015.2829

**114 But oncology as a whole** Buyse M, Molenberghs G., Paoletti X, et al. Statistical evaluation of surrogate endpoints with examples from cancer clinical trials. *Biom J* 2015;58:104-132 doi:10.1002/bimj.201400049

**115 On this point we are in agreement** file:///Users/owner/Downloads/cancer-treatment-and-survivorship-facts-and-figures-2016-2017.pdf

**115 But in recent years** Fauber J, Chu E. The slippery slope: Is a surrogate endpoint evidence of efficacy? *MedPage Today,* October 26, 2014 https://www.medpagetoday.org/special-reports/slipperyslope/48244?vpass=1 Accessed: January 2020.

**115 In drug development, every month** Abraham J. Sociology of pharmaceuticals development and regulation: a realist empirical research programme. In: *Pharmaceuticals And Society: Critical Discourses And Debates.* 28 August 2008 https://doi.org/10.1111/j.1467-9566.2008.01101.

**116 A very important JAMA** Mailankody S, Prasad V. Five years of cancer drug approvals: innovation, efficacy, and costs. *JAMA Oncol* 2015;1(4):539–540. doi:https://doi.org/10.1001/jamaoncol.2015.0373

**116 In a 60-year period** Parikh, Ravi. New cancer therapies offer great hope, but there can be surprising complications. *Washington Post,* April 14, 2019.

**116 The National Cancer Institute website now lists** https://www.cancer.gov/about-cancer/treatment/drugs, and https://www.fda.gov/drugs/resources-information-approved-drugs/hematologyoncology-cancer-approvals-safety-notifications Accessed: January 2020

**117 In response to this pressure** Johnson JR, Ning YM, Farrell A, et al. Accelerated approval of oncology products: The Food and Drug Administration experience. *J Natl Cancer Inst* 2011;103(8):636-44. doi: 10.1093/jnci/djr062. Epub 2011 Mar 21.

**117 Sometimes a drug receives** Food and Drug Administration news release. FDA approves an oncology drug that targets a key genetic driver of cancer, rather than a specific type of tumor. New drug Vitrakvi targets specific receptor kinase that promotes tumors November 26, 2018. Accessed: January 2020.

**118 Since it usually takes** https://www.upcounsel.com/how-long-does-a-drug-patent-last

**118 A similar situation is found** Herder, Matthew. The FDA and Sarepta: a window into the real world of drug regulation, *STATNews.com,* September 3, 2019. https://www.statnews.com/2019/09/03/fda-sarepta-real-world-drug-regulation/ Accessed: January 2020.

**118 Or, as ProPublica put it** Chen, Caroline. FDA repays industry by rushing risky drugs to market. *Medscape Oncology.* July 02, 2018. https://www.medscape.com/viewarticle/898782 Accessed: January 2020.

**119 One of the more bizarre** Taylor, Nick Paul. ChemRen website. AstraZeneca pays Sobi $95M for priority review voucher. August 23, 2019. https://www.chemren.com/news/2192_AstraZeneca-pays-Sobi-95M-for-priority-review-voucher. Accessed: January 2020.

**120 In 1992, under the terms** Ibid. (Taylor).

**120 We all think we know** Gutman SI, Piper M, Grant MD, et al. Progression-free urvival: what does it mean for psychological well-being or quality of life? Rockville, Maryland: Agency for Healthcare Research and Quality (US); 2013 Apr. Available from: https://www.ncbi.nlm.nih.gov/books/NBK137759/ Accessed: January 2020.

**121 And according to a 2013** Villaruz LC, Socinski MA. The clinical viewpoint: definitions, limitations of RECIST, practical considerations of measurement. *Clin Cancer Res* 2013 May 15;19(10):2629-36. doi: 10.1158/1078-0432.CCR-12-2935.

**122 As Mary Chris Jaklevic** Mary Chris Jaklevic. How one bit of medical jargon fuels public confusion about cancer treatments. *HealthNewsReview,* October 22, 2019. https://www.healthnewsreview.org/2019/10/how-one-bit-of-medical-jargon-fuels-public-confusion-about-cancer-treatments/ Accessed: January 2020.

**122 In each and every case** https://twitter.com/VincentRK/status/1175827263675424769 Accessed: January 2020.

**123 We first learned this** Moertel CG, Hanley JA. The effect of measuring error on the results of therapeutic trials in advanced cancer. *Cancer* 1976;38(1)388-394. doi: 10.1002/1097-0142(197607)38:1<388::aid-cncr2820380156>3.0.co;2-a

**123 To summarize: overall survival and** Sridhara R, Johnson JR, Justice R, et al. Review of oncology and hematology drug product approvals at the US Food and Drug Administration between July 2005 and December 2007. *J Natl Cancer Inst.* 2010;102(4):230-43. doi: 10.1093/jnci/djp515.

**123 In a devastating** Kovic B, Jin X, Kennedy SA, et al. Evaluating progression-free survival as a surrogate Outcome for health-related quality of life in oncology: A systematic review and quantitative analysis. *JAMA Intern Med.* 2018;178(12):1586–1596. doi:10.1001/jamainternmed.2018.4710

**124 To quote an analysis** James Miessler. Cancer trials: Is progression-free survival enough? *CenterWatch*, October 8, 2018. https://www.centerwatch.com/articles/12479

**125 Despite its inferiority:** Gutman SI, *op. cit.*

**126 In fact, FDA's Guidance** Food and Drug Administration. *Clinical Trial Endpoints for the Approval of Cancer Drugs and Biologics Guidance for Industry.* December 1018. https://www.fda.gov/media/71195/download Accessed: January 2020.

**126 A comprehensive review** Prasad V, Kim C, Burotto M, et al. The strength of association between surrogate end points and survival in oncology: A systematic review of trial-level meta-analyses. *JAMA Intern Med* 2015;175(8):1389–1398. doi:https://doi.org/10.1001/jamainternmed.2015.2829

**127 I would say to a patient** Chen, Caroline. FDA repays industry by rushing risky drugs to market. ProPublica, June 26, 2018. https://www.propublica.org/article/fda-repays-industry-by-rushing-risky-drugs-to-market. Accessed: January 2020.

**127 A search of PubMed** Carlson RH. Stronger correlation of surrogate endpoints with survival needed. *Lancet Oncology.* 2016;17(7):e273. doi: 10.1016/S1470-2045(16)30210-8.

**127 One odd fact** Chen EY, Raghunathan V, Prasad V. An overview of cancer drugs approved by the US Food and Drug Administration based on the surrogate end point of response rate. *JAMA Intern Med.* 2019;179(7):915–921. doi:https://doi.org/10.1001/jamainternmed.2019.0583

**128 Huseyin Naci, PhD, MPH of the London School** Naci H, Wouters OJ, Gupta R, et al. Timing and characteristics of cumulative evidence available on novel therapeutic agents receiving Food and Drug Administration accelerated approval. *Milbank Q* 2017;95(2):261-290. doi: 10.1111/1468-0009.12261.

## Section III, Chapter 2

**128 Independent researchers** Christina Bennett, MS. FDA proposal threatens transparency on cancer drug safety and efficacy. *Cancer Therapy Advisor.* November 4, 2019. https://www.cancertherapyadvisor.com/home/cancer-topics/general-oncology/cancer-drug-safety-efficacy-fda-proposal-threatens-transparency/2/ Accessed: January 2020.

**129 In 2019, Alyson Haslam** Haslam A, Hey SP, Gill J, et al. A systematic review of trial-level meta-analyses measuring the strength of association between surrogate end-points and overall survival in oncology. Eur J Cancer. 2019;106:196-211. doi: 10.1016/j.ejca.2018.11.012.

**129 In fact, in at least** Kumar S, Harrison SJ, Cavo M, et al. A Phase 3 study of venetoclax or placebo in combination with bortezomib and dexamethasone in patients with relapsed/refractory multiple myeloma. *Clinical Lymphoma, Myeloma and Leukemia.* 2019:19(10):e31

**129 Median overall survival was not reached:** https://www.ascopost.com/News/60166 Accessed: January 2020.

**129 To quote an editorial in the** Editorial. Gauging the validity of cancer drug trials: a call for collaboration. *BMJ* September 18, 2019. https://blogs.bmj.com/bmj/2019/09/18/gauging-the-validity-of-cancer-drug-trials-a-call-for-collaboration/ Accessed: January 2020.

**130 Big drug companies are multinational** Davis C, Naci H, Gurpinar E, et al. Availability of evidence of benefits on overall survival and quality of life of cancer drugs approved by European Medicines Agency: retrospective cohort study of drug approvals 2009-13. *BMJ*. 2017;359:j4530. doi: 10.1136/bmj.j4530.

**130 There's not much evidence** Rapaport, Lisa. Little evidence new cancer drugs improve survival. *Reuters Health News,* October 13, 2017. https://www.reuters.com/article/us-health-cancer-drugs/little-evidence-new-cancer-drugs-improve-survival Accessed: January 2020.

**130 A 2019 follow-up study** Naci H, Davis C, Savovi J, et al. Design characteristics, risk of bias, and reporting of randomised controlled trials supporting approvals of cancer drugs by European Medicines Agency, 2014-16: cross sectional analysis. *BMJ* 2019;366:l5221.doi:10.1136/bmj.l5221

**132 Daniel S. Greenberg** https://www.healthaffairs.org/doi/pdf/10.1377/hlthaff.21.3.274 Accessed: January 2020.

**133 No surprise, then** Booth CM, Cescon DW, Wang L, et al. Evolution of the randomized controlled trial in oncology over three decades. *J Clin Oncol* 2008;26(33):5458-64. doi: 10.1200/JCO.2008.16.5456.

**133 This is among the biggest** Weeks JC, Catalano PJ, Cronin A, et al. Patients' expectations about effects of chemotherapy for advanced cancer. *N Engl J Med* 2012;367(17):1616-25. doi: 10.1056/NEJMoa1204410.

**135 According to a 2018 report** Oxfam. *Prescription for Poverty.* Drug companies as tax dodgers, price gougers, and influence peddlers. September 17, 2018. https://www.oxfamamerica.org/explore/research-publications/prescription-for-poverty/ Accessed: January 2020.

**135 In the U.S., DTCPA** Ventola CL. Direct-to-consumer pharmaceutical advertising: therapeutic or toxic? *P&T: A Peer-Reviewed Journal For Formulary Management* 2011;36(10):669-84.

**135 The average American TV viewer** Frosch DL, Krueger PM, Hornik RC, et al. Creating demand for prescription drugs: a content analysis of television direct-to-consumer advertising. *Ann Fam Med* 2007;5(1):6–13. doi:10.1370/afm.611; and Donohue J. A history of drug advertising: the evolving roles of consumers and consumer protection. *Milbank Q* 2006;84(4):659-99. doi: 10.1111/j.1468-0009.2006.00464.x; and Epstein, Ella. The dangers of DTCPA: A legal analysis. *Columbia Undergraduate Law Review.* November 19, 2017. https://blogs.cuit.columbia.edu/culr/2017/11/19/the-dangers-of-dtcpa-a-legal-analysis/; and Schwartz LM, Woloshin S. Medical marketing in the United States, 1997-2016. *JAMA.* 2019;321(1):80–96. doi:https://doi.org/10.1001/jama.2018.19320

**136 This included a total of** Mole, Beth. Big Pharma shells out $20B each year to schmooze docs, $6B on drug ads persuading doctors and direct-to-consumer ads land 1-2 punch for knockout sales. *ArsTechnica,* January 11, 2019. https://arstechnica.com/science/2019/01/healthcare-industry-spends-30b-on-marketing-most-of-it-goes-to-doctors/; and Shannon Brownlee. Health, hope and hype. Why the media oversells medical 'breakthroughs.' *Washington Post,* August 3, 2003.

**138 We focus here on the FDA** Lehman R, Gross CP. An international perspective on drugs for cancer: The best of times, the worst of times. *JAMA Intern Med* 2019;179(7):913–914. doi:https://doi.org/10.1001/jamainternmed.2019.0458

**138 The function of the formal** Junod, Suzanne White. FDA and clinical drug trials: A short history. In: *A Quick Guide to Clinical Trials.* Davies, Mahdu, Kerimani, Faiz, eds. Washington: Bioplan, Inc.: 2008, pp. 25-55. https://www.fda.gov/media/110437/download Accessed: Jan. 2020.

**139 Each of these criteria** Frieden, Joyce. Clinical trials need to be more inclusive, experts say. Children, seniors, and chronic disease patients need more options. *MedPage Today,* April 17, 2018. https://www.medpagetoday.com/publichealthpolicy/clinicaltrials/72400. Accessed: January 2020.

**139 That's quite a few people** Redfearn. Suz. Clinical trial patient inclusion and exclusion criteria need an overhaul, say experts. April 23, 2018. https://www.centerwatch.com/articles/12622-clinical-trial-patient-inclusion-and-exclusion-criteria-need-an-overhaul-say-experts Accessed: January 2020.

**139 One can easily find** Anon. Broader inclusion criteria could double the number of patients with lung cancer eligible for clinical trials. *Healio HemOnc Today.* June 5, 2019. https://www.healio.com/hematology-oncology/lung-cancer/news/online/%7B0c781cf2-4ed3-49a0-89a2-ad14ddd8545f%7D/broader-inclusion-criteria-could-double-the-number-of-patients-with-lung-cancer-eligible-for-clinical-trials Accessed: January 2020.

**139 Stringent inclusion and exclusion** Farooq V, Serruy PW. Cherry-picking patients for randomized controlled trials: Reliving the past. *J Am Coll Cardiol.* 2013;61(24):2492.

**139 Clinical trials involve selected** James S, Rao S. Granger C. Registry-based randomized clinical trials—a new clinical trial paradigm. *Nat Rev Cardiol* 2015;12:312–316. doi:10.1038/nrcardio.2015.33

**139 Extrapolating results from adult** Naka F, Strober B, Shahriari M. Clinical trials: Kids are not just little people. *Clin Dermatol* 2017;356):583-593. doi: 10.1016/j.clindermatol.2017.08.008.

**139 Results from novel therapeutics** Sam D, Gresham G, Abdel-Rahman O. et al. Generalizability of clinical trials of advanced melanoma in the real-world, population-based setting. *Med Oncol* 2018;35:110. doi:10.1007/s12032-018-1167-7

## Section III, Chapter 3

**139 Results from clinical trials** Knauf W, Aldaoud A, Hutzschenreuter U, et al. Survival of non-transplant patients with multiple myeloma in routine care differs from that in clinical trials-data from the prospective German Tumour Registry Lymphatic Neoplasms. *Ann Hematol* 2018;97(12):2437–2445. doi:10.1007/s00277-018-3449-8

## Section III, Chapter 4

**139 One very significant** Ibid. (Knauf)

**140 Yet it has often been noted** Murthy VH, Krumholz HM, Gross CP. Participation in Cancer Clinical Trials: Race-, Sex-, and Age-Based Disparities. *JAMA* 2004;291(22):2720–2726. doi:https://doi.org/10.1001/jama.291.22.2720; Chen MS Jr, Lara PN, Dang JH, et al. Twenty years post-NIH Revitalization Act: enhancing minority participation in clinical trials (EMPaCT): laying the groundwork for improving minority clinical trial accrual: renewing the case for enhancing minority participation in cancer clinical trials. *Cancer* 2014;120 Suppl 7(0 7):1091–1096. doi:10.1002/cncr.28575

**141 This underrepresentation** Robbins NM, Bernat JL, Minority representation in migraine treatment trials. *Headache: The Journal of Head and Face Pain* 2017;57:525-533. doi:10.1111/head.13018

**141 Minority U.S. populations** Nazha B, Mishra M, Pentz R, et al. Enrollment of racial minorities in clinical trials: Old problem assumes new urgency in the age of immunotherapy. *American Society of Clinical Oncology Educational Book* 2019 :39, 3-10.

**141 Suboptimal race reporting** Loree JM, Anand S, Dasari A, et al. Disparity of race reporting and representation in clinical trials leading to cancer drug approvals from 2008 to 2018. *JAMA Oncol* 2019;5(10):e191870. doi:https://doi.org/10.1001/jamaoncol.2019.1870

**141 There is another important variable** White MC, Holman DM, Boehm JE, et al. Age and cancer risk: a potentially modifiable relationship. *Am J Prev Med.* 2014;46(3 Suppl 1):S7–S15. doi:10.1016/j.amepre.2013.10.029; and Cinar D, Tas D. Cancer in the elderly. *North Clin Istanb.* 2015;2(1):73–80. doi:10.14744/nci.2015.72691

**141 At the same time, seniors** Seattle Cancer Care Alliance. Myths vs. facts about clinical studies, n.d. https://www.seattlecca.org/guide-clinical-trials/making-decision/myths-vs-facts-about-clinical-trials. Accessed: January 2020; and Murthy VH, Krumholz HM, Gross CP. Participation in cancer clinical trials: Race-, sex-, and age-based disparities. *JAMA.* 2004;291(22):2720–2726. doi:https://doi.org/10.1001/jama.291.22.2720

**141 What impact does advanced** Anon. *PRA Health Sciences.* The need for more elderly patients in cancer clinical trials. https://prahs.com/insights/the-need-for-more-elderly-patients-in-cancer-clinical-trials Accessed: January 2020.

**142 The prevalence of adverse** Lavan AH, Gallagher P. Predicting risk of adverse drug reactions in older adults. *Ther Adv Drug Saf* 2016;7(1):11-22. doi: 10.1177/2042098615615472.

**142 There is evidence that many** van Beek MWH, Roukens M, Jacobs WCH, et al. Real-world adverse effects of capecitabine toxicity in an elderly population. *Drugs Real World Outcomes.* 2018;5(3):161-167 doi: 10.1007/s40801-018-0138-9.

**142 In 2012, Doctors Scher and Hurria** Scher KS, Hurria H. Under-representation of older adults in cancer registration trials: Known problem, little progress. *Journal of Clinical Oncology* 2012;30:17:2036-2038

**142 A 2018 study** Galsky MD, Pal SK, Lin SW, et al. Real-world effectiveness of chemotherapy in elderly patients with metastatic bladder cancer in the United States. Bladder Cancer. 2018;4(2):227–238. Published 2018 Apr 26. doi:10.3233/BLC-170149. Herrera AP, Snipes SA, King DW, et al. Disparate inclusion of older adults in clinical trials: priorities and opportunities for policy and practice change. *Am J Public Health.* 2010;100 Suppl 1(Suppl 1):S105-12. doi: 10.2105/AJPH.2009.162982

**143 Another important factor** West H, Jin JO. Performance status in patients with cancer. *JAMA Oncol* 2015;1(7):998. doi:https://doi.org/10.1001/jamaoncol.2015.3113

**143 Ian F. Tannock, MD** Zhang S, Liang F, Li W, et al. Comparison of eligibility criteria between protocols, registries, and publications of cancer clinical trials, *JNCI: Journal of the National Cancer Institute,* 2016;108(11) doi: djw129, https://doi.org/10.1093/jnci/djw129

**143 In a bluntly honest ASH** Anon. Reader beware: Interpreting clinical trial data. *ASH Clinical News.* April 1, 2019. https://www.ashclinicalnews.org/spotlight/reader-beware-interpreting-clinical-trial-data/ Accessed: January 2020.

**144 In fact, we know that** Ecke TH, Gerullis H, Bartel P, et al. Palliative chemotherapy with gemcitabine, paclitaxel, and cisplatin as first-line treatment following gemcitabine monotherapy for patients with transitional cell carcinoma of the urothelium. *Minerva Urologica e Nefrologica* 2009;61(1):1-8.

**144 Italian oncologists similarly explained** Gebbia V, Galetta D, De Marinis F. Non small cell lung cancer patients with ECOG PS2: unsolved questions and lessons from clinical trials, *Annals of Oncology* 2005;16)S4):iv123-iv131 doi: https://doi.org/10.1093/annonc/mdi921

**144 By stratifying they mean** Pirker R, Pereira JR, Szczesna A, et al. Prognostic factors in patients with advanced non-small cell lung cancer: Data from the phase III FLEX study. *Lung Cancer* 2012 Aug;77(2):376-82. doi: 10.1016/j.lungcan.2012.03.010.

**144 Further confirmation came** Aspinall SL, Zhao X, Geraci MC, et al. Targeted therapies in Veterans with RCC Study Group. Use of targeted therapies for advanced renal cell carcinoma in the Veterans Health Administration. *Cancer Med.* 2019 Nov;8(15):6651-6661. doi: 10.1002/cam4.2531.

**145 Narrower criteria should only be used** Harvey RD, Rubenstein WS, Ison G, et al. Impact of broadening clinical trial eligibility criteria for advanced non-small cell lung cancer patients: Real-world analysis. *Journal of Clinical Oncology* 2019 37:18_suppl, LBA108-LBA108 doi: 10.1200/JCO.2019.37.18_suppl.LBA108

**145 Income as a Factor** Anon. Are Americans Financially Healthy? *New York Times.* Paid for and posted by the Financial Health Network. https://www.nytimes.com/paidpost/financial-health-network/are-americans-financially-healthy.html Accessed: January 2020.

**145 Almost half of all Americans exist** https://www.commondreams.org/views/2017/10/16/yes-half-americans-are-or-near-poverty-heres-more-evidence

**145 15 million American workers earn less than $10 an hour** https://money.cnn.com/2015/02/23/news/economy/15-million-american-workers-earn-10-dollars-or-less-an-hour/

**145 Four in ten American adults** https://money.cnn.com/2018/05/22/pf/emergency-expenses-household-finances/index.html

**145 87 million Americans are medically uninsured** Unger JM, et al. Patient income level and cancer clinical trial participation: A prospective survey study. *JAMA Oncol.* 2016 Jan;2(1):137-9.

doi: 10.1001/jamaoncol.2015.3924; and https://www.commonwealthfund.org/sites/default/files/2019-02/Collins_hlt_ins_coverage_8_years_after_ACA_2018_biennial_survey_tables.pdf#page=1.

**146 Participants in clinical trials are five** Gross CP, Filardo G, Mayne ST, et al. The impact of socioeconomic status and race on trial participation for older women with breast cancer. *Cancer* 2005;103:483-491. doi: 10.1002/cncr.20792; and O'Connor JM, Sedghi T, Dhodapkar M, et al. Factors associated with cancer disparities among low-, medium-, and high-income US Counties. *JAMA Netw Open.* 2018;1(6):e183146. doi:https://doi.org/10.1001/jamanetworkopen.2018.3146

**146 For various reasons** Briggs B. Patients treated at cancer centers live longer: study. *Fred Hutch News Service.* November 6, 2015. https://www.fredhutch.org/en/news/center-news/2015/11/cancer-center-patients-live-longer.html Accessed: January 2020.

**146 To quote the veteran science journalist** Begley, Sharon. Do cancer clinical trials exaggerate the real-world benefits of drugs? *STATNews.com,* November 21, 2016. https://www.statnews.com/2016/11/21/cancer-clinical-trials/

**147 In a 2015 California study** Bristow RE, Chang J, Ziogas A, et al. Impact of National Cancer Institute Comprehensive Cancer Centers on ovarian cancer treatment and survival. *J Am Coll Surg* 2015;220(5):940-50. doi: 10.1016/j.jamcollsurg.2015.01.056.

**147 Community hospitals and practices** Mehmet Sitki Copur, et al. ReCAP: Impact of the National Cancer Institute Community Cancer Centers program on clinical trial and related activities at a community cancer center in rural Nebraska. *Journal of Oncology Practice* 2016 12:1, 67-68

**147 Over the years there** Murthy VH, Krumholz HM, Gross CP. Participation in cancer clinical trials: Race-, Sex-, and Age-Based Disparities. *JAMA* 2004;291(22):2720–2726. doi:https://doi.org/10.1001/jama.291.22.2720; and Chen MS Jr, Lara PN, Dang JH, et al. Twenty years post-NIH Revitalization Act: enhancing minority participation in clinical trials (EMPaCT): laying the groundwork for improving minority clinical trial accrual: renewing the case for enhancing minority participation in cancer clinical trials. *Cancer.* 2014 Apr 1;120 Suppl 7(0 7):1091-6. doi: 10.1002/cncr.28575; and Scher KS, Hurria A. Under-representation of older adults in cancer registration trials: Known problem, little progress. *Journal of Clinical Oncology* 2012 30:17, 2036-2038

**149 Cancer clinical trials, wrote Australian** Pearce A, Haas M, Viney R, et al. Incidence and severity of self-reported chemotherapy side effects in routine care: A prospective cohort study. *PLoS One* 2017;12(10):e0184360. doi: 10.1371/journal.pone.0184360.

**149 Patients who are at risk** Pearce A, Haas M, Viney R, et al. Incidence and severity of self-reported chemotherapy side effects in routine care: A prospective cohort study. *PLoS One* 2017 Oct 10;12(10):e0184360. doi: 10.1371/journal.pone.0184360.

**149 Safety monitoring is more intensive** Rothwell PM. External validity of randomised controlled trials: "to whom do the results of this trial apply?" *Lancet* 2005 Jan 1-7;365(9453):82-93.

**149 The reporting of chemo's side effects** Pitrou I, Boutron I, Ahmad N,et al. Reporting of safety results in published reports of randomized controlled trials. *Arch Intern Med.* 2009 Oct 26;169(19):1756-61. doi: 10.1001/archinternmed.2009.306.

**149 Side effects in clinical trials** Basch E. Patient versus clinician symptom reporting using the National Cancer Institute Common Terminology Criteria for Adverse Events: results of a questionnaire-based study. *Lancet Oncol* 2006;7(11):903-9.

**149 In 2015, there was an article in JAMA** Seife, Charles. Research misconduct identified by the US Food and Drug Administration: out of sight, out of mind, out of the peer-reviewed literature. *JAMA Intern Med.* 2015;175(4):567–577. doi:https://doi.org/10.1001/jamainternmed.2014.7774

## Section III, Chapter 5

**151 On very rare occasions the FDA** Herder, Matthew. The FDA and Sarepta: a window into the real world of drug regulation. *STATNews.com,* September 3, 2019. https://www.statnews.com/2019/09/03/fda-sarepta-real-world-drug-regulation/

**151 For decades, Avastin has been a huge** https://www.fiercepharma.com/special-report/6-avastin Accessed: January 2020.

**151 But, in an unusual move, FDA officials** Gray R, Bhattacharya S, Bowden C, et al. Independent review of E2100: a phase III trial of bevacizumab plus paclitaxel versus paclitaxel in women with metastatic breast cancer. *J Clin Onco*l 2009 ;27(30):4966-72. doi: 10.1200/JCO.2008.21.6630.

**151 Avastin soon became one of the** Mukherjee, Sy. Amgen Is taking on a $3 billion cancer drug. But will it cut costs for patients? *Fortune.* September 15, 2017. https://fortune.com/2017/09/15/amgen-roche-avastin-biosimilar-price/; and Frederick C. Tucker, Jr. Drugs and profits. *New York Time*s [op-ed]. May 24, 2011.

**152 Then two subsequent trials of Avastin** Pivot X, Schneeweiss A, Verma S, et al. Efficacy and safety of bevacizumab in combination with docetaxel for the first-line treatment of elderly patients with locally recurrent or metastatic breast cancer: Results from AVADO. *Eur J Cancer*

2011;47(16):2387-95. doi: 10.1016/j.ejca.2011.06.018. Epub 2011 Jul 15.

152 **No statistically significant differences** Robert NJ, Diéras V, Glaspy J, et al. RIBBON-1: Randomized, double-blind, placebo-controlled, phase III trial of chemotherapy with or without bevacizumab for first-line treatment of human epidermal growth factor receptor 2–negative, locally recurrent or metastatic breast cancer. *Journal of Clinical Oncology* 2011(29):10:1252-1260.

152 **As she stated at the time** ASCO Post Staff. FDA Commissioner announces decision on bevacizumab . Drug not shown to be safe and effective in breast cancer patients, November 15, 2011, https://www.ascopost.com/issues/november-15-2011/fda-commissioner-announces-decision-on-bevacizumab/

153 **The mainstream media was its compliant self** Associated Press. FDA revokes approval of Avastin for breast cancer. *The Star Press* (Muncie, Indiana) 19 Nov 2011, p. 16.

153 **This publicity blitz was followed** Fang, Lee. Big Pharma funds “independent” advocacy groups attacking drug-price reduction bill. *The Intercept,* April 10 2017. https://theintercept.com/2017/04/10/drug-price-astroturf/

154 **In 2015, Hamburg was replaced** Herper, Matthew. Robert Califf could transform the FDA—the right way. Sep 16, 2015. https://www.forbes.com/sites/matthewherper/2015/09/16/robert-califf-could-transform-the-fda-the-right-way/#2c7f263f3486 Accessed: January 2020.

154 **According to government documents** https://openpaymentsdata.cms.gov/physician/300432/general-payments

## Section III, Chapter 7

155 **A long time ago** U.S. Department of Health and Human Services, Food and Drug Administration Oncology Center of Excellence, Center for Drug Evaluation and Research (CDER) Center for Biologics Evaluation and Research (CBER). *Clinical Trial Endpoints for the Approval of Cancer Drugs and Biologics Guidance for Industry,* December 2018. https://www.fda.gov/media/71195/download Accessed: January 2020.

155 **In 2015, FDA approved the drug, Lynparza** Geoffrey Kim, et al. FDA Approval Summary: Olaparib monotherapy in patients with deleterious germline BRCA-mutated advanced ovarian cancer treated with three or more lines of chemotherapy. *Clin Cancer Res* 2015(21):4257-4261; doi: 10.1158/1078-0432.CCR-15-0887

155 **In 2017, FDA approved the drug Rubraca** Balasubramaniam S, Beaver JA, Horton S, et al. FDA approval summary: Rucaparib for the treatment of patients with deleterious BRCA mutation–associated advanced ovarian cancer. *Clin Cancer Res* 2017(23):7165-7170; doi: 10.1158/1078-0432.CCR-17-1337

155 **In 2019, FDA approved Yescarta** Bouchkouj N, Kasamon YL, de Claro RA, et al. FDA approval summary: Axicabtagene ciloleucel for relapsed or refractory large B-cell lymphoma. *Clin Cancer Res* 2019(25):1702-1708; doi: 10.1158/1078-0432.CCR-18-2743

156 **Breast Cancer (2008): No endpoint could** Burzykowski T, Buyse M, Piccart-Gebhart MJ, et al. Evaluation of tumor response, disease control, progression-free survival, and time to progression as potential surrogate end points in metastatic breast cancer. *J Clin Oncol* 2008;20;26(12):1987-92. doi: 10.1200/JCO.2007.10.8407.

156 **Breast Cancer (2016): No endpoint was judged** Fiteni F, Bonnetain F. Surrogate end points for overall survival in breast cancer trials: A review. *Breast* 2016;29:44-8. doi: 10.1016/j.breast.2016.06.005

156 **Gastro-Esophageal (GE) Cancer (2017)** Petrelli F, Tomasello G, Barni S. Surrogate end-points for overall survival in 22 neoadjuvant trials of gastro-oesophageal cancers. *Eur J Cancer* 017;76:8-16. doi: 10.1016/j.ejca.2017.01.032.

156 **Immune Checkpoint Drugs (2017):** Roviello G, Andre F, Venturini S, et al. Response rate as a potential surrogate for survival and efficacy in patients treated with novel immune checkpoint inhibitors: A meta-regression of randomised prospective studies. *Eur J Cancer* 2017;86:257-265. doi: 10.1016/j.ejca.2017.09.018.

156 **Lung Cancer (2017): With certain exceptions** Fiteni F, *op.cit.*

156 **Lung Cancer (2018): In previous studies,** Hashim M, Pfeiffer BM, Bartsch R. et al. Do surrogate endpoints better correlate with overall survival in studies that did not allow for crossover or reported balanced post-progression treatments? An application in advanced non–small cell lung cancer. *Value in Health*. 2018;21(1):9-17. doi: 10.1016/j.jval.2017.07.011

156 **The oncologist Vinay Prasad** Chen EY, Raghunathan, Prasad V. An overview of cancer drugs approved by the US Food and Drug Administration based on the surrogate end point of response Rate. *JAMA Intern Med* 2019;179(7):915-921. doi: 10.1001/jamainternmed.2019.0583.

## Section IV, Chapter 1

159 **An article in Health Affairs** Kleutghen P, Mitchell PD, Kesselheim AS, et al. Drugs don’t work if people can’t afford them: the high price of tisagenlecleucel. February 8, 2018. https://www.healthaffairs.org/do/10.1377/hblog20180205.292531/full/

159 **Kite Pharma, a division of Gilead** Clarke T, Berkrot B. FDA approves Gilead cancer gene

therapy; price set at $373,000. *Reuters Health News,* October 18, 2017. https://www.reuters.com/article/us-gilead-sciences-fda/fda-approves-gilead-cancer-gene-therapy-price-set-at-373000-idUSKBN1CN35H Accessed: January 2020.

**159 In 2013, Duke University scientists** Zafar SY, Abernethy AP. Financial toxicity, Part I: a new name for a growing problem. *Oncology (Williston Park)* 201327(2):80-149.

**160 According to the head of Roche's pharmaceuticals** Roland, Denise. Cancer-drug giant roche loses edge as rivals grow. *Wall Street Journal,* April 28, 2019. https://www.wsj.com/articles/cancer-drug-giant-roche-loses-edge-as-rivals-grow-11556449201?mod=searchresults&page=1&pos=4 Accessed: January 2020.

**160 In fact, six of the 15** https://www.genengnews.com/a-lists/top-15-best-selling-drugs-of-2018/ Accessed: January 2020.

**161 Twenty-five years ago, a drug industry newsletter** https://www.thepha

**161 George Lundberg, MD, long-time editor** George D. Lundberg. *Severed Trust: Why American Medicine Hasn't Been Fixed.* New York, NY: Basic Books, 2001.

**162 Drs. Oldham and West did some** Boly, William. Cancer enterprise. *Washington Post,* Feb. 14, 1989.

**162 Some in the nonprofit sector** Raeburn, Paul. Expensive scam or equal opportunity. *The Scientist,* December, 1988.

**162 Biotherapeutics was publicly traded** Bylinsky Gene and Moore, Alicia Hills. The anticancer company expands. *Fortune,* November 23, 1987. https://archive.fortune.com/magazines/fortune/fortune_archive/1987/11/23/69876/index.htm; and Ed Gregory. Many symptoms sink firm. *The Tennessean* (Nashville, Tennessee), March 12, 1990, p. 30.; and Peters WP, Eder JP, Henner WD, et al. High-dose combination alkylating agents with autologous bone marrow support: a Phase 1 trial. *J Clin Oncol* 1986;4(5):646-54.

**163 The drug industry's response to anger** Blankenship, Kyle. Pharma lobbyists flood the zone in D.C., with Pfizer and Amgen leading the way. *FiercePharma.com,* April 23, 2019. https://www.fiercepharma.com/pharma/pharma-lobbyists-flood-zone-d-c-as-congressional-scrutiny-grows Accessed: January 2020.

**163 In part because of this systematic undermining** https://www.kff.org/health-reform/poll-finding/kff-health-tracking-poll-february-2019-prescription-drugs/ Accessed: January 2020.

**163 In part because of this systematic** Szabo L. Cascade of costs could push new gene therapy above $1 million per patient. *Kaiser Health News,* October 17, 2017. https://khn.org/news/cascade-of-costs-could-push-new-gene-therapy-above-1-million-per-patient/ Accessed: January 2020.

**164 This has resulted in an unusual:** https://www.wsj.com/articles/the-rights-left-turn-on-drug-prices-11566157320; and https://www.opensecrets.org/news/2019/06/efforts-to-reduce-drug-prices-stall-amid-pharmaceutical-lobbying/ Accessed: January 2020.rmaletter.com/article/oligopoly-the-future-for-the-pharma-industry Accessed: January 2020.

**164 The outrageous pricing** https://www.iqvia.com/newsroom/2018/05/iqvia-institute-for-human-data-science-study-spending-on-cancer-meds-in-the-us-doubled-from-2012-201; and Linda Marsa. Here's how to lower prescription drug prices. *AARP,* April 30, 2019. https://www.aarp.org/politics-society/advocacy/info-2019/5-point-prescription-drug-plan.html Accessed: January 2020.

**164 Treating the side effects** Hernandez I, Prasad V, Gellad WF. Total costs of chimeric antigen receptor T-cell immunotherapy. JAMA Oncol. 2018 Jul 1;4(7):994-996. doi: 10.1001/jamaoncol.2018.0977; and Healio.com, April 26, 2018; and Hernandez I. Analysis determines true cost for CAR T-cell therapy Healio Hem-Onc Today. https://www.healio.com/hematology-oncology/practice-management/news/online/%7B0c1d1a07-647d-4c69-9264-42f68526b0a9%7D/analysis-determines-true-cost-for-car-t-cell-therapy Accessed: January 2020.

**164 For example, Leonard B. Saltz** Szabo L. Cascade of costs could push new gene therapy above $1 million per patient. *Kaiser Health News,* October 17, 2017. https://khn.org/news/cascade-of-costs-could-push-new-gene-therapy-above-1-million-per-patient/ Accessed: January 2020

**165 Another oncologist who has called out** Kantarjian H, Raikumar SV. Why are cancer drugs so expensive in the United States, and what are the solutions? Mayo Clin Proc. 2015;90(4):500-4. doi: 10.1016/j.mayocp.2015.01.014..

**165 In 2013, in an unprecedented move** Experts in Chronic Myeloid Leukemia. The price of drugs for chronic myeloid leukemia (CML) is a reflection of the unsustainable prices of cancer drugs: from the perspective of a large group of CML experts. *Blood.* 2013;121(22):4439-42. doi: 10.1182/blood-2013-03-490003.

**166 National Institutes of Health funding** Galkina Cleary E, Beierlein JM, Khanuja NS1 leary EG, et al. Contribution of NIH funding to new drug approvals. *Proceedings of the National Academy of Sciences* 2018;115(10)2329-2334; doi: 10.1073/pnas.1715368115; and Kacik A. Fewer drug rep visits lead to lower drug costs. *Modern Healthcare,* May 3, 2017. https://www.modernhealthcare.com/article/20170503/NEWS/170509961/fewer-drug-rep-visits-lead-to-lower-drug-costs Accessed: January 2020.

**167 The NCI spent a total of $32 million** Garber K. Battle over generic Taxol concludes, but controversy continues, *JNCI: Journal of the National Cancer Institute,* 2002;94(5-6):324–326. https://doi.org/10.1093/jnci/94.5.324

**167 NCI cultivated what it called** Goodman, Jordan and Walsh, Vivien. *The Story of Taxol: Nature and Politics in the Pursuit of an Anti-Cancer Drug.* Cambridge, U.K.: Cambridge University Press, 2001.

**168 The whole thing was a sweetheart deal** Petersen, Melody and Walsh, Mary Williams. States accuse Bristol-Myers of fraud on Taxol. *New York Times,* June 5, 2002.

**168 According to a 2019 CNBC Report** Konish, Lorie. This is the real reason most Americans file for bankruptcy. Feb. 11, 2019. https://www.cnbc.com/2019/02/11/this-is-the-real-reason-most-americans-file-for-bankruptcy.html Accessed: January 2020.

**170 "I promise you, if I'm elected"** Wulfsohn, John A. Joe Biden promises to 'cure cancer' if elected president. *Foxnews.com,* June 11, 2019. https://www.foxnews.com/politics/joe-biden-cure-cancer-president Accessed: January 2020.

**170 Then, a few days later,** Hannon, Elliott. Trump kicks off 2020 reelection bid by promising to cure cancer, land on Mars, *Etc.* June 19, 2019. https://slate.com/news-and-politics/2019/06/trump-kicks-off-2020-reelection-bid-promising-to-cure-cancer-land-on-mars.html; and Merrill Goozner, Big databases: Outcomes research begins to yield results, *JNCI: Journal of the National Cancer Institute,* 2010;1-2(4):2010. https://doi.org/10.1093/jnci/djq034

**170 The NCI once asked the Institute** American Society of Clinical Oncology and Institute of Medicine Workshop; Institute of Medicine; National Cancer Policy Forum; Board on Health Care Services. *Implementing a National Cancer Clinical Trials System for the 21st Century:* Second Workshop Summary. Washington (DC): National Academies Press (US); 2013 Sep 27. Available from: https://www.ncbi.nlm.nih.gov/books/NBK202108/ doi: 10.17226/18362; and Institute of Medicine (US) Committee on Cancer Clinical Trials and the NCI Cooperative Group Program; Nass SJ, Moses HL, Mendelsohn J, editors. *A National Cancer Clinical Trials System for the 21st Century: Reinvigorating the NCI Cooperative Group Program.* Washington (DC): National Academies Press (US); 2010.

**170 The NCI once asked** Piana, Ronald. Demanding more from clinical trials. *ASCO Post,* May 15, 2014. https://www.ascopost.com/issues/may-15-2014/demanding-more-from-clinical-trials/ Accessed: January 2020.

### Section IV, Chapter 2

**172 A doctor once called** Leff, Richard S. A Sign of the times: ASCO's relationship with the pharmaceutical industry. Jun 05, 2012. https://connection.asco.org/discussion/sign-times-ascos-relationship-pharmaceutical-industry Accessed: January 2020.

**172 The traditional structure** Cox, John Vernon. The JOP provides increased visibility through NLM indexing. *ASCO Connection,* Jan 15, 2013. https://connection.asco.org/blogs/jop-provides-increased-visibility-through-nlm-indexing

**172 Dr. Cox alluded to** Polite B, Conti RM, Ward JC. Reform of the buy-and-bill system for outpatient chemotherapy care Is inevitable: Perspectives from an economist, a realpolitik, and an oncologist. *Am Soc Clin Oncol Educ Book* 2015;e75-80. doi: 10.14694/EdBook_AM.2015.35.e75.

**173 In the U.S., at that time** Chustecka, Zosia. How do oncologist salaries compare with Other Specialties? *Medscape.com,* April 24, 2019 Accessed: January 2020.

**173 The "chemotherapy concession" was named** Reynolds T. Salary a major factor for academic oncologists, study shows, *JNCI: Journal of the National Cancer Institute,* Volume 93, Issue 7, 4 April 2001, Page 491, https://doi.org/10.1093/jnci/93.7.491

**174 Professor Joseph P. Newhouse of Harvard University** Abelson, Reed. Doctors recouped cuts in Medicare pay, study finds. *New York Times,* June 17, 2010.

**174 340B required drug companies** Pollack, Andrew. Dispute develops over discount drug program. *New York Times,* February 12, 2013.

**174 The chemotherapy concession further declined** Hoffman, Jan. $260 Million opioid settlement reached at last minute with big drug companies. *New York Times,* Oct. 21, 2019.

**175 The Medicare Modernization Act of 2003.** Jacobson M, Earle CC, Price M, et al. How Medicare's payment cuts for cancer chemotherapy drugs changed patterns of treatment. *Health Affairs,* July 2010. https://doi.org/10.1377/hlthaff.2009.0563p. 213

**176 "We're just trying to break even"** Abelson. Reed. Drug sales bring huge profits, and scrutiny, to cancer doctors. *New York Times,* January 16, 2003.

**176 In 2010, the New York Times published** Berenson, Alex and Pollack, Andrew. Doctors reap millions for anemia drugs. *New York Times,* May 9, 2007.

**177 According to Dr. Angell** Peter Whoriskey. Honest research vs. drug company bias. *The Washington Post.* December 2, 2012.

**177 These researchers think what these companies** Seife, Charles. How drug company money is undermining science. *Scientific American,* November 21, 2012 https://www.comtrea.org/files/users/melaniecole/HowDrugCompanyMoneyisUnderminingScience-ScientificAmerican.pdf Accessed: January 2020.

**178 Finally, Richard Smith, MD** https://www.thetimes.co.uk/article/how-worthy-is-research-3xdchdwf3xk

**179 Professor Charles Seife expanded** Seife, Charles. How drug company money Is undermining science. *Scientific American,* November 21, 2012 https://www.comtrea.org/files/users/melaniecole/HowDrugCompanyMoneyisUnderminingScience-ScientificAmerican.pdf Accessed: January 2020.

**180 Similarly, Justin E. Bekelman** Bekelman JE, Li Y, Gross CP. Scope and impact of financial conflicts of interest in biomedical research: A systematic review. *JAMA* 2003;289(4):454–465. doi:https://doi.org/10.1001/jama.289.4.454

## Section IV, Chapter 3

**182 For details on payments** Richards SE. Everyone's conflicted: How Open Payments did little to discourage conflicts of interest in oncology. *Cancer Therapy Advisor,* October 21, 2019. https://www.cancertherapyadvisor.com/home/cancer-topics/general-oncology/oncology-cancer-open-payment-do-not-discourage-conflicts-interest-coi/ Accessed: January 2020.

**182 Dr. Vinay Prasad has called** Prasad V. The 'cancer growing in cancer medicine': pharma money paid to doctors. *STATNews.com,* October 30, 2019. https://www.statnews.com/2019/10/30/cancer-growing-in-cancer-medicine-pharma-money-doctors/ Accessed: January 2020.

**184 There are even KOL management** Anon. Key opinion leaders: who are they and why do they matter? https://www.lianatech.com/resources/blog/key-opinion-leaders-who-are-they-and-why-do-they-matter.html' Accessed: January 2020; and Carr D, Welch HG. Industry payments to physician directors of National Cancer Institute-designated cancer centers, 2015-2017. *JAMA Intern Med* 2019 Aug 5. doi: 10.1001/jamainternmed.2019.3098

**184 Spin, in a medical context** Boutron I, Dutton S, Ravaud P, et al. Reporting and interpretation of randomized controlled trials with statistically nonsignificant results for primary outcomes. *JAMA.* 2010;303(20):2058–2064. doi:https://doi.org/10.1001/jama.2010.651

**185 In articles on cancer treatment** Vera-Badillo FE, Shapiro R, Ocana A, et al. Bias in reporting of end points of efficacy and toxicity in randomized, clinical trials for women with breast cancer, *Annals of Oncology* 2013;24(5):1238–1244, https://doi.org/10.1093/annonc/mds636

**185 A follow-up study of cancer trials** Vera-Badillo FE, Napoleone M, Krzyzanowska MK, et al. Bias in reporting of randomised clinical trials in oncology. *Eur J Cancer.* 2016;61:29-35. doi: 10.1016/j.ejca.2016.03.066. https://www.; and Jagsi R., Sheets N, Jankovic A, et al. Frequency, nature, effects, and correlates of conflicts of interest in published clinical cancer research. Cancer, 2009;115: 2783-2791. doi:10.1002/cncr.24315

## Section IV, Chapter 4

**187 In a 2017 paper of which** Baselga J, Zamagni C, Gómez P, et al. RESILIENCE: Phase III randomized, double-blind trial comparing sorafenib with capecitabine versus placebo with capecitabine in locally advanced or metastatic her2-negative breast cancer. *Clin Breast Cancer* 2017;17(8):585-594. doi: e4. doi: 10.1016/j.clbc.2017.05.006; and Piccart M, Goldhirsch A, Wood W. et al. Keeping faith with trial volunteers. *Nature* 2007;446:137–138 doi:10.1038/446137a; and Phil Taylor. AstraZeneca unveils reorg, hires controversial José Baselga as cancer chief. *PM Live,* January 8, 2019. http://www.pmlive.com/pharma_news/astrazeneca_announces_reorg,_hires_controversial_jose_baselga_as_cancer_chief_1274244 p.225 Accessed: January 2020.

**188 Our findings are proof that** Anon. 2018 ASCO: Phase III SANDPIPER trial evaluates taselisib plus fulvestrant in advanced breast cancer. *The ASCO Post.* June 2, 2018. Last Updated: June 6, 2018. https://www.ascopost.com/News/58901 Accessed: January 2020.

**188 Memorial Sloan-Kettering Cancer Center Physician-in-chief José Baselga** Stallard J. Targeted therapy slows growth of most common type of advanced breast cancer. June 2, 2018. https://www.mskcc.org/blog/asco18-drug-slows-growth-most-common-type-advanced-breast Accessed: January 2020.

**188 Roche dumps...its effort** Carroll J. Roche dumps its PhIII PI3K effort on taselisib after researchers track poor survival edge, harsh side effects for breast cancer. *Endpoints News,* June 3, 2018. https://endpts.com/roche-dumps-its-phiii-pi3k-effort-on-taselisib-after-researchers-track-poor-survival-edge-harsh-side-effects-for-breast-cancer/; and https://openpaymentsdata.cms.gov/physician/223663/summary Accessed: January 2020.

**189 Dr. Baselga was publicly criticized** Ornstein C, Thomas K. Cancer center's board chairman faults top doctor, saying he "crossed lines." *The New York Times* (with *Propublica).* Oct. 1, 2018. https://www.propublica.org/article/cancer-centers-board-chairman-faults-top-doctor-saying-he-crossed-lines Accessed: January 2020.

**189 Then it turned out that** https://openpaymentsdata.cms.gov/physician/71137/summary Accessed: January 2020.

## Section IV, Chapter 5

**191 In particular, the FDA's decisions:** https://www.statista.com/topics/1719/pharmaceutical-industry/ Accessed: January 2020.

**191 Instead of a regulator and a regulated industry** Chen C (ProPublica). FDA increasingly approves drugs without conclusive proof they work. *PBS News Hour,* Jun 26, 2018. https://www.pbs.org/newshour/health/fda-increasingly-approves-drugs-without-conclusive-proof-they-work Accessed: January 2020.

**191 "Partnership" and "friendliness"** Venable V. Regulatory capture of the Food and Drug Administration as a result of new right neoliberalism. May 2016. https://www.academia.edu/27074415/Regulatory_Capture_of_the_Food_and_Drug_Administration_As_a_Result_of_New_Right_Neoliberalism Accessed: January 2020.

**192 A 2018 study in Science** Piller C. FDA's revolving door: Companies often hire agency staffers who managed their successful drug reviews. *Science,* July 5, 2018. https://www.sciencemag.org/news/2018/07/fda-s-revolving-door-companies-often-hire-agency-staffers-who-managed-their-successful Accessed: January 2020.

**192 Top pharmaceutical CEOs** Facher L. As Congress considers lowering drug costs, pharma CEOs target key senators with campaign cash. *STAT News,* September 3, 2019. https://www.statnews.com/2019/09/03/pharma-executives-campaign-donations-influential-gop-senators/ Accessed: January 2020.

**193 This kind of revolving door** https://www.usatoday.com/story/news/politics/2019/07/03/elizabeth-warren-tells-scott-gottlieb-resign-pfizer-board/1637789001/ Accessed: January 2020.

**193 2006: Lester M. Crawford, MD, who pleaded guilty** Stout, David. Ex-F.D.A. chief pleads guilty in stock case. *New York Times,* October 18, 2006.

**194 A Kaiser Health News article** Lupkin S. Big pharma greets hundreds of ex-federal workers at the 'revolving door', *Kaiser Health News,* January 25, 2018. https://www.statnews.com/2018/01/25/pharma-federal-workers-revolving-door/ Accessed: January 2020.

**194 Science's investigative reporter, Charles Piller** Piller C. FDA's revolving door: Companies often hire agency staffers who managed their successful drug reviews. *Science,* July 5, 2018. https://www.sciencemag.org/news/2018/07/fda-s-revolving-door-companies-often-hire-agency-staffers-who-managed-their-successful

**194 One prominent critic** https://www.npr.org/sections/health-shots/2016/09/28/495694559/a-look-at-how-the-revolving-door-spins-from-fda-to-industry Accessed: January 2020.

**194 Dr. Prasad asked the following** Lupkin S. A look at how the revolving door spins from FDA to industry. *NPR.org.* September 28, 2016. https://www.npr.org/sections/health-shots/2016/09/28/495694559/a-look-at-how-the-revolving-door-spins-from-fda-to-industry Accessed: January 2020.

**194 David S. Egilman, MD, a professor of family medicine** Egilman DS, Presler AH, Valentin CS. Avoiding the regulatory capture of the Food and Drug Administration. *Arch Intern Med.* 2007;167(7):732–733. doi:https://doi.org/10.1001/archinte.167.7.732-b

**195 Professor John Abraham of King's College** Abraham J. Sociology of pharmaceuticals development and regulation: a realist empirical research programme. *Sociology of Health and Illness.* 2008;30(5):869-885 https://doi.org/10.1111/j.1467-9566.2008.01101.x

**195 A key turning point** Ceccoli, Stephen J. *Pill Politics: Drugs and the FDA.* Boulder, CO: Lynne Rienner Publishers, 2004.

**195 According to Professor Donald W. Light** Light DW, Lexchin J, Darrow JJ. Institutional corruption of pharmaceuticals and the myth of safe and effective drugs. J Law Med Ethics 2013:41(3):590–600. https://doi.org/10.1111/jlme.12068

**196 As of 2019, the fee for a** Hilts PJ. Senate passes bill to charge makers for drug approval. *New York Times,* October 8, 1992.

**196 According to a 2018 investigation** Chen C. FDA repays industry by rushing risky drugs to market. *ProPublica,* June 26, 2018. https://www.propublica.org/article/fda-repays-industry-by-rushing-risky-drugs-to-market; Miller C, You J. Hidden conflicts? Pharma payments to FDA advisers after drug approvals spark ethical concerns. *Science,* July 5, 2018. https://www.sciencemag.org/news/2018/07/hidden-conflicts-pharma-payments-fda-advisers-after-drug-approvals-spark-ethical

**198 The FDA rarely overrides its chief** https://www.linkedin.com/in/phuong-khanh-morrow-97113b117 Accessed: January 2020.

**198 FDA has determined that members** https://www.fda.gov/media/112893/download Accessed: January 2020.

**199 Congress has authorized FDA** https://www.fda.gov/media/112893/download Accessed: January 2020.

**200 While at Eli Lilly, Azar** Associated Press. Health secretary nominee reaped big earnings from drug industry tenure. November 20, 2017 Accessed: January 2020.

**201 There is little difference between** https://mronline.org/2019/07/23/the-ruling-class-does-rule/ Accessed: January 2020.

**201 Open Secrets shows that** https://www.opensecrets.org/industries/lobbying.php?cycle=2018&ind=H04 Accessed: January 2020.

## Section IV, Chapter 7


**202 Revelations from Goldman Sachs** Richter S. *The Genome Revolution*. Goldman Sachs website. June 25, 2018. https://www.goldmansachs.com/insights/pages/genome-revolution.html Accessed: January 2020.

**202 Her answer was no.** Kim T. Goldman Sachs asks in biotech research report: 'Is curing patients a sustainable business model?' CNBC.com., April 11, 2018. https://www.cnbc.com/2018/04/11/goldman-asks-is-curing-patients-a-sustainable-business-model.html Accessed: January 2020.


## Section V, Chapter 1


**203 Open up the clinical trial system** Unger JM, Cook E, Tai E, et al. The role of clinical trial participation in cancer research: barriers, evidence, and strategies. *Am Soc Clin Oncol Educ Book*. 2016;35:185-98. doi: 10.1200/EDBK_156686. and Harvey RD, Rubinstein WS, Ison G, et al. Impact of broadening clinical trial eligibility criteria for advanced non-small cell lung cancer patients: Real-world analysis. *2019 ASCO Annual Meeting*, June 3, 2019. https://meetinglibrary.asco.org/record/178360/abstract Accessed: January 2020

**203 Institute a single-payer Medicare for All** https://thehill.com/hilltv/what-americas-thinking/412545-70-percent-of-americans-support-medicare-for-all-health-care Accessed: January 2020

**206 "I would be willing to accept almost..."** Quoted in Patterson John T, *The Dread Disease*, Cambridge: Harvard University Press, 1987, p. 118.

**206 On July 18, 2019, JAMA Oncology** Neff I. Beyond parity and toward socially owned anticancer drug research. *JAMA Oncol* 2019;5(9):1260–1261. doi:https://doi.org/10.1001/jamaoncol.2019.2291

**206 The American Medical Association, under Dr. Morris Fishbein,** Quoted in Miller I, *American Health Care Blues: Blue Cross, Hmos, and Pragmatic Reform Since 1960*. New Brunswick, New Jersey: Transaction Publishers, 2000, p. 20.; and https://www.cbsnews.com/news/a-history-of-corporate-nationalization/

**207 The government also forced** https://www.thebalance.com/aig-bailout-cost-timeline-bonuses-causes-effects-3305693 Accessed: January 2020

**207 For the majority of poor people** https://socialsecurityworks.org/2019/03/26/social-security-polling/ Accessed: January 2020.

**207 The movement for placing** Quoted as testimony against the National Health Act of 1945. https://tinyurl.com/fishbein1945 Accessed: January 2020.

**208 In Canada, as of 2019** https://www.cbc.ca/news/health/glybera-lpld-rare-drug-orphan-disease-nrc-cbc-price-1.5312177 Accessed: January 2020.

**209 The National Research Centre of Canada** National Research Council Canada. Health challenge: disruptive technology solutions for cell and gene therapy. https://nrc.canada.ca/en/research-development/research-collaboration/programs/health-challenge-disruptive-technology-solutions-cell-gene-therapy-0; and https://www.inquirer.com/philly/health/20130630_Medication_shortages___Truly_a_public_health_crisis_.html Accessed: January 2020.

**209 Companies have very little incentive** Keshavan M. With one manufacturer and little money to be made, supplies of a critical cancer drug are dwindling. *STATnew.com*. February 20, 2019. https://www.statnews.com/2019/02/20/supplies-bladder-cancer-drug-bcg-dwindling/ Accessed: January 2020.

**210 In fact, cancer drug development** Thielking M. NIH funding contributed to 210 approved drugs in recent years, study says. February 12, 2018. https://www.statnews.com/2018/02/12/nih-funding-drug-development/ Accessed: January 2020.

# Index

## About the Author

Ralph W. Moss, PhD, has written or edited fourteen books and collaborated on four film documentaries on cancer. Born in Brooklyn, New York, Dr. Moss is an honors graduate of New York University and Stanford University. In the 1970s, he was assistant director of public affairs at Memorial Sloan-Kettering Cancer Center.

For over forty years he has been evaluating cancer treatments. He writes the Moss Reports, which are up-to-date book-length reports on the most common cancers, for laypeople. He has also written the chapter on complementary and alternative medicine for the *Encyclopedia Britannica* and for a legal series, *Courtroom Medicine: Cancer.* He co-edited the first medical textbook on *Complementary Oncology*.

His writings have appeared in the *Journal of the National Cancer Institute, Journal of Clinical Oncology, Journal of the American Medical Association, New Scientist,* and many others. His invited op-ed "Patents Over Patients" appeared in the *New York Times.*

Dr. Moss was a founding member of the National Institutes of Health's Alternative Medicine Program Advisory Council, and of the Complementary and Alternative Medicine panel. He has also served as a peer reviewer for a dozen medical journals.

He has been invited to lecture at Memorial Sloan-Kettering Cancer Center, Johns Hopkins University, Howard University, University of Arizona, Department of Energy, American Cancer Society, Penn State Hershey Medical Center, and many other institutions. He led the History of Science Seminar at the National Library of Medicine on the life and work of his mentor, the Nobel laureate Albert Szent-Györgyi, MD, PhD.

He has received lifetime achievement awards from the American College for the Advancement of Medicine, Cancer Control Society, National Foundation for Alternative Medicine, Center for Advancement in Cancer Education, and Wellness Forum, and has been honored with visiting professorships at the Shanxi Province Anticancer Research Institute, Chang'An Hospital in Xi'an, and Friendship Hospital in Guangzhou, China.

He gave the keynote address at the International Clinical Hyperthermia Society meeting in Guangzhou. He was honored there with a Grand Award for Special Contribution to Natural Medicine and was made a standing director of the World Federation of Chinese Medicine Societies. He was also made a guest professor at the Southern Medical University in Dongguan.

Moss has made 18 separate tours of cancer clinics in Germany, as well as in Austria, Mexico, Turkey, Holland, Israel, Hungary, the Czech Republic, Ireland, Russia, Switzerland, Denmark, Italy, Bahamas, Honduras, Great Britain, and most states of the U.S. and provinces of Canada. He and his team continue to tour clinics around the U.S. and the world looking for advanced cancer treatments.

Made in the USA
Monee, IL
04 November 2026

67385341R00138